To Shelagh Ferguson-Miller

In appreciation for
your efforts on behalf of the
Biochemistry Department, the
University of Missouri - Columbia.

January 1996

# The University of Missouri

# The University

# of Missouri

## AN ILLUSTRATED HISTORY

James and Vera Olson

University of Missouri Press
Columbia, 1988

Copyright © 1988 by
The Curators of the University of Missouri
University of Missouri Press, Columbia, Missouri 65211
Printed and bound in Japan

Library of Congress Cataloging-in-Publication Data
Olson, James, 1917–
   The University of Missouri
   Includes index.
   1. University of Missouri—History.  I. Olson,
Vera, 1918–    .  II. Title.
LD3468.047   1988   378.778'29   88–1158
ISBN 0-8262-0678-6 (alk. paper)

∞™ This paper meets the minimum requirements of
the American National Standard for Permanence of Paper
for Printed Library Materials, Z39.48, 1984.

To all the faculty, staff, students,
alumni, and friends who are a part
of the history of this great university

# PREFACE

As the oldest public institution of higher learning west of the Mississippi River, the University of Missouri has a significant place in the history of American higher education. It has been a major force in the economic, social, and cultural development of the state of Missouri. The story of its transformation from a tiny academy in an isolated frontier village into a large, multicampus, statewide university is a major chapter in the history of both American higher education and the state of Missouri.

This book, published on the eve of the sesquicentennial, represents an effort to survey in words and pictures the history of the University of Missouri from its founding in 1839 to the present. Themes in Missouri history can be traced in the history of its state university. From the beginning the university was the victim of the sectional disputes that characterized Missouri society. After the Civil War, which threatened the existence of the institution, sectional jealousies made it difficult for the university to exercise statewide influence. For many years it was looked upon as primarily a Columbia institution.

The state was slow to assume responsibility for the support of the university. Even after the General Assembly started appropriating funds for its annual maintenance, the amounts were never equal to the institution's needs, let alone its aspirations. The caution epitomized in the state's "show me" attitude, combined with the Jeffersonian view that government should be both limited and inexpensive, made it difficult for the university to persuade the people of the state that they should provide generously for the institution's support. The struggle with the budget has been an enduring theme of the university's history. Somewhat paradoxically, another enduring theme has been the commitment to quality. This commitment enabled the university to develop into an institution of the first rank in its region and early on to take its place with the leading research universities of the country.

In 1963, the university established campuses in St. Louis and Kansas City. This was without a doubt the most far-reaching development in the history of the university. Establishing these two campuses transformed the university from an institution isolated in the middle of the state with a detached and even more isolated school of mines and metallurgy into an institution positioned to serve the state's major population centers. At this writing, a quarter of a century later, the university is still coming to grips with its new structure.

This book is by no means a definitive history of the University of Missouri. The limits of space and the availability of photographs made that impossible. A word of explanation is in order with regard to the photographs. The reader will note that there are relatively few portraits of individuals. As we got into the work we discovered that the availability of negatives or of high-quality prints was so uneven as to make it difficult to portray adequately many persons who played a significant role in the history of the institution and who are mentioned in the text. Moreover, had we used even such photographs as were available, much of the book would have had the appearance of the class pages in a college annual. As much as possible, we have tried to limit ourselves to photographs that show the university in action.

We also wish to acknowledge our personal relationship to parts of this history. Eight years in the chancellor's residence in Kansas City and eight in the president's home in Columbia inevitably influenced the objectivity with which we could approach the university's history during those years. We have tried to be as objective as possible.

During the years in which we were active in the day-to-day life of the university, we were impressed with the quality and devotion of hundreds of faculty and staff members with whom we were privileged to work. Likewise, in our research for this book we have been impressed with the same quality and devotion on the part of those who have gone before. We wish we might have dealt with more of them. The people of the university have served Missouri well. We hope that this story will contribute to an understanding of that service.

J. C. O.
V. B. O.
January 1988

# ACKNOWLEDGMENTS

During our work on this book we have incurred many debts, and we are pleased to acknowledge them here. We have relied heavily on a number of books written about various aspects of the University's history. Frank V. Stephens, *A History of the University of Missouri* (Columbia: University of Missouri, 1962), is the standard work for the early years, but it is seriously out of date. Jonas Viles, *The University of Missouri: A Centennial History* (Columbia, 1939), is older and less useful. Lawrence O. Christensen and Jack B. Ridley, *UM-Rolla: A History of MSM/UMR* (Columbia, 1983), provides an excellent overview of the history of the Rolla campus and is particularly well-balanced in its treatment of the relationship between the Missouri School of Mines and the University of Missouri. Bonita H. Mann and Clair V. Mann, *The History of Missouri School of Mines and Metallurgy* (Rolla, 1941), is ponderous and prejudiced but contains much valuable detail. Carleton F. Scofield, *A History of the University of Kansas City* (Kansas City, 1976), is useful for the early years of the Kansas City campus, but nothing has been published on the years since 1963. Blanche M. Touhill, *The Emerging University: The University of Missouri-St. Louis, 1963–1983* (Columbia, 1985), provides a highly useful year-by-year account of the first twenty years on the St. Louis campus.

Various campus publications were helpful. On the Columbia campus *The Missouri Alumnus* and its predecessor, *The Missouri Alumni Quarterly, Savitar, Columbia Missourian, The Missouri Review,* and *Maneater;* on the Rolla campus *MSM-UMR Alumnus, Rollamo,* and *Missouri Miner;* on the Kansas City campus *Alumni Magazine, Tempo, Kangaroo,* and *University News;* on the St. Louis campus *Riverman* and various special publications.

Many people have provided generous assistance. James W. Goodrich, Director at the State Historical Society of Missouri, and members of the staff, especially Elizabeth Bailey and Ed Parker, Reference Librarians, Fae E. Sotham, Secretary in the Editorial Department, and Mark Thomas, Newspaper Librarian. At the University of Missouri were Director Ralph S. Havener, Jr., Archivist, University Archives; Catherine Hunt, Secretary to the Board of Curators; and Robert Mussman, Director of Public Information. D. J. Wade, Reference Specialist at the University Archives, provided invaluable help in guiding us through the resources of the University Archives and in locating hard-to-find photographs.

We would also like to thank for their support at the University of Missouri–Columbia Dean James Atwater, School of Journalism; Laura Bullion, Senior Manuscript Specialist, Western Historical Manuscripts Collection; Joe Castiglione, Assistant Director of Athletics; Sue Engel, Senior Secretary, Agricultural Editor's Office; Don Faurot; Margaret Howell, Special Collections Division Head, Ellis Library; Forrest McGill, Director of the Museum of Art and Archaeology; Susan Merkel, President, Theta Chapter, Kappa Kappa Gamma; Annette Range, Administrative Assistant to the Dean of the School of

Education; Mary Robertson, Administrative Assistant to the Dean of
the School of Law; Betty Rottman, Coordinator, Visitor and Guest
Relations; Carolus Taylor, Student Services Advisor, Residential
Life/Greek Life; Robert Stevens, Morgue Librarian, *Columbia Missourian*; and Larry Boehm, Senior Information Specialist, and Jeff
Adams, Senior Photographer, *Missouri Alumnus*. Michael DeSantis,
Photographer, Academic Support Center, used his expertise in pho-
tographing delicate and faded old documents so that they could be
reproduced here. In Columbia we would like to thank Mrs. Thomas
Botts and Janice Summers, Librarian, *Columbia Daily Tribune*. We
would also like to extend thanks to the late James A. Finch of Jefferson City and to Ann Milgram of Kansas City.

For their assistance at the University of Missouri–Kansas City we
wish to acknowledge David Boutros, Acting Associate Director,
UMKC Archives, and Marilyn Burlingame, Archives Assistant; John
Dunn, Supervisor, Audiovisual Services, and Larry Pape, Photographer; Barbara Smith, Director, University Communications, and
staff; the Conservatory of Music; and Marilyn Cannaday and Delores
Wilson, Office of the President Emeritus.

For their assistance at the University of Missouri–Rolla we would
like to thank Wayne M. Bledsoe, University Archives; Ronald Bohley,
Director, and staff of the Curtis Laws Wilson Library; Ernest Gutier-
rez, Senior Information Specialist, News and Publications; Lynn
Waggoner, Director, Public Affairs; and Sally White, Editor, Alumni
Development Publications.

For their assistance at the University of Missouri–St. Louis we
would like to thank Patricia Adams, Associate Archivist; Thomas B.
Corbett, Reference Specialist, University Archives; Sean Johnson,
Sports Information Department; Kathy Osborn, Director of Alumni
Relations; Mary Proemsey, Senior Secretary, Office of News Services.
We would like to acknowledge the assistance of the *St. Louis Post-
Dispatch* Picture Library; Duane R. Sneddeker, Curator of Photo-
graphs and Prints, Missouri Historical Society, and Bryan Stephen
Thomas, Tutorial Assistant, Photographs and Prints, in St. Louis.

Through the leadership of Henry Bloch, President and Chief Executive Officer of H&R Block, Inc., assisted by Barbara Allmon and
Terrence Ward of his staff, many of our friends in Kansas City, indi-
vidually or through their companies, provided the University Press
with financial assistance to help defray the cost of publishing this
book, and it is a particular pleasure to acknowledge their goodwill
and generosity.

Major underwriters include The H&R Block Foundation, Hallmark
Corporate Foundation, Jones & Babson, Inc., Kansas City Southern
Industries, Inc., Payless Cashways, Inc., The Sosland Foundation,
and United Telecommunications, Inc.

Underwriters include American Multi-Cinema, Inc., John and Phy-
llis Anderson, Arthur Young & Company, Joan and Bert Berkley, Blue
Cross and Blue Shield of Kansas City, Business Men's Assurance Co.,
Butler Manufacturing Company, Clarkson Construction Company,
Commerce Bank Foundation, Commercial Lithographing Company,

Deacy and Deacy, J. E. Dunn Construction Company, Employers
Reinsurance Corporation, Faultless Starch/Bon Ami Company, The
Parker B. Francis III Foundation, Gage & Tucker, Pitt and Al
Hoffman, Howard Needles Tammen & Bergendoff, Mr. and Mrs.
Robert P. Ingram, International Business Machines Corporation,
Interstate Brands Corporation, Cliff C. Jones, David Woods Kemper
Memorial Foundation, Kenneth Kalen, Kansas City Chiefs Football
Club, Inc., Kansas City Power & Light Company, John Latshaw,
Alfred Lighton, McLiney & Company, Marion Laboratories, Inc., The
Marley Company, Massman Construction Company, Mercantile Bank
of Kansas City, Mobay Corporation, John A. Morgan, The Mutual
Benefit Life Insurance Company, Nichols Company Charitable Trust,
Peat Marwick Main & Co., Gerard B. Rivette, Mr. Byron T. Shutz,
Edward and Beth Smith, Mr. and Mrs. Gad Smith, Smith, Gill,
Fisher & Butts, Southwestern Bell Telephone Company, Stinson, Mag
& Fizzell, Herman and Helen Sutherland, Tivol, Inc., Touche Ross
and Company, Trans World Airlines, Avis Green Tucker, UtiliCorp
United, Yellow Freight System, Inc., and The Zimmer Companies.

# CONTENTS

Preface, vii

Acknowledgments, ix

COLUMBIA

1. The First Half Century, 3

2. An Emerging Public University, 29

3. War, Uncertainty, Depression, and War, 53

4. A Time of Growth, 77

5. University of Missouri–Columbia, 101

ROLLA

6. Beginnings at Rolla, 131

7. Missouri School of Mines, 153

8. University of Missouri–Rolla, 171

KANSAS CITY

9. University of Kansas City, 193

10. University of Missouri–Kansas City, 215

ST. LOUIS

11. University of Missouri–St. Louis, 241

UNIVERSITY OF MISSOURI

12. The Statewide University, 267

Index, 283

Photo Credits, 295

Columbia

# 1 THE FIRST

## HALF CENTURY

In the United States, public universities were frequently founded with land grants. The history of the University of Missouri can be said to have its beginning in a clause in the Act of 1820, admitting Missouri to the Union, which granted to the new state two townships, "for the use of a seminary of learning."

It was not until the 1830s that the legislature sold the land and sentiment mounted for the establishment of a university with the proceeds. By 1839, the fund amounted to about $100,000—enough, it was believed, to endow a university—and in that year the General Assembly passed two acts that provided for the establishment and location of the University of Missouri. The first, passed in part because of the influence of Representative David Rice Atchison of Clay County, who later won fame as a controversial United States senator from Missouri, and the persuasive arguments of James S. Rollins, a young legislator from Boone County, provided for the location of the university in one of six counties in the central part of the state (Cooper, Cole, and Saline on the south side of the Missouri River; Howard, Boone, and Callaway on the north) that offered the greatest inducements in land and money.

The bill that established the university was introduced by Representative Henry S. Geyer of St. Louis. It created a seminary fund

James S. Rollins, recognized by the board of curators in 1872 as *"Pater Universitatis Missouriensis."* Rollins and Lathrop are commemorated by bronze reliefs that adorn the columns at the north entrance to the campus.

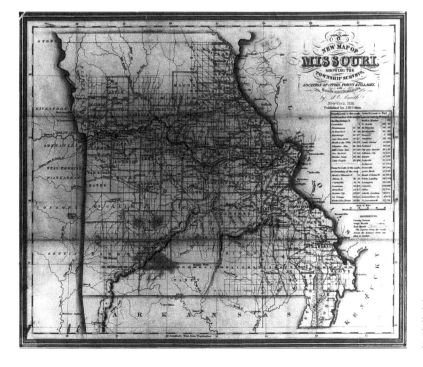

In 1838 most of the population of Missouri was concentrated in and around St. Louis and along the Mississippi and Missouri rivers.

3

from the proceeds of the land sales and vested control of the university in a board of curators. It envisioned a statewide university with campuses located in various parts of the state and required that only students who could read in Latin the first book of the *Aeneid,* who had studied the higher branches of English, and who had advanced beyond the common-school level in English grammar, geography, and arithmetic should be admitted. Not more than one professor could be selected from any one religious denomination. Although these latter provisions were soon abandoned, the basic form of governance by a board of curators remains in force, and the legislature continues to

The site selected for the university included the land on which Columbia College, founded in 1834, already stood. The university's first classes were conducted in the Columbia College building.

Eli E. Bass, pioneer member of a prominent Boone County family, served as curator on a number of occasions during the 1840s and 1850s and exerted a moderating influence during periods of factional and political strife.

Dr. A. W. Rollins, also a member of the first board of curators. Although somewhat overshadowed by his famous son, James S. Rollins, he was devoted to the university and served it well. When he died in 1845, he left $10,000 to aid in the education of needy students from Boone County. The fund grew and today remains an important source of student aid.

Reverend Thomas S. Allen, a prominent member of the Disciples of Christ Church, was the first president of the board of curators.

appropriate interest from the seminary fund for the benefit of the
university.

Each of the designated counties except Cooper worked aggressively to secure the university. Boone County's bid, $82,300 in cash
plus land valued at $36,000, was the highest, and Columbia, the coun-
ty seat, with a population of about 900, was awarded the prize. Pre-
dictably, the outcome brought hard feelings, and for many years the
university was handicapped by being thought of as a "Boone County
institution."

The first board of curators contained names still familiar in Missouri. Eli E. Bass, reputed to be the wealthiest man in Boone County,
served on the building committee; Irvine O. Hockaday, whose family
became related by marriage to the Rollins, represented Callaway
County; Dr. A. W. Rollins, father of James, was an important influence on the board; Thomas S. Allen of Boone County served as the
board's first president. Perhaps the most valuable of the early board
members was Warren Woodson of Columbia, the university's first
treasurer, who also served as president of the board.

The first board held its initial meeting 10 October 1839 on the site
selected for the university. Its two major tasks were to construct a
building and to hire a president. They were highly successful in both.

Early in 1840 the board approved plans for the construction of "a
magnificent edifice" at a cost not to exceed $75,000. The building,
designed by Stephen Hills, the architect of the state capitol, became at
the time of its completion the most impressive educational building in
the Mississippi Valley. The cornerstone was laid 4 July 1840, and fifty
years later T. J. Lowry, dean of engineering, recalled the day: "Exu-
berant with liberty, transported by the thought of planting the state
tree of higher education in Missouri, Boone County, Columbia, soil,
an immense concourse of reverent Missourians, with loving hands,
laid the (northeast) corner stone of the (original) main building of the
university with great pomp and ceremony."

With the building under construction, the board members turned
to the business of hiring a president. After some difficulty, they se-

Warren Woodson, the university's first
treasurer, also served for a term as
president of the board of curators. He
was a strong supporter of President
Lathrop and an equally strong oppo-
nent of President Shannon. In 1853 he
wrote to Shannon that if the curators
"had fully known your history, there
would have been no more probability
of your election to the Presidency than
of procuring ostrich feathers from the
back of a goat."

Academic Hall, the university's first
building (from a drawing of 1843).

John Hiram Lathrop, first president of
the university, resigned in 1849 to
become the first chancellor of the University of Wisconsin. In 1860 he was
appointed president of Indiana University, returning to Missouri in 1862
as a professor of English. He became
chair of the faculty and was appointed
president in 1865, serving until his
death in 1866. During his second term
as president he presided over the re-
opening of the university after the
Civil War.

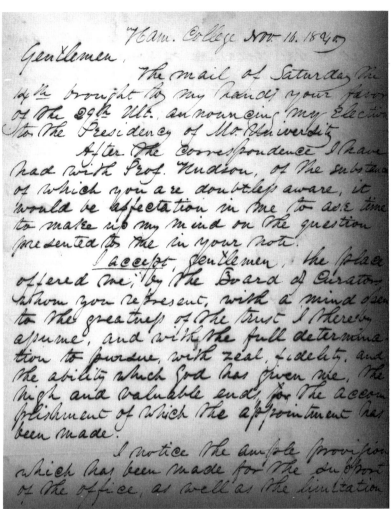

John H. Lathrop accepts the presidency of the University of Missouri, 16
November 1840.

William W. Hudson, member of the
first faculty as a professor of mathematics and president of the university
from 1856 to his death in 1859.

lected John Hiram Lathrop, a graduate of Yale University, who was
serving as professor of law, civil polity, and political economy at Hamilton College in New York. Lathrop accepted immediately. The new
president arrived in January 1841, and in March issued a handbill
announcing that classes would begin on 14 April. Also in the spring
of 1841, the board of curators provided $4,500 from the building fund
to be used for the construction of a "family house" just east of the
university building for the use of the president. This house burned in
1865, and the present home was built on the same spot two years later.

Lathrop faced almost insurmountable problems as he worked to
establish a university in what was still a frontier state. The citizens
had little appreciation for or understanding of higher education and
the requirements of university life. The institution's financial condition remained desperate—the legislature failed to appropriate any
funds whatsoever, interest on the seminary fund was not always paid
on time, and the lands donated in lieu of cash failed to yield anything

approaching their appraised value. Lathrop and other members of the faculty frequently went without pay to keep the institution open.

On 4 July 1843, just three years after the cornerstone ceremony, the completed university building was dedicated with as much patriotic pomp as the town of Columbia could muster. A procession, headed by a band, was formed in the vicinity of the courthouse. When it reached the university building, the gallery of the chapel, reserved for ladies, was already filled. In an hour-long address, President Lathrop urged the importance of scholarship and devotion to teaching as the central criteria in the selection of faculty.

On 28 November 1843, the university held its first Commencement. Although it was scheduled to be held in the chapel of the new building, one of the graduates recalled fifty years later, "As the finances of the institution were not equal to the purchase of stoves to heat the Chapel, the Commencement exercises were held in the Christian Church." There were only two graduates, but there were ten speeches, and the ceremonies went on for about three hours. The two graduates were cousins, Robert L. Todd and Robert B. Todd.

The "Scheme of Exercises" for Commencement was an important feature of the first university catalog, issued in 1843. That catalog also contained the names of the students—numbering seventy-seven in all—and of the members of the faculty, consisting of four professors in addition to President Lathrop. Two members of that first faculty, William W. Hudson and Robert S. Thomas, had taught at Columbia College. Hudson, who was professor of mathematics and related subjects, became president of the university in 1856. Thomas, who was professor of languages, resigned in 1853 to become the first president of William Jewell College. George C. Pratt, who was assistant professor of languages, had been principal of Bonne Femme Academy

Robert S. Thomas, member of the first faculty as professor of languages. In 1853 he became the first president of William Jewell College.

Robert L. Todd, one of the first two graduates, served for twenty-five years as secretary to the board of curators.

Robert B. Todd, the other member of the first graduating class, became a judge of the Louisiana Supreme Court.

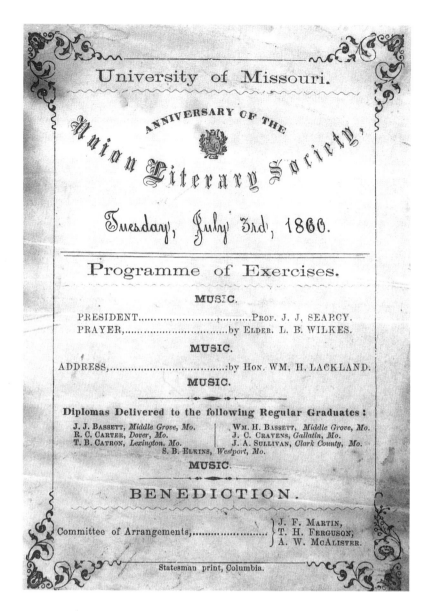

Statesman print, Columbia.

The programs of the literary societies—important events on the campus during the university's early years—consisted of declamations, essays, and formal debates on topics assigned in advance.

south of Columbia. Edward H. Leffingwell, who had been a student at Yale during Lathrop's years, became professor of chemistry, mineralogy, and geology and later taught in the Medical School.

Two literary societies, the Union Literary Society and the Athenaean Society, were organized in 1842 and were extremely important to the early intellectual life of the university. Their organization had been encouraged by President Lathrop, who had observed the importance of literary societies in the student life of eastern universities. Both societies were secret organizations, but they frequently admitted the public to their meetings. The societies had their own meeting rooms and libraries, and they provided students in these early years with valuable reading materials as well as with experience in parliamentary procedure, composition, and public speaking. Late in life, Stephen B. King, who graduated in 1856, reminisced about the role of the two societies:

Judging from the first reception I had at the University Town one would conclude that debating societies were the leading industries of the school for I had no more than alighted at the hotel from the Stage that conveyed me from home, when I was besieged by bevies of boosters boosting their society. The Athenean [*sic*] boosters finally bootlegged me into their society. The main difference of these societies was that the membership of the Athenean, as a rule, was composed of those who were under the lure of becoming politicians, while those of the Union Literary seemed to be under the lure of becoming preachers. The former as a rule were rather "High rollers" while the latter as a rule were rather sedate—the one having somewhat the spirit of, "on with the dance" while the others were led by the spirit of the Sunday School. In spite of the shortcomings of the society I joined, I, in after years, found great profit in what I acquired there, for it served me all my life in athletic exercises on fields of mental contests and reasoning together.

The Society of Alumni was thought of as a third literary society. The society was organized on 3 July 1852, and the *Missouri Statesman* covered the event. Odon Guitar, who became prominent in state and local affairs, was elected president at the society's second meeting.

During the years before the Civil War, enrollments were small—the highest enrollment prior to 1865 was 181—and the university building easily accommodated the needs of the institution. During the 1850s, however, there were a number of additions to the campus. The president's house, which had been so poorly built as to be almost uninhabitable, was remodeled into a handsome, substantial building.

An interesting, and for the time unusual, addition was an observatory, the first built west of the Allegheny Mountains. President Hudson, who had a great interest in astronomical sciences, was largely responsible for the construction of the observatory, but the curators also were pleased with "this beautiful addition to our campus."

To accommodate the primary school, established in 1856, the curators constructed a frame building at the northwest corner of the cam-

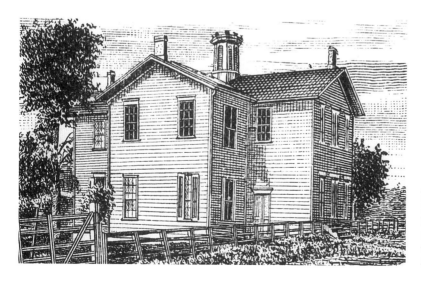

The Normal School, described by the *University Missourian* as "a pile of bad lumber [which] shivered itself into a severe looking building." At various times it housed the departments of art and English and the medical school.

The palatial home of William W. Hudson, south of Columbia. After Hudson's death, the home served as the residence of the dean of the College of Agriculture. At various times it and the adjoining cottages provided housing for women students.

pus. The normal school, as it came to be known, housed a number of departments over the years, including, after the Civil War, the first department of art, presided over by George Caleb Bingham, and, later, the Medical School. Also during the fifties, the grounds were fenced to keep out wandering livestock, young trees were planted, and a cinder walk was constructed from the main building to the north entrance of the campus.

But these years of some progress were also a time when the university found itself embroiled in partisan politics. The membership of the board of curators came to be dominated by the pro-slavery wing of the Democratic party, which also controlled the legislature. After eight difficult years, Lathrop resigned to become the first president of the University of Wisconsin. Virtually everyone associated with the university—aside from the ruling faction on the board, which was particularly suspicious of Lathrop's Yankee origins—was sorry to see him leave, and in 1862, after having moved from Wisconsin to become president of Indiana University, he returned to Missouri as professor of English.

In selecting a president to succeed Lathrop the board chose one of its own kind, James Shannon, a Disciples of Christ preacher who was serving as president of Bacon College in Kentucky. Shannon, an eloquent, articulate speaker learned in both Latin and Greek, was really more interested in preaching and politics than in performing the duties of the presidency. He traveled extensively, recruiting students, speaking at political meetings, and preaching in Christian churches. He lectured frequently on the Bible justification of slavery, and at one time participated in a student meeting to encourage volunteers for the invasion of Kansas!

James Shannon, president of the university from 1850 to 1856, was also a Disciples of Christ preacher. He was an eloquent orator who spoke extensively throughout the state. Strongly pro-slavery in opinion, he involved the university in bitter political controversies.

When Shannon resigned in 1856 to devote all his time to preaching, he was succeeded by William W. Hudson, a faculty member since the university was established. Hudson was a wealthy slaveholder, but he was moderate in his views and not inclined to engage in either political or religious controversy. Unfortunately, poor health caused him to limit his activities, and on 14 June 1859 he died.

Hudson's death precipitated what was perhaps the greatest crisis the university had faced. The board offered the presidency to Alfred

Taylor Bledsoe of Virginia, but after deliberating the matter for several weeks he declined. Meanwhile, the faculty submitted a plan to the curators that would organize the university into departments, with the professor in charge reporting directly to the board. Rather than having a president the university would be administered by a rotating chair of the faculty. The legislature responded to the highly controversial plan by dismissing both the board and the faculty.

The new board, mercifully free of the partisanship that had characterized its predecessors for more than a decade, elected a new faculty—only George H. Matthews, professor of ancient languages, was reelected—and began the search for a president. The search culminated in the election of Benjamin B. Minor, a Richmond, Virginia, lawyer who had been editor and publisher of the *Southern Literary Messenger.*

Minor had little opportunity to make much of an impact on the university because in March 1862 the board, faced with a financial crisis and the ravages of the Civil War, suspended operations. Federal troops occupied the main building, officers used the president's house, and the normal school became a hospital. The campus enclosure was used for the stabling of horses. The university was reopened in the fall of 1862, but the troops stayed on for several months—indeed, until the end of the Civil War the university was open but hardly functioned as an educational institution.

The board took the position that members of the faculty were terminated with the suspension of operations unless specifically reelected, and they refused to reelect Minor, who, though he was very moderate in his views and had taken the oath of allegiance, was looked on with suspicion because he was a Virginian. Instead, they turned to Lathrop, who had returned to Missouri in 1862 as professor of English, making him chair of the faculty. At their June meeting in 1865, the curators changed Lathrop's title to president. He served in this capacity for little more than a year. In the summer of 1866 he was stricken with typhoid fever and died on 2 August.

Colonel William F. Switzler, editor and publisher of the *Missouri Statesman,* an early Columbia newspaper, and a close observer of university affairs, wrote, "Patiently, courageously, and successfully, and with the wisdom of a great scholar and the self-sacrifice of a Christian gentleman President Lathrop quickened into life in a pioneer population a desire for higher learning and greater culture, and laid the foundations of the great university super-structure which is now the pride and boast of the State."

Lathrop's second career at the university was devoted to trying to save the institution from the ravages of war. He did keep it open, although only about fifty students were enrolled at any one time. By his last year, though, there was definite improvement in the instructional program, and, with the war over, there was some hope for continued progress.

The university's future, however, was far from secure. The legislature had never made an appropriation for its support; in 1865 the president's house had been destroyed by fire; the main building was

William F. Switzler, editor and publisher of the *Missouri Statesman,* was a lifelong, if at times somewhat critical, supporter of the university. He served for a number of years on the board of curators. Switzler Hall is named in his honor.

The Columbia residence of Colonel and Mrs. William F. Switzler.

Daniel Read, president of the university from 1866 to 1876. Read actually performed the duties of the presidency for several months before formally accepting the position. He wanted certain commitments from the board and the legislature before formally accepting. Read's administration brought substantial expansion, and the admission of women for the first time.

in need of extensive repairs. Moreover, there was strong hostility to Columbia in the legislature because of its presumed "disloyalty" during the Civil War. The university's prospects were so uncertain that when Daniel Read of the University of Wisconsin was elected president he announced that he would accept only if the legislature indicated support for the institution. Under the leadership of Rollins—who was now serving as member of the legislature and as president of the board of curators—the session of 1867 appropriated funds for rebuilding the president's house, repairing the main building, and establishing a normal school; the legislators also agreed to a regular annual allotment for the university from the general funds of the state. With these assurances, Read accepted the presidency and was inaugurated at the 1867 June Commencement.

Thus began a decade of expansion under an able and forceful leader. Most of the members of the faculty who participated in the expansion were brought in by Read, but among those who were at the university when he arrived were George Matthews; Joseph Ficklin, professor of mathematics, and later of astronomy; Joseph G. Norwood, formerly state geologist of Illinois, who was appointed as professor of natural philosophy and natural science and who later became the first dean of the Medical School; and Oren Root, brother of Elihu Root and

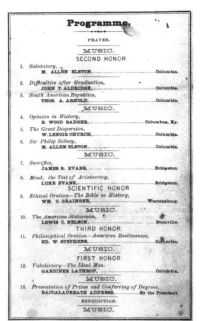

The cover and contents of an early Commencement program. Graduation Day was the highlight of the year. The ceremonies were long and elaborate.

a graduate of Hamilton College, Lathrop's school, who served for a short time as professor of English.

Two of Read's important appointees were Dr. Paul Schweitzer and James K. Hosmer. Schweitzer was the first member of the faculty to devote himself solely to the teaching of chemistry, and for thirty years he set high standards in his dedication to research, teaching, and sound scholarship. Hosmer, after two successful years at Missouri, left for Washington University in St. Louis, where he developed a national reputation for his writings on the Civil War and on Mississippi Valley history.

Carrying out one of their promises to Read, the curators in September created a normal school. E. L. Ripley of the Michigan State Normal School was selected as head of the new school. The *Missouri Statesman* described the "model school," established to provide practical experience, in glowing terms as "an essential element of success in the Normal College, [which] occupies a prominent and important position in the great educational programme upon which our University has entered . . . . A model in study, progress, efficiency, discipline, and facilities of instruction, worthy of the imitation of all the common schools in the county and State." The model school was a revolutionary trend in education.

The normal school provided Read with an opportunity to advance one of his leading interests—the education of women. He argued, "Women are better teachers of children than men. It is their mission— their God-appointed work." Women were admitted to the normal school from its beginning, and in 1870 Mary Louise Gillette became the first graduate.

Women were not permitted in other areas of the campus, however, and could use the library only during periods that were especially set aside for them. In 1870 they were allowed to attend chapel. Sarah

Eliza Gentry, an 1871 graduate of the normal school. Thirteen members of the Gentry family had graduated from the university by 1906.

Gentry Elston, one of twenty-two young ladies admitted in 1868, later described that experience:

> We were formed into a line at the Normal Building, with Professor Ripley at the head and Mrs. Ripley forming the rear guard, we . . . passed under the great columns and into the august building, not to be seated, however, on the same floor as the men, but given a place in the gallery above.

Gradually, women were permitted to enroll in courses outside the normal school. In the university catalog for 1873, President Read pronounced the admission of women a success:

> Finding . . . that the young women at "the Normal" did no manner of harm, we very cautiously admitted them to some of the recitations and lectures in the University building itself, providing always that they were to be marched in good order, with at least two teachers, one in front and the other in the rear of the column, as guards. . . .
> By degrees, and carefully feeling our way, as though explosive material was all around us, we have come to admit them to all the classes in all the departments, just as young men are admitted.

Another of Read's goals was to establish a School of Agriculture. While farmers for years had been asking for specialized scientific training, the political problems concerning the location of the college were enormous. After the passage of the Morrill Act in 1862, enemies of Columbia saw an opportunity to move the university out of that community; every politician seemed to want the College of Agriculture for his district. Finally, during the session of 1870, Rollins worked out a compromise that resulted in the location of the College of Agriculture in Columbia as a part of the university, and the establishment of a School of Mines in Rolla—a unique "Missouri Compromise" in the implementing of the Morrill Act.

To meet the growing demand for instruction in science, and particularly in agriculture, the curators used what remained of the Boone County funds supplemented by an appropriation from the legislature

Sarah Gentry, who graduated from the normal school in 1872.

The president's house, Academic Hall, the observatory, and the Scientific Building as they appear in an 1874 engraving.

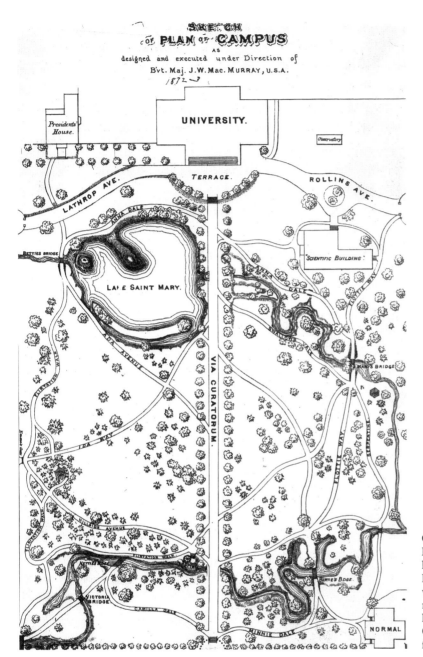

Campus plan, 1872. "Lake Saint Mary," in front of the president's house and named in honor of Mary Read, daughter of President Read, was a favorite resort for students—note "Flirtation Walk" leading to the lake. With the development of the Quadrangle in the 1890s the lake was filled in.

to construct a science building. Coincident with the construction of the Scientific Building, substantial improvements were made to the campus itself, including rustic bridges and paths leading to the north end of campus.

The deans of the College of Agriculture have always played important roles in the university and the state—and the early ones clearly established the prominence of the position. To organize the college, the curators chose George C. Swallow. Swallow was nothing if not controversial. Although he was popular with the students and some of the farmers of the state, he did not get along well with many of his colleagues and with a significant portion of the state's agricultural leadership. Above all, he was consistently at odds with Read's suc-

STATE UNIVERSITY, Columbia, Mo.

The campus of 1875 included, in addition to Academic Hall, the president's house, the observatory, the Scientific Building, and the normal school. Chalybeate Spring, with its pagoda, was a favorite student meeting place. The lake near the president's house was used for boating and ice skating.

cessor, President Samuel Spahr Laws—never one to shrink from controversy—and in 1882 Laws told the board that either he or the dean of agriculture would have to resign. Swallow refused to resign, and the board, sticking with the president, declared the deanship vacant. Although the College of Agriculture failed to live up to the rosy expectations Swallow had painted for it, the fact that it was kept going at all during a period of woefully inadequate support is something of a tribute to Swallow's abilities. His service to the university was recognized in 1930 when the building that housed the museum was named for him.

To succeed Swallow, the curators appointed Dr. J. W. Sanborn of the New Hampshire College of Agriculture. Sanborn was nationally recognized for his research and brought considerable attention to the university. Sanborn, like Swallow, was controversial, and the controversy also involved President Laws. This time, however, the president and the dean of agriculture were on the same side of the issue; indeed, Laws's stubborn—and unsuccessful—defense of Sanborn against criticism from the legislature and the board of his administration of the College of Agriculture was a factor in his own resignation.

In an effort to increase the professional offerings of the university,

As had been true in the case of Swallow, the board in later years honored Sanborn in the naming of a university facility, the experimental field he had established in 1888. It exists today in the center of the campus as one of the oldest experimental fields in the country and is noted nationally as containing the plot from which aureomycin was produced. This photograph, taken in 1926, shows F. B. Mumford, Sanborn, and M. F. Miller.

The bell tower of Switzler Hall, completed in 1872 and still standing, second only to the chancellor's residence as the oldest building on the campus. When the board of curators declared that the newly installed bell should not be rung at night, the *University Missourian,* in reporting the action, concluded with, "We shall see."

President Read repeatedly urged the curators to establish a College of Law. In 1867 they announced their intention to do so, and on 9 October 1872, the School of Law was officially opened with Judge Philemon Bliss as its first dean. Judge Bliss, a former congressman from Ohio, served as dean until his death in 1889, greatly influencing the development of the law school. Another important force during the

Early "clinical training" in the medical school.

early years was Boyle Gordon, a prominent Columbia lawyer who served as a full-time professor from the founding of the law school until 1882.

The establishment of the law school completed Read's initial plan for the expansion of the university. Among physicians in Columbia, however, there was a strong interest in establishing a medical school. Prior to the Civil War the university had offered some medical instruction in St. Louis, but this had been abandoned. Everyone recognized that it would be difficult to operate a clinical program in a small town like Columbia, but the local physicians persisted and in 1873 the board of curators, although divided on the issue, established a School of Medicine.

Dr. Joseph G. Norwood, who had been professor of natural science since 1860, was appointed dean, and the school announced that the degree of Doctor of Medicine would be conferred "whenever the student is found worthy to receive it." Dr. Andrew W. McAlester, a leading member of the Boone County Medical Society, was appointed to the first faculty, as was another Columbia physician, Dr. Thomas A. Arnold.

The campus in winter.

Unlike the law school, which was generally popular, the medical
school was buffeted by controversy. Had it not been for McAlester,
the school might not have survived. He provided the clinic and de-
fended the school against false accusations. Friends of the College of
Agriculture, for example, charged that money appropriated for agricultural instruction was used to support the travel of medical school
faculty in Europe!

From the beginning, there seems to have been pride in the university's library. As early as 1858, the student publication *The Collegian*
reported holdings of about 2,500 books. Adding the 1,500 volumes of
the two literary societies, 4,000 volumes were available to students
and faculty. It is not clear where the books were stored, or where the
students used them, but by 1870, with the library having grown to
10,000 volumes, the university catalog announced plans for "the Forum for the Library and reading room. This room is over seventy feet
in its greatest length, has lofty ceilings, is well lighted, and is admira-
bly adapted to the intended purpose."

The establishment of courses in military science, as required by
the Morrill Act of 1862, provided an important addition to student life.
All students were required to take the basic course in military tactics.
General R. W. Johnson, the first officer assigned to the university by
the Army, was highly qualified but left after only a year, and for almost a decade the university was unable to secure the services of a
really satisfactory officer to head its military program. In 1879, however, Lt. Francis Preston Blair, of St. Louis, son of the noted Missouri
General Francis Preston Blair, was appointed. He reorganized the
military department, and in addition to courses in military tactics he

Lieutenant Francis Preston Blair, son
of the noted Civil War general and
postwar political leader, served as professor of military science from 1879 to
1881, when he resigned to practice law
in St. Louis.

Lt. Enoch H. Crowder. In addition to his distinguished military career, Crowder served as an associate justice of the supreme court of the Philippines and as the first American ambassador to Cuba. The ROTC building is named for him.

Coed drill company, 1880.

Officers of the cadet corps, in an "informal" pose, 1893.

taught descriptive geometry and completed work for a degree in law. In 1881, he resigned from the army to practice law in St. Louis. He was succeeded by another Missourian, Lt. John J. Haden, whose service also gave great satisfaction, and who assisted Professor Schweitzer in the chemistry department.

A new era dawned with the appointment, in 1885, of another Missourian, Lt. Enoch H. Crowder, to head the military department. Lieutenant Crowder, who was to have a distinguished career in the army, invigorated and popularized military training at the university. Under his direction the first military band was formed, with the state furnishing instruments, sheet music, and uniforms. Enrollments increased, and the women students petitioned for and were granted the privilege of forming a separate company that "drilled with light gear and without corsets."

Military training for both men and women was just one—and perhaps a minor—aspect of the developing student life that characterized the university in the years following the Civil War. In the postwar

Members of the agricultural boarding club pose with their cook, ca. 1883.

The first dormitory, called the University Club-House, completed in 1890.

years, living units and purely social organizations became increasingly important.

Prior to the war, students who were not residents of Columbia boarded with townspeople. This worked well, because enrollments remained small—as late as 1868, the graduating class consisted of only six young men. In that year, however, the university announced the construction of three cottages to serve as boarding clubs for men. These cottages, built just east of Hitt Street near the southeast corner of the campus, housed nineteen students. By the middle seventies, two clubs, each accommodating forty students, were located in clusters of small buildings about a third of a mile apart.

Actually, the university was slow to provide housing for students, partly because of fiscal restraints and partly because President Laws felt that students were better off living with "refined families" than with other students. It was not until 1890 that the first dormitory was built, a handsome three-story brick structure that, according to the catalog, could house "twenty-five or thirty lodgers." The dining room

The insignia of Phi Delta Theta, 1891.

Charter members of Theta Chapter, Kappa Kappa Gamma, 1875, the first sorority established on the campus. Members pictured here are, clockwise from top left, Miss L. Johnson, Miss Ina Aldrich, Miss E. Dimmitt, Miss L. Peters, Miss N. E. Goula, and Miss M. B. Harbison.

could accommodate sixty.

These facilities were for men only. Although a few women found board and room in the former home of President Hudson, which served primarily as the residence of the Dean of Agriculture, and in two small cottages that surrounded it, throughout the nineteenth century women were required to find accommodations with townspeople. Indeed, as late as 1898, President Richard H. Jesse commented ruefully, "I desire to express regret that there is no club-house for women. By the aid of the club-house, the sons of Missouri may get most comfortable board, with heat and light, for a maximum cost of $2 a week, while their sisters pay for the same in private families $4 a week. In this matter, the state is permitting women to be discriminated against, and is making the attainment of an education more difficult for them than for the young men."

Along with the boarding clubs, Greek letter organizations came to the campus. The Phi Kappa Psi fraternity was established in 1869, followed by Phi Delta Theta in 1870. The Kappa Kappa Gamma sorority was established in 1875. Despite considerable faculty and administrative opposition—President Laws was particularly hostile to "secret societies"—the Greek letter organizations flourished, particularly among the more affluent students. Their members dressed with style and took the lead in campus activities. At first—and this is strange, considering official attitudes—the organizations were given rooms in Academic Hall for their meetings, but by the turn of the century they had established their own houses.

Not all students, or even a majority, were affluent, and almost from the beginning there was the realization that many young people needed financial help to attend the university. The boarding clubs were organized in part to reduce costs, and various kinds of student aid funds were established. Dr. A. W. Rollins had provided for a student aid fund in his will. In 1867 the board established the curators scholarships, to be presented in each county to some "worthy young man." The curators scholarships continue to the present time, without, of course, the discriminatory clause.

A popular former student, Eugene Field, and his brother, R. M.

The men of Zeta Phi (now Beta Theta Phi), 1887-1888. Enoch Crowder, third from left, back row, is flanked by Edward Rollins and Curtis Rollins. Everett Bass is second from left, second row.

Members of the faculty, 1873, together with the presidents of Columbia College and Stephens College.

Field, established a scholarship fund for the best students in "declamations," American constitutional history, and law. Eugene Field is remembered as the first editor of the *University Missourian,* whose editorial policy was then, as it is now, defiantly independent of university officialdom.

As was true of an unfortunately high percentage of the early presidents of the university, Daniel Read's tenure was terminated in part for political reasons. Read's strong pro-Union views had appealed to many legislators at the time he was appointed, but by the mid-seventies, conservative Democrats, many of whom had had pro-slavery leanings, had gained control of the legislature. They were unhappy with Read and made it clear to the curators that he would have to go. Moreover, many felt that Read was getting too old for the job—he would be seventy-one by the time his term ended, the oldest person ever to serve as president of the university. Despite his record of achievement, therefore, the board decided that he would be replaced at the end of his term.

To succeed Read, the board chose Samuel Spahr Laws, a man who was almost the complete opposite. Where Read was easy-going, Laws

In many respects Eugene Field was the quintessential student. He was in school only from 1870 to 1872, but he became well known as a fun-loving prankster. He began to write poetry while still a student.

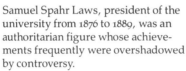

Samuel Spahr Laws, president of the          Mrs. Samuel Spahr Laws.
university from 1876 to 1889, was an
authoritarian figure whose achievements frequently were overshadowed
by controversy.

was autocratic. Where Read had been pro-Union, Laws was pro-
Southern and, indeed, had been arrested for disloyalty during the
Civil War, being briefly imprisoned in St. Louis and released on the
condition that he would leave the country. Laws was serving as the
first president of Westminster College in Fulton when he was arrested. After spending the war in Europe he returned to New York,
where he invented the stock ticker and became vice president of the
New York Stock Exchange.

Laws was controversial from the beginning. Several important faculty members resigned or were dismissed. In addition to Swallow,
Dean E. L. Ripley of the normal school resigned when Laws abolished
the preparatory department and the model school. Indeed, Laws had
strong views on the education of teachers and carried on a running
battle with the State Superintendent of Public Instruction. He also
engaged in a public controversy with Dean Bliss of the law school on
the nature of sovereignty in a democratic society. The students dis-
liked him because of his hostility toward fraternities, sororities, and
boarding clubs, and for his efforts to regulate virtually all aspects of
student life, including the attire of women students, whom he believed did not belong at the university anyway.

Despite the controversy surrounding the president—and in some
instances because of it—the university made significant progress during the Laws administration. Enrollments increased steadily, reaching
a high of 580 in 1889. The School of Engineering was established in
1877, due largely to the work of Thomas Jefferson Lowry, a graduate of
the university who had served in the United States Coast Survey and
who served as dean of the school until his retirement in 1893. He did
much to build interest in engineering at the university and throughout the state.

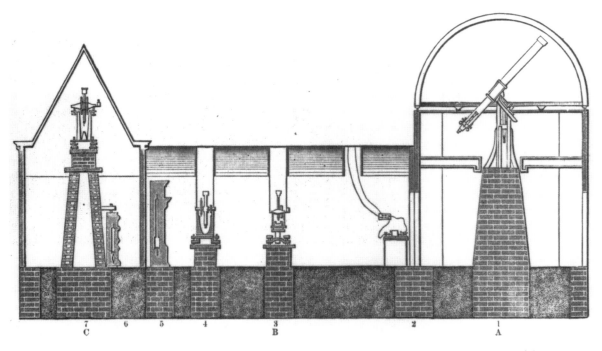

The university catalog for 1857 introduced the observatory with a cross-section drawing and a description of the instruments mounted in it: "The Observatory stands west of the University edifice. It is forty-four feet long, fourteen feet wide, fourteen feet high in the equational room, and ten feet high in the transit room."

President Laws was much interested in the observatory. He paid for a new telescope with his own funds and also paid for the construction of a new building to house it. The new telescope was mounted 13 March 1880, and the new building was named the Laws Observatory.

The University Building (Academic Hall), 1885, with the wings added during the Laws administration.

Laws's interest in science resulted in the acquisition of a fine new telescope and a reconstructed, relocated observatory. Laws paid for the telescope with his own funds and also paid for the construction of a new building on the northeast corner of the campus to house it. The new telescope was mounted on 13 March 1880, and the new building was named the Laws Observatory.

Perhaps Laws's most important achievement was securing an appropriation from the legislature to enlarge Academic Hall. It and the Scientific Building had been built with funds from Boone County, but that money had run out and it was clear that if the university were to expand the state would have to provide money for the necessary buildings. Laws worked hard to convince the legislature of the need and finally was successful. He was so excited when a messenger brought the news to him that he called to his wife, "Anna, hand that boy a quarter."

The new wings, completed in 1885, were sources of great pride. The size of the building was more than doubled. The west wing was devoted to the natural history museum and to the departments of law, modern languages, and physics. In the east wing, the first floor was occupied by the chapel and the second floor by the library. The construction of the chapel was "similar to that of the most handsome opera houses and auditoriums. . . . This is the only room in which there is any attempt at ornamentation, and here, indeed, it is pardonable and proper."

One of Laws's opportunistic efforts that did not turn out well concerned the carcass of the great elephant "Emperor." This elephant, belonging to a traveling circus and believed to be second in size only to "Jumbo," died while the circus was in Liberty. Laws, seeing an opportunity to secure a spectacular specimen for the university museum, got possession of the carcass and had it sent to a taxidermist in Rochester, New York, for mounting. When the curators reimbursed Laws for the cost, after the legislature had specifically refused to appropriate money for the purpose, there was a great uproar in Jefferson City and around the state. As has been pointed out, Laws was in

University cadets in front of Academic Hall, late 1880s.

The class of 1883, consisting of twenty-seven young men and women, affect an air of informality for the photographer.

deep trouble because of his defense of Sanborn and the College of Agriculture, but as he later wrote to the *Kansas City Star*, "This elephant business had something to do in creating the disgust that caused me to resign."

The curators took almost two years to find a new president. In the meantime, A. F. Fleet, professor of Greek and "Acting Senior Professor," and later M. M. Fisher of the Latin department administered the university.

Laws's resignation under fire fifty years from the date the university was founded brought to an end a turbulent half century characterized by a bitter Civil War that closed the institution and by periodic

The faculty sat for an informal photograph in 1890—a distinguished, contented-looking group. The "chaperone of women students" was in the picture, but appropriately for the time she was seated off at one side.

political controversies that threatened to destroy it. Yet the university had progressed from a situation in which its future seemed constantly threatened, in which the state recognized no financial responsibility, to one in which the legislature was appropriating funds regularly for operating expenses and occasionally for construction projects. Its enrollment numbered more than five hundred students from all over the state, and its future seemed secure.

# 2 AN EMERGING
# PUBLIC UNIVERSITY

After a leisurely search, the board of curators selected Richard Henry Jesse, professor of Latin at Tulane, as the university's seventh president. He was only thirty-eight at the time of his appointment—younger than any of his predecessors. His inaugural, held during Commencement week in 1891, was an auspicious occasion, marking what everyone seemed to sense was a new era for the university. Governor David R. Francis spoke, as did Gideon Rothwell, president of the board of curators, and Curtis B. Rollins, president of the Alumni Association. The new president's address was felicitous and well received.

"It is with a deep sense of responsibility," Jesse began, "that I assume the office of president of the University of Missouri. The institution seems about to enter into stronger life and wider usefulness. The pride of the people has been touched; their enthusiasm has been kindled; and the liberality of the 36th General Assembly demonstrates a widespread demand for progress in higher education. My administration seems to begin with greater opportunities; and, therefore, with graver responsibilities." The young president was unaware how those "graver responsibilities" would age him during the seventeen years of his administration—and the process began within six months of his inauguration.

On the evening of 9 January 1892, as the Athenaean Society was preparing for a program in the chapel, the central chandelier suddenly crashed to the floor, amid the assembling audience. Academic Hall began to burn. There was no hope of saving the great building—Columbia's primitive water supply was wholly inadequate—but students, faculty, and townspeople worked valiantly to save books, furniture, paintings, and museum pieces—even the notorious elephant was dragged to safety. Much was lost, however, including the Bingham portraits of James S. Rollins and Governor Francis. Left standing were the six Ionic columns that remain today as an eloquent monument to the university's beginnings.

President Jesse sent an immediate message to parents, patrons, and friends of the university: "The main building of the University of the State of Missouri was totally destroyed by fire on Saturday evening, 9 January, but the University itself—its learning, its skill, its zeal, its enthusiasm—remains untouched, and its work will go on without interruption." And, indeed, classes resumed without interruption, in buildings all over town.

The board went to work immediately on plans to rebuild and to enlarge the institution. Four days after the fire, Dr. C. M. Woodward, a board member and director of the "manual training school" at Washington University, sent Gideon Rothwell a letter and diagram detailing specific plans and suggestions for the university.

Richard Henry Jesse, president of the university from 1891 to 1908, a period of time characterized both by growth and by an improvement in quality.

Mrs. Richard Henry Jesse. Despite the burden of caring for six young children, Addie Jesse entertained frequently in the president's house, particularly students.

About the destruction of Academic
Hall George Wauchope, professor of
English, wrote, "That great, roaring
palate of fire with its red-litten win-
dows, its flame-wrapped cornices, its
fire-crowned dome, standing out
against the black shadows of the
night, and the white waste of snow,
formed a picture which can never be
forgotten."

The Columns, shortly after the fire.

The campus before the rebuilding of Academic Hall. The buildings are, from left to right, the law school; the chemical laboratory; the president's house; the museum, biology, and geology building; the Agricultural College; the physics and engineering building; the Manual Training School; and the Power House.

The law building, completed in 1893 as one of the new buildings constructed after the fire. Known affectionately as the "Law Barn" the building contained a large library room, two classrooms, moot court and club rooms, quiz rooms, and offices for the dean and faculty. The building now houses the sociology department.

Governor Francis, a strong supporter of the university, called the legislature into special session, and, after a short delay caused by enemies of Columbia attempting to use the fire as an excuse to move the institution, that body appropriated $250,000 to rebuild the university—but only after Columbia put $50,000 into the building fund and filed a bond to guarantee the construction of an adequate water supply.

By fall construction was underway, and within a year six new buildings were in place—at a total cost of $204,651. The first to be completed was the Manual Training Building. The Law Building—soon to be known affectionately as the "Law Barn"—was completed early in 1893

The laboratory for chemistry and physics, ca. 1902.

The auditorium or chapel in the new Academic Hall, later renamed Jesse Hall. This was replaced by the present Jesse Hall Auditorium in the 1950s.

The library in Academic Hall apparently was a popular place at the turn of the century.

Students in agriculture dressed carefully, even for work in the greenhouse.

A summer school class in agriculture, 1903.

near the northeast corner of the campus, and the others—a chemistry laboratory; a biology, geology, and museum building; a physics and engineering building; and a power plant—were ready for use by the fall semester 1893.

Rebuilding Academic Hall required an additional appropriation of $250,000, but that was forthcoming, and on Commencement Day 1895, Woodward, who was now president of the board, officially accepted the new buildings on the quadrangle, later to be named in honor of Governor David R. Francis. The new academic building (later named Jesse Hall) was situated at the end of the quadrangle and, together with the columns, became its dominant feature. Like

From the early years of the College of Agriculture, the "short course" provided an opportunity for farmers to receive training in specific subjects, as they are doing here in livestock judging, with Missouri mules as the laboratory materials.

John Connaway's research at the agricultural experiment station led to the eradication of the cattle tick, carrier of the dread Texas fever. He also played an important part in the effort to control hog cholera.

Academic Hall, the chapel occupied the building's east end, and the library was situated in the west end.

As the university developed its campus during the 1890s, it also developed organizationally. To accommodate the demand particularly from public school teachers, summer schools were organized in science, language, and mathematics. The legislature provided funds in 1895, and in 1898 the various summer schools were combined and announced as "The Missouri University Summer School."

Early on, the university began to offer courses through extension. Courses for teachers were taught, and the faculty of the College of Agriculture took part in fifty farmers' institutes in various parts of the state. By 1908 courses were being offered in Carthage, Joplin, Kansas City, Mexico, Nevada, St. Joseph, St. Louis, and Webb City. In 1910 the University Extension Division was created, the institution's tenth. In 1913 funds were appropriated for extension, and with the appointment of Charles H. Williams as director, the division grew rapidly.

Of even greater importance was the development of graduate work, which evolved from vague arrangements for the awarding of master's degrees to specific requirements for the Ph.D. Graduate work was initially controlled by individual departments, but by 1910 the graduate school was organized. From the beginning, graduate work at Missouri received national recognition. The institution was admitted to the Federation of Graduate Clubs at its second meeting in 1896. In 1908, the university became the twenty-second member of the prestigious Association of American Universities, organized in 1900.

None of this would have been possible without the presence of a high-quality faculty, and one of Jesse's major accomplishments was recruiting a number of outstanding professors. John R. Connaway was appointed professor of veterinary science in 1888 but earned his

Isidor Loeb temporarily took charge of the history department when political economy was separated from history. He served at various times as acting dean of the schools of commerce and education, as dean of faculties, and as acting president.

During the years he served the philosophy department before he left for Princeton, Frank Thilly was a leader among a group of young Ph.D.s who were building the university's reputation for scholarship. Among his other achievements was the establishment of the *University of Missouri Studies.*

John Pickard, a native of New England with a Ph.D. from Munich, laid the groundwork for a distinguished program in art and art history. When the old chemistry building was restored and remodeled as a museum it was appropriately named Pickard Hall.

reputation during Jesse's tenure. George A. Wauchope joined the English faculty in 1891 and is remembered for the words of the first university song, "Old Missouri, Fair Missouri." His tenure was brief, and he was replaced by Henry M. Belden of Johns Hopkins, who devoted his career to the university and was widely known for his writings on the literature of the frontier. Another long-time member of the department, and one who was particularly active in campus affairs, was Edward A. Allen, who came to the university from Central College in Fayette. Arthur H. R. Fairchild, of Yale University, added to the English department in 1904, became one of the country's leading Shakespearean scholars.

Frederick C. Hicks from the University of Michigan was appointed chair of the new Department of History and Political Economy in 1891. His classes were so popular that almost immediately an assistant was appointed. The assistant, Isidor Loeb, joined the faculty as professor of history and served the university in many capacities during his career. Norman Trenholme of Harvard became chair of the history department in 1902, and Jonas Viles also of Harvard was appointed as instructor. Both men devoted their careers to Missouri.

In 1892, a separate Department of Philosophy was established, and Frank Thilly from Cornell University was appointed as its first professor. John Pickard, appointed professor of Greek in 1892, later became chair of the newly formed Department of Classical Archaeology and the History of Art. George Lefevre, a young Ph.D. from Johns Hopkins, became professor of zoology in 1899, serving as chair of the Department of Zoology until his death in 1923. Curtis Fletcher Marbut, an instructor in the Department of Geology and Mineralogy, became its chair in 1895.

George Lefevre, a brilliant teacher and respected scholar, was held in high regard by both students and colleagues. He served on many important committees and was editor of the *University of Missouri Studies.* He was largely responsible for planning and promoting the new biology building, and it was named for him after his death.

Curtis F. Marbut, who established the geology camp near Lander, Wyoming, is shown here with M. F. Miller east of Columbia, 1914.

F. B. Mumford teaching a class, ca. 1901. Mumford served as dean of the College of Agriculture from 1909 to 1938.

The sciences were further strengthened in 1901 when Frederick H. Seares of the University of California was appointed head of the Department of Astronomy. Astronomy had been taught in one form or another since the founding of the university, but Seares elevated it to an important scientific study. Harlow Shapley, who became director of the Harvard Observatory and later chancellor of Washington University, began his studies under Seares. In 1909 Seares left Missouri to work in the newly constructed Mount Wilson Solar Observatory in California.

In 1902 Herman Schlundt joined the Department of Chemistry. Schlundt spent his entire life at Missouri and came to be recognized as one of the university's great teachers. In addition, he was nationally known for his work in physical chemistry and as an authority on radioactivity. After his death in 1937 the then new chemistry building was named in his honor.

Perhaps nowhere did Jesse's appointments have a greater impact than in the College of Agriculture, where he added M. F. Miller, F. B. Mumford, Henry J. Waters, and J. C. Whitten. Waters, a native Missourian, became dean and served with great effectiveness until 1909 when he resigned to become president of Kansas State College of Agriculture. Mumford, from Michigan, taught animal husbandry until he succeeded Waters as dean in 1909. He served in that capacity until 1938, the longest tenure of any dean of agriculture, and it was under his leadership that the modern College of Agriculture took shape. Miller, after a long period as professor of soils and director of the Missouri Soil Survey, concluded his career by serving for seven years as dean, following Mumford's retirement. Whitten, professor of horticulture, had a profound impact on fruit growing in Missouri. Waters, Mumford, and Whitten all have buildings named for them, and at the turn of the century a delightful path across the quadrangle was known as Whitten's Walk.

Henry J. Waters, dean of the College of Agriculture from 1895 until 1909, when he resigned to become president of the Kansas State College of Agriculture.

Governor Alexander Dockery lays the cornerstone of Waters Hall, 1900.

John R. Scott's elocution class, ca. 1890. Public speaking became a part of the curriculum as interest in the literary societies declined, and as fraternities, sororities, and athletics began to absorb more student time. Note that part of Tennyson's "Charge of the Light Brigade" has been put on the blackboard.

During the nineties, recognizing the importance of public speaking in the curriculum, the university appointed John R. Scott to teach classes in oratory to supplement and later to replace the experience provided by the literary societies, where the practice of public speaking had been students' principal extracurricular interest. As fraternities and sororities began offering students less demanding and more accessible social activity, interest in the literary societies waned.

During the early years, student publications came and went. There was the short-lived *University Magazine* in 1848, and the *Collegian* in 1858. The *University Missourian*, started in 1871, continued until 1887, when students suspended it rather than submit to what the editors perceived as undue faculty censorship. The *Savitar* made its first appearance in 1895. Also published in the nineties were *The Index*, *The Tiger*, *The Argus*, and *The M.S.U. Independent*. In 1905 the students maintained and managed four periodicals, *The Independent* (weekly), the *Savitar* (annual), *The Missouri Agricultural College Farmer* (monthly), and *The Asterisk* (quarterly).

The young men who in 1904 formed the Asterisk Club of "original writers" constituted a rather remarkable group, and some members gained considerable fame in later years. Charles G. Ross, who for a time was a member of the faculty of the School of Journalism, served as press secretary for his boyhood friend from Independence, President Harry S. Truman. Herbert Carl Crow began his writing career on the *Columbia Missourian*. In 1911 he went to Shanghai to begin a long tradition of University of Missouri journalists in China—names such as J. B Powell and Edgar Snow—first as an editor of the *China Press* and later as the founder of the *Shanghai Evening Post*.

Perhaps the best known of the founding Asterisks was Homer Croy, who served as editor of the *Savitar* in 1906. After leaving the university he became a well-known novelist, frequently using Missouri themes, as in *West of the Water Tower*. The 1908 *Savitar* contained the work of a young artist, Thomas Hart Benton, that would make it a much-prized collector's item.

Military training continued to be an important feature of both the curriculum and the extracurricular activities. The cadet band provided music for its ceremonies and, in addition, gave regular concerts—it would be a while, though, before it evolved into "Marching Mizzou."

One of the more important developments in student life during Jesse's administration was the emergence of football as an absorbing passion. Intercollegiate athletics dated back to 1873, when a university team played baseball with Westminster College. The game created wide interest, and each spring thereafter the varsity baseball team challenged teams from nearby towns. Baseball, however, was soon surpassed by football.

Edgar Snow, a young journalism student, en route to China, 1928. He wrote on this snapshot, "Start of journey—I grew it [presumably a mustache] in 2 weeks—and cut it off at Honolulu in 2 seconds." Snow, through such books as *Red Star Over China* and many articles, became one of the world's leading authorities on the Communist Revolution in China.

A caricature of Homer Croy by Monte Crews, who became a well-known New York illustrator, published with a story Croy wrote for the *Savitar* in 1914. The caption for this drawing reads, "The only way that I could get a girl to talk to during the evening was to get her into a corner and pen her with my feet."

The 1908 *Savitar* contained a number of illustrations by a young Missouri artist named Thomas Hart Benton.

The cadet corps drawn up in formation alongside the columns, with a goodly number of spectators, ca. 1905. The president's house is in the background.

The varsity football team, 1891.

Intercollegiate football began at Missouri with a game against Washington University in St. Louis on Thanksgiving Day, 1890. Missouri lost 28 to 0, but that did not seem to dampen enthusiasm for the sport. The Football Association cleared one hundred dollars, and an old grad suggested that the team be called the "Tigers," a name that had been given to a Boone County vigilante committee during the Civil War. The curators set aside six acres of the college farm for a football field, named Rollins Field in recognition of the effort expended by the Rollins brothers in grading and improving it. In 1891 a regular schedule of football games was arranged with nearby colleges and universities, and interest in the game steadily increased.

Almost from the beginning the big game of the year was against Kansas. Traditionally it was played in Kansas City on Thanksgiving Day. As the *Missouri Alumni Quarterly* of September 1905 observed, "Socially the Missouri-Kansas game is the athletic event of the year here; financially it is the source of fifty per cent of the income of both

Members of the 1901 "MSU" women's basketball team pose for a group shot.

the athletic associations concerned."

As interest in athletics increased, so did support from the university. With the appointment of Clark W. Hetherington as director of the gymnasium, facilities expanded. The university catalog for 1907–1908 boasted of the gymnasiums, including Rothwell Gymnasium built in 1900, the golf links, also built in 1900, and a main athletic field—Rollins Field—with five playing fields, four outdoor basketball courts, four handball courts, and fourteen tennis courts plus the varsity field sporting two grandstands.

Hetherington had also taken the lead in organizing the Missouri Valley Conference. He resigned in 1910 and was succeeded by Chester L. Brewer from Michigan State University. Brewer, with an interruption from 1917 to 1923, served as director of athletics until 1935 and became a legendary figure at Missouri. His teams frequently won conference championships, and when in 1911 the conference ruled that all games had to be played on the campuses—moving the Kansas game out of Kansas City—he successfully developed the idea of "homecoming" to sell the game in Columbia. At first, homecoming was celebrated only on alternate Thanksgivings, when Kansas played in Columbia, but after World War I homecoming developed into an annual celebration of major significance with mass meetings, rallies, bonfires, parades, house decorations, and ultimately queens.

Henry Schulte coached both football and track during the years prior to the war and then went to the University of Nebraska to build an outstanding career as a track coach. Among the standout players during those years were Anton J. Stankowski, the diminutive quarterback from St. Joseph, who remained at the university as a coach and then as director of the intramural program; and Crosby Kemper, a "walk-on" who became a star and later achieved prominence as a leading Kansas City banker.

The university began the new century with its name officially established as the University of Missouri. It had been founded as the University of the State of Missouri, but this cumbersome name was seldom used. The institution was variously called Missouri State University, Missouri University, and the University of Missouri. President Laws for a time arbitrarily referred to it as the Missouri Agricultural College and University. While they were establishing the name once and for all, the curators also adopted a seal, and declared that the

Henry Schulte, who coached football and track before World War I, and Chester Brewer, legendary football coach and athletic director, flank R. C. Wilson, captain of the 1913–1914 football team.

The new century brought an expansion of academic traditions. As this photograph from 1906 shows, graduating seniors began to wear caps and gowns at Commencement.

Lathrop Hall as it looked in 1909. This dormitory, the second to be built for men, was completed in 1899.

founding date of the institution was 11 February 1839, the date on which the Geyer Act was passed.

By the turn of the century, enrollment had reached 1,050, with students coming from "42 states, territories and foreign countries." In 1906 a special convocation was held to celebrate the fact that the student body numbered two thousand. As enrollment grew, so did the need for student housing. In 1899 a second men's dormitory, Lathrop Hall, was added, and in 1903 the university finally provided a dormitory for women. This building, named in honor of Daniel Read,

A room in the men's dormitory at the turn of the century. The styles were different, but the clutter and the decorations seem timeless.

Women's gymnastics, with Schweitzer Hall in the background.

marked the expansion of the campus east of Hitt Street as well as a departure in architecture. Bedford limestone replaced brick in Read Hall and in a new horticulture building (later named Whitten Hall), thus giving rise to the "White Campus." Growth had impact on other areas as well.

Students generally and medical students in particular benefited greatly from Parker Memorial Hospital, built with $15,000 given by William L. Parker of Columbia and $10,000 appropriated by the state. The hospital opened in 1901, and it was soon followed by a new laboratory building for medical classes, named McAlester Hall in honor of the early dean of the medical school. A training school for nurses graduated its first class in 1904.

A cooking class in the "domestic economy" laboratory, 1908.

Students in the College of Agriculture strike a pose in front of the old Agricultural Hall, ca. 1900, possibly to promote the Farmers Fair. When a new building for the College of Agriculture was completed in 1909, the old building was named Switzler Hall and for a time was occupied by the School of Journalism.

Attendance by women increased notably in the College of Agriculture, where courses in home economics were offered. As the College of Agriculture expanded its program under the leadership of Dean Waters, it also boosted its reputation. James Wilson, Secretary of Agriculture, described Missouri's College of Agriculture as, "in some respects the best College of Agriculture in the United States."

With the growth in enrollment, student organizations proliferated. In 1904 students in the College of Agriculture organized the Ag Club, and a year later, to advertise the college, they staged the first Farmers Fair. Taken by surprise, President Jesse protested the students' arrival at chapel the morning of 7 April in farmers' attire, carrying pitchforks and hoe handles, but he later apologized when the event was explained to him. The morning parade through downtown Columbia and the burlesque county fair of the afternoon became an annual spring rite that continued until 1958. An Ag Club tradition that endures to the present time is the annual fall barnwarming, dating from 1906 when the main barn on the college farm was completed.

Another traditional celebration became Engineers Week in 1903 when students "discovered" that Saint Patrick was an engineer. The annual Saint Patrick's Day celebration was soon adopted by engineering students at other universities around the country.

In 1901 Missouri was granted a charter for the Alpha chapter of Phi Beta Kappa, and in 1905 received a charter for Sigma Xi, the honorary scientific fraternity. The select QEBH senior society, organized in 1897 and limited to ten men, was followed by the Mystical Seven in 1907. Literary clubs had grown from the original two in 1842 to seventeen by 1901, and the M.S.U. Debating Club was formed in 1895. The 1890 university catalog announced the organization of the Young Men's Christian Association with 150 members, and in 1907 the Young Women's Christian Association began to meet in Read Hall. In 1906 university women secured a chapter of the Association of Collegiate Alumni that in 1921 became the American Association of University Women. L.S.V., an organization for senior women, was formed to

An entry in the Farmers Fair parade, 1919.

Barnwarming was always a jolly occasion, but crowning the Harvest Queen at Barnwarming, 1916, seems to be mighty serious business.

Engineers Week is still grandly observed with ceremonies, lectures, and discussions, but these tend to get lost in the parades, the "kowtowing," shown here from observances of 1906, and the parties associated with the cult of Saint Patrick.

Dramatizing Missouri's contributions to the nation, the university in 1902 gave honorary degrees to five distinguished native sons: Secretary of the Interior Ethan Allen Hitchcock, Secretary of Agriculture James Wilson, Assistant Secretary of Agriculture Beverly T. Galloway, Robert Brookings, founder of the Brookings Institution, and Mark Twain. Twain spoke at a banquet given by Phi Beta Kappa, and, according to the *Columbia Herald*, "kept the audience in a constant roar of laughter, which reached at times the explosive stage."

New students arrive in Columbia, 1911.

recognize women's roles on campus.

Higher standards in all aspects of the university characterized Jesse's administration. In addition to enlarging the faculty and improving its quality, Jesse increased admissions standards and gave much attention to the development of graduate work. He also worked hard to develop local alumni associations throughout the state. Moreover, he was in great demand as a speaker and participated actively in both state and national organizations. He carried out his many responsibilities with virtually no help—during the early years of his administration he did not even have a secretary—with the result that his health, once robust, began to fail. Finally, in December 1907, on the advice of his physician, he submitted his resignation, to take effect the following summer.

The board lost little time in choosing a successor, selecting A. Ross Hill, who a few months earlier had left Missouri to become dean of the College of Arts and Science at Cornell University. Hill was a Canadian, born in Nova Scotia and educated in Canada, Europe, and the United States. He was professor of philosophy at the University of Nebraska when Jesse, in 1903, persuaded him to become head of the Normal Department. Later he served as the first dean of the Teachers College. He was thirty-seven at the time of his appointment—the youngest person ever to be appointed president of the university.

In June 1908 the *Missouri Alumni Quarterly* announced a development that would greatly enhance the university's reputation, the establishment of the School of Journalism. Classes began in September 1908 in rooms on the second floor of the academic hall, with seventy-two students. Walter Williams, editor of the *Columbia Herald* and a member of the board of curators, was appointed dean. Charles G. Ross, an alumnus of the university, came from the *St. Louis Republic* to teach and a few months later Frank L. Martin of the *Kansas City Star* joined the faculty.

Bowling at the YMCA, ca. 1912. By 1909 the YMCA had a fine building at Eighth and Elm streets that for several years served as the center of student life and activities.

A. Ross Hill, president of the university from 1908 to 1922. Prior to his appointment as president he had served as the first dean of the Teachers College. Appointed president at the age of thirty-seven, he was the youngest person ever to serve as president of the university.

Ice skaters, ca. 1905, on Hinkson Creek, a favorite spot in all seasons for generations of Missouri students.

A journalism class, 1913.

The initial issue of the re-established *University Missourian* came off the press the first day of classes. According to the lead editorial, the paper was to be "the laboratory, the clinic, the practice school of the Department of Journalism." Throughout its history, *The Missourian* has frequently been controversial, and from time to time the very existence of a newspaper published by a state institution has been questioned, but Williams established a separate corporation to publish the paper in order to fend off would-be attackers and at the same time give the publication freedom from university control.

In its second year, the School of Journalism held a week-long conference during which faculty and visiting journalists delivered public lectures. The conference became an annual event known as Journalism Week and developed considerable international importance. Beginning in 1930, Journalism Week was enhanced with the awarding of the Missouri Medal of Honor, soon to become one of journalism's most prestigious prizes.

Mary Paxton Keeley at the time of her graduation from the School of Journalism.

Among the early graduates of the School of Journalism was Mary Paxton Keeley, who received her degree in 1910, becoming the first woman graduate. Howard Lamade, a graduate of 1913, and his brother George, a graduate of 1916, became publishers of *Grit*, the weekly newspaper read by millions of rural Americans. Another 1913 graduate, Ward Neff, in 1918 donated funds for a journalism building.

The School of Education, which had been greatly expanded during Hill's deanship, continued to flourish under the leadership of W. W. Charters. Charters did a great deal to bring the school under the influence of John Dewey.

The School of Commerce, established in 1914, grew rapidly in enrollment and reputation. The Department of Economics, on which it

The campus from the north, ca. 1900. The pagoda in the lower left was over Chalybeate Spring, a romantic spot.

At Commencement 1929, the university dedicated two bronze reliefs at the north entrance to the campus, one in honor of James S. Rollins, generally referred to as "the father of the university," and the other in honor of John Hiram Lathrop, the first president. Here the Rollins and Lathrop families pose for the photographer, flanked on the left by President Stratton D. Brooks and on the right by John Pickard, professor of classical archaeology and the history of art.

was based, was one of the strongest in the country at the time. Herbert J. Davenport, who had joined the department from the University of Chicago in 1908, became the first dean; he was an effective administrator as well as a widely reputed scholar. It was Davenport who brought the noted economist Thorstein Veblen to Missouri. Veblen was on the faculty for seven years before he resigned to join the New School for Social Research in New York. He published some of his most important work during his Missouri years and brought significant recognition to the institution. With the departure of Davenport for Cornell, veteran teacher and administrator Isidor Loeb became dean of the school, and it was enlarged and renamed the School of Business and Public Administration.

The university celebrated its seventy-fifth anniversary in 1914. Presiding over the anniversary ceremonies, President Hill reflected on the history of the institution, suggesting that it could be divided roughly into three twenty-five-year segments. The first, concluding with the end of the Civil War, was a struggle for existence by a small classical college; the second, ending with the fiftieth anniversary, saw the development of the "college into a university"; and the third, culminating in the seventy-fifth year, saw the maturing of the institution into a full-fledged public university with broad programs of education, research, and service. Whereas enrollment had never

A 1921 view of the University Library, completed in 1914. The library, although soon requiring expansion, symbolized the university's emergence as a major educational institution.

exceeded 100 students during the first 25 years, nor 500 during the second 25, there were now 3,400 students attending the university; annual income had increased from $7,500 to $75,000 to more than $1,000,000.

By 1912 the outlines of the modern campus were beginning to take shape, with Francis Quadrangle, the white campus, and the agricultural complex showing some development. Everything south of Rollins Avenue was given over to athletics and student housing. Chalybeate Spring still flowed near the Eighth Street entrance to the campus, but the curators had ordered the removal of the 1870s pagoda that covered it. A sunken garden graced the area south of the academic hall.

At the corner of Ninth and Lowry streets a fine new building on the white campus had been built for the Bible College of Missouri, a private institution established in 1896 with close ties to the university—students could get university credit for Bible College courses.

Signaling the end of an era, the board of curators in 1915 decided to use funds that had been received from the federal government in compensation for damage done by Union soldiers during the Civil War to build an ornamental gate at the north entrance to the campus. The cornerstone of the original Academic Hall became a part of the west pillar of the new stone gateway, and in 1929 the board erected bronze reliefs on the two entrance columns, one commemorating Lathrop and the other James S. Rollins.

The university's emergence as a major institution of higher education was graphically demonstrated by the construction of a new library, completed in 1916, to replace overcrowded and inadequate quarters in the academic hall. Neoclassical in style, the library was built of Bedford limestone with its main entrance on Lowry Street. A fine new reading room on the second floor had a seating capacity of 250. The State Historical Society, which had been established by the Missouri Press Association in 1898, was housed with the library. In the new building the society was given its own reading room, newspaper room, and offices on the first floor.

Even as the library was being occupied, however, the attention of the nation, the state, and the university was being focused increasingly on the war in Europe. When the United States formally entered the conflict, the university, in common with all other institutions, found itself caught up in a world at war.

# 3 WAR, UNCERTAINTY,

## DEPRESSION, AND WAR

Until the United States entered the war, the conflict in Europe had little impact on the university. Enrollment actually increased, classes were held as usual, and intercollegiate athletics flourished. About the only evidence of war-related change was an increased emphasis on ROTC as the university responded to President Wilson's preparedness drive.

The American Declaration of War, however—6 April 1917—profoundly affected all aspects of university life. By fall, classes were depleted as students and faculty members left the campus for military service or for work in war industries. Military training was greatly expanded; fraternity houses and dormitories were used as barracks. Intercollegiate athletics were greatly curtailed, and in 1918 were abandoned altogether. Student social life virtually disappeared.

The nationwide influenza epidemic of 1918 further affected the campus. All public events were canceled, and the university itself was closed for three weeks in October. It was not long after the end of

A unit of the cadet corps, drawn up alongside the president's house. Over the years, Francis Quadrangle has been the favored site for dress parades and reviews.

The artillery class out for practice on a Boone County road.

The girls' rifle team, carrying forward a tradition of military training for women dating back to the 1880s when women students "drilled with light gear and no corsets."

When this photo of "co-eds hamming it up" was taken in the 1920s, college life appeared to have been getting back to normal.

the war, however, that life on campus returned to a normal pace.

The state took great pride in the fact that General John J. Pershing, who had led the American Expeditionary Forces to victory in Europe, was a native Missourian. The university expressed that pride by awarding him an honorary degree during Commencement 1920.

After leading the university through the difficult wartime years, President Hill resigned in 1921 to take charge of the foreign operations of the American Red Cross. Though he had been controversial both on the campus and in the state, he had a substantial national reputation as an educational reformer, and he had further developed the university's reputation for quality.

The board turned to J. Carleton Jones to serve as acting president. A veteran professor of Latin, he was filling the newly created post of vice-president in addition to serving as dean of the College of Arts and Science, a position he had held for many years. Jones retired before Hill's permanent replacement was found, and for a few months in 1923 Isidor Loeb served as acting president.

Finally, the board chose Stratton D. Brooks, president of the University of Oklahoma. Brooks, a native Missourian, had been educated in Michigan, and before going to Oklahoma he had served for a number of years as superintendent of schools in Boston.

General John J. Pershing, the native Missourian who commanded the American Expeditionary Forces in World War I, was given an honorary degree in 1920.

Students crowding the main entrance of Jesse Hall, 1924. They seem to be a happy lot, bundled up for winter weather.

After his resignation as president, J. Carleton Jones headed the fund-raising drive for Memorial Stadium and Memorial Union until his death in 1930.

Stratton D. Brooks was appointed president of the university in 1923. A native Missourian, he had been educated in Michigan and eventually served as president of the University of Oklahoma before returning to the state.

The "White Campus" provided many pleasant vistas, as in front of Mumford Hall.

During the early twenties the legislature was fairly generous with the university, providing money for some badly needed buildings as well as increased funds for operations. A women's gymnasium—later named for Mary McKee, long-time instructor in physical education—was built just south of Read Hall on Hitt Street. To the north, the increasing needs of agriculture were accommodated by the construction of Mumford Hall. A new chemistry building, later named Schlundt Hall in honor of Professor Herman Schlundt, was erected on University Avenue, and a new hospital—named for G. L. Noyes, like Mumford a still active dean—was built on the west side of the campus.

A new law school, built on the southeast corner of the old campus, provided an early example of partial funding of buildings from private sources. Mr. and Mrs. Frank R. Tate of St. Louis donated $75,000 for a new law building, to be named in memory of their son, Lee R. Tate, a graduate of the law school. The legislature was slow in providing matching funds, and Tate Hall was not completed until 1927.

Building projects receiving the most attention in the twenties were Memorial Tower and Memorial Stadium, sponsored by the Alumni Association and built in honor of university students who had given their lives in the Great War. Memorial Tower, conceived as part of a student union building, was dedicated on homecoming day 1926. Chiseled on the interior walls of the great arch at the base of the tower are the names of 116 students who lost their lives in the war. From the

A class in vegetable gardening, 1923. By this time ag students were dressing a little less formally than their counterparts of an earlier generation.

A chemistry laboratory, 1923.

beginning that arch has been a special place on campus, and for as long as students wore hats, they tipped them as they walked through. In 1936 a carillon was installed in the tower as a gift of Charles Baird of Kansas City.

The new stadium—seating 25,000 with room for expansion—was ready for use in the fall of 1926. The Tigers closed out Rollins Field 14 November 1925, with a 16 to 14 win over Oklahoma, and Memorial

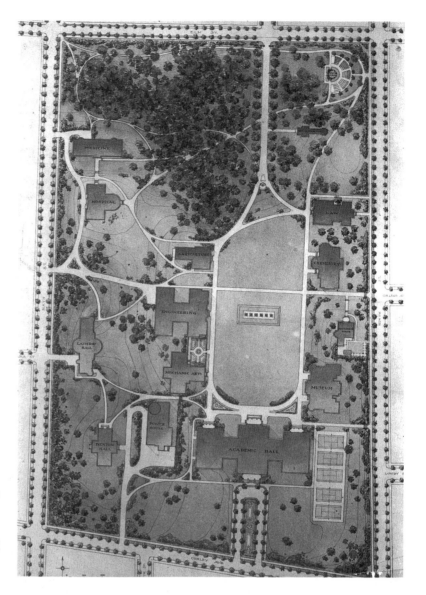

A sketch of the campus, 1925. Note the tennis courts east of Academic Hall, occupying part of the ground where Tate Hall would soon be built. Academic Hall had been named Jesse Hall in 1921, even though the older name appears on this sketch.

A horse show on Rollins Field, held as part of Commencement festivities in the 1920s.

Memorial Tower beginning to rise from the ground.

The intricate construction of Memorial Tower required skilled workmen.

Stadium was dedicated 2 October 1926, with a scoreless tie in a game with Tulane.

By the first game of the 1927 season, the freshman class had constructed the big stone "M" at the north end of the stadium. Described by contemporary accounts as "a tradition in the making," the project took 250 freshmen one hour to complete. For many years the freshman class maintained the tradition by whitewashing the rocks at the beginning of each season.

These were the days when Missouri students helped give meaning to the word "sophomoric," as each sophomore class sought to outdo

Looking east along Lowry Street in the fall of 1925. The Missouri School of Religion (now Lowry Hall) is at the left. Memorial Tower, nearing completion, is at one end of the street, and Francis Fountain, named for former governor David R. Francis, is at the other.

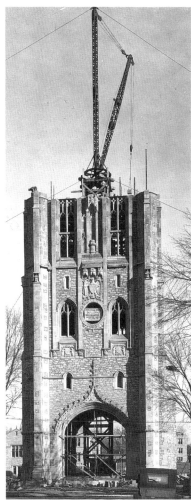

Memorial Tower nearing completion.

Memorial Tower as it looked in 1927. Dedicated at homecoming in 1926, it was conceived as part of a Memorial Union, but it stood alone until the 1950s when the north wing was built.

its predecessor in devising new ways to initiate the freshmen into campus life. A freshman tradition that developed without the benefit of sophomore coercion was that carried on by the "Thundering Thousand," a freshman pep club that marched "in lock step" from the columns to the stadium before each home game. The "Thundering Thousand" was led by Jesse Wrench, who himself became legendary during his more than forty years at Missouri. Founder of the Missouri Archaeological Society in 1936, Wrench was elected president of the organization every year until his death in 1958. Carl Chapman, a student at the time—and the first person to receive a degree in archaeology from the university—joined Wrench in the enterprise. Chapman eventually joined the faculty and distinguished himself as *the* authority on the archaeology of Missouri.

With the construction of Memorial Stadium and the need to pay off bonds from gate receipts, pressure to win steadily mounted. During the twenties, under Coach Gwinn Henry, the Tigers did well, win-

The Homecoming Committee, 1936, caught in a relaxed stance. Missouri students usually have been fairly relaxed in front of the photographer, but compare these students with some of those pictured in Chapter 1, who were separated by little more than half a century.

Paul Christman, named All-American in 1939 and 1940, provided the spark that gave Don Faurot many of his early victories. Generally recognized as the best quarterback in the history of the Big Eight Conference, he is a member of the College Football Hall of Fame.

ning three conference championships in six years and producing the school's first All-American, Ed Lindenmeyer. Henry resigned in the spring of 1932. The board's choice of a successor, Frank Carideo, a two-time All-American from Notre Dame, was most unfortunate. Carideo was generally unpopular, and in three years he won only a single major game. He resigned in 1934 and was replaced by Don Faurot.

Faurot revitalized football at Missouri. In 1936 the Tigers finished second in the Big Six (which had been formed from the old Missouri Valley Conference in 1928), enjoying their first winning season since 1929. Then came the glory years, with the team winning conference championships in 1939 and 1941 and playing in the Orange Bowl in 1940 and the Sugar Bowl in 1942. Faurot, inventor of the Split-T, relied primarily on Missouri boys, and they included two-time All-American Paul Christman and All-Americans Bob Steuber and Darold Jenkins.

Football was the activity generating the greatest student and alumni enthusiasm, but there was more to athletics than football. To accommodate other sports—and particularly basketball, in which George R. Edwards consistently fielded winning teams—Brewer Field House, named for the popular director of athletics, was constructed in the late twenties. The Tigers won the 1930 conference title in their first season in Brewer.

Missouri teams did fairly well in both baseball and track, although the university provided inadequate facilities for both sports. Anton Stankowski produced a conference championship in baseball in 1936. John "Hi" Simmons began his long and illustrious career as baseball coach with a conference championship in 1937 and another in 1940. Henry Schulte and Chauncey Simpson coached track on a part-time basis during the twenties and thirties, and Tom Botts began his long,

The Men's Glee Club, winners of a national contest and awarded a U.S. tour, appear here on the White House grounds on 14 March 1927 with President Coolidge. Other notables include General Pershing and Secretary of War Davis.

For many years field work under the leadership of Carl Chapman was an important feature of archaeological instruction at Missouri. He is shown here with a group of students at a prehistoric Indian site in 1949.

During his many years as director of the University Theater, Donovan Rhynsburger gave drama students an opportunity to act in the great classics of the stage. This is a scene from Eugene O'Neill's *The Hairy Ape,* performed in March 1932.

Theater stage crew at work, ca. 1930.

highly successful tenure as full-time track coach in 1946.

The twenties brought considerable expansion in the arts. With the arrival of James T. Quarles in 1923, a new Division of Fine Arts was created. Lathrop Hall, the old dormitory for men, was converted into a home for the new division, and in 1929 the division became a separate college, although this status lasted only until 1935, when fine arts were placed in the College of Arts and Science. In the thirties Fred Shane began a distinguished career as artist, teacher, and administrator that would influence the university for more than three decades.

In theater, the Workshop, a drama group developed during the twenties, continued to stage important productions. One of the most significant was John Drinkwater's *Abraham Lincoln*. Playing the role of Lincoln was Donovan Rhynsburger, who remained at Missouri for forty-eight years, as director of the Workshop and chair of the Department of Theater. Among the students in the Workshop was George C. Scott, whose first role was in the 1949 Workshop performance of *The Winslow Boy*. Scott credited Rhynsburger with telling him, "Don't act, just be."

The University Glee Club, under the direction of Herbert Wall, won regional and national honors. Best known of the singers from this period was Jane Froman, "Blues-singing co-ed from the University of Mo.," who built a remarkable career on the stage, and in radio and television.

Although the number of visiting scholars and literary figures would seem small to a generation accustomed to a steady parade of lecturers from all parts of the world, each year the university brought a few outstanding speakers to the campus—among them, Robert Frost, Irvin S. Cobb, Will Irwin, Edna St. Vincent Millay, and Bernard De Voto.

From its earliest years the university had fostered student interest in forensics and debate. In the twenties, the Women's Forum and the men's old debating organizations, the Athenaean Society and the Missouri State University Debating Society, joined together as the Uni-

Jane Froman always attracted admirers on her return to the campus. She continued her successful career despite an airplane accident, while traveling overseas for the USO, which left her partially paralyzed. Late in life she returned to Columbia to live.

versity Committee on Forensic Activity. Outstanding among the debaters of the period was Rosemary Lucas, who was captain of women's varsity debate in 1931. She graduated in 1933, became prominent in Republican politics, and as Rosemary Lucas Ginn was appointed ambassador to Luxembourg in 1976.

The twenties were years of relative calm, but also of relatively little progress for the university. With the exception of agriculture, Missouri's economy enjoyed reasonable prosperity. That prosperity, however, was not reflected in support for the university. Enrollment increased but appropriations did not. As a result, the university stagnated when it should have been developing.

President Brooks began to have difficulty with both faculty and members of the board. His troubles came to a head in 1929 in connection with a questionnaire circulated by a graduate student in sociology who was doing a paper on the influence of women's economic status on their sexual relations with men. The "sex questionnaire" was sensationalized in the Columbia newspapers and created an uproar throughout the state. The board, on Brooks's recommenda-

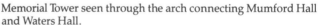
Memorial Tower seen through the arch connecting Mumford Hall
and Waters Hall.

Walter Williams, dean of the School of
Journalism since its founding in 1908,
was chosen to succeed Stratton Brooks
as president in 1930.

tion, dismissed the graduate student and two professors, including
Max Meyer, generally seen as one of the university's best teachers and
a national leader in the emerging field of behaviorist psychology. The
incident brought an investigation by the American Association of
University Professors and much criticism from thoughtful people
both on campus and around the state. The board, in reconsidering its
action, concluded that Brooks was creating too many problems and
relieved him from duty 5 June 1930. Meyer, unfortunately, never returned to the university.

To succeed Brooks, the board chose Walter Williams, who had been
dean of the School of Journalism since its founding in 1908. Although
he had not attended college, he was cultivated and widely read. A former publisher, he had served for a number of years on the board of
curators. He was well liked and highly respected, both on campus
and off. During his term, the impact of the Great Depression on the

Aerial view of the campus, looking west from College Avenue, ca. 1932. Memorial Tower and Jesse Hall dominate the scene, but Schweitzer, Schlundt, Stewart, Stanley, the library, the School of Religion, and Tate are visible along the walks and through the trees.

university was extremely severe. There had been no growth during the twenties that could be cut back in hard times. As a result, essential programs had to be reduced, faculty had to be dismissed wherever possible, and those who remained had to take substantial salary cuts. That all this could be accomplished without more serious erosion than occurred—or, indeed, without a faculty rebellion—was a tribute to Williams and an unusually competent body of deans.

At the time of his appointment, however, Williams was sixty-six years of age and not in robust health. Although he did a remarkable job of maintaining the university in the midst of a devastating economic depression, his health further declined, and on 27 July 1934, at a meeting that had to be held in his house because he could not venture out, he submitted his resignation. He died a year later, on 29 July 1935.

The curators conducted a national search for Williams's successor, but from the beginning of the process there was a strong feeling that the logical choice was Frederick A. Middlebush, dean of the School of Business and Public Administration, who was serving as acting president. Born in Michigan and educated at its state university, he established himself as a leader in campus affairs, and when Williams became too ill to carry on, he was appointed acting president. He became president on 30 June 1935, the date Williams's resignation took effect.

Middlebush's early years were characterized by both growth and improvement. Enrollment was increasing, larger appropriations made possible the restoration of faculty salaries, and the assistance of

Frederick A. Middlebush, president of the university from 1935 to 1954, in his office, 1940. Middlebush came to Missouri from Knox College in 1922 as associate professor of political science. Three years later he was appointed dean of the School of Business and Public Administration. His tenure as president was the longest in the history of the university.

Workmen constructing a fence for the women's athletic field on Hitt Street. This was one of a number of campus improvements completed with federal works funds in the 1930s.

Workmen constructing a gate to the athletic field near Brewer Fieldhouse.

the federal Public Works Administration brought about one of the most extensive building programs in the university's history. To accommodate the needs of the library a new west wing was added to the building of 1914. A new building for the School of Education was dedicated in 1937 just west of Jesse Hall.

A separate student health center was built near Noyes Hospital. Since 1909 the School of Medicine had functioned only as a two-year school, but its quality was high and graduates had no difficulty in finding places to complete their training. Two students of this period became important figures in medicine: Dr. Howard Rusk, for whom the Rusk Rehabilitation Center is named, and Dr. Frederick A. Robbins, Nobel Laureate in physiology and medicine.

The need for student housing was critical. A men's dormitory, named in honor of Luther M. Defoe, a former mathematics instructor who was very popular with the students, was built south of the gymnasium on Hitt Street. A second women's dormitory, named for Eliza Gentry, was built just north of Read Hall. This did not provide many additional rooms for women, because when Gentry was completed, Read Hall was converted into a student union—Memorial Union was still a dream.

While most of the buildings constructed during this period were paid for entirely by state funds, Curtis Hall, on the south side of the developing white campus quadrangle, was paid for by the Rockefeller Foundation to support R. J. Stadler's work in corn genetics. The building was named for Winterton C. Curtis, who had joined the zoology

Lewis J. Stadler, famed geneticist, at work in a university greenhouse, 1938. Stadler Hall, on the campus of the University of Missouri-St. Louis, is named in his honor.

When Walter Williams Hall was built in the 1930s to provide additional space for the School of Journalism, this arch, constituting the northeast entrance to Francis Quadrangle, connected the new building to Neff Hall, which had been occupied by the school since 1920.

One of the first female radio announcers on KFRU in 1941, then the School of Journalism's laboratory station.

Frank Luther Mott, Dean of the School of Journalism, 1942–1952, autographing copies of *Golden Multitudes.* Mott wrote extensively and was recognized as the nation's preeminent authority on the history of American magazines.

department in 1901, and who as dean of Arts and Science had been instrumental in securing the Rockefeller grant.

The thirties saw the arrival of some notable additions to the science faculties, including Henry E. Bent from Harvard, who joined the chemistry department in 1936. Also in 1936 Newell Gingerich from the Massachusetts Institute of Technology added stature to the physics department. Further developments occurred in zoology and engineering. The Department of Zoology secured a wildlife unit during the late thirties, and the College of Engineering, still operating out of Switzler Hall, obtained a new laboratory annex.

Among the students in zoology was Marlin Perkins of NBC's *Wild Kingdom.* Also during these years, Charles and Elizabeth Schwartz were students in biology and zoology, laying the foundations for their later notable publications combining art, nature, and conservation— such as *Wild Mammals of Missouri,* published by the University of Missouri Press in 1959.

The burgeoning School of Journalism received additional space when Walter Williams Hall was built on Ninth Street, joined to Neff Hall by the arch that constitutes the northeast entrance to Francis Quadrangle. Frank L. Martin, Williams's successor as dean of the School of Journalism, who had done much to further cement the school's China connection, died in 1941. He was succeeded by Frank Luther Mott, who brought a distinguished reputation with him from the University of Iowa—a reputation that he further enhanced at Missouri.

Among the students in journalism were Walter D. Scott, who became president and chief executive officer of NBC; Elmer Lower, who became head of ABC News and in retirement returned to the faculty, serving for a time as acting dean; Donald W. Reynolds, who built a publishing and television empire in the Southwest; Hal Boyle, colorful columnist; and Craig Claiborne, noted food editor and author of best-selling cookbooks. Also a student in the J-School during the thirties was Avis Green, who as Avis Tucker built a wide reputation in journalism, business, and public service. She became the first woman to serve as president of the board of curators.

The College of Agriculture continued to be scattered about the campus, but a new dairy building, constructed just west of the agricultural engineering laboratory southeast of Sanborn Field, hinted at the development of an agricultural complex in that area. The building was named for C. H. Eckles, a faculty member since 1901 who had been responsible for considerable progress in milk production. Near Memorial Tower, Gwynn Hall, the home economics building that had stood unfinished for fifteen years, was finally completed.

The College of Agriculture also experienced a change in leadership. After thirty years in the deanship Frederick B. Mumford retired and was replaced by Merritt F. Miller, who had been professor of soils since 1904. Professor Charles Edmund Marshall came from the University of Leeds in England to join the Department of Soils and served the university with distinction until his retirement some forty years later. William C. Etheridge, appointed to the faculty in 1916 and

Cattle grazing contentedly on the lawn in front of Eckles Hall, the new dairy building, ca. 1940.

The College of Education's laboratory school building, with the dome of Jesse Hall in the background. This building, completed in 1937, made it possible to combine the elementary and secondary training programs in one building and greatly facilitated the training of teachers. Later it was named for Loran Townsend, dean of the college from 1945 to 1963.

responsible for the introduction and promotion of soybeans and les-pedeza in Missouri, was at the peak of his career. Among students of the period was Cordell Tindall, who as editor of the *Missouri Ruralist* became influential in Missouri agriculture and politics.

In the School of Law, J. L. Parks, appointed dean in 1928, died suddenly in 1934. His position was not filled permanently until 1939, when Glenn A. McCleary, a member of the faculty since 1929, was appointed. McCleary served as dean for twenty years.

The floats in the Farmers Fair parade frequently inspired photographers, as did this one in 1938.

During these years there were a number of students from southeast Missouri who were to play important roles in the life of the university and the state. One of them was James A. Finch, president of the student body in 1931; he served for nine years as president of the board of curators before being appointed to the Missouri Supreme Court in 1966. Another was John W. Oliver, president of the student body in 1935. When he received his law degree, he followed in the footsteps of his father, his grandfather, and his two brothers. In 1962 he became a federal district judge for western Missouri. John Hall Dalton, son of a 1923 graduate who became governor in the sixties and was a key figure in the establishment of the University of Missouri system, graduated in 1949 and in the seventies served as president of the board of curators.

Another student leader who served as president of the board of curators in the seventies was Irvin Fane of Kansas City, business manager of the *Savitar*—Fane recalled that he helped construct the rock "M" at the north end of Memorial Stadium. Busy working his way through school was a Columbia boy who would become one of the wealthiest men in America. Sam Walton demonstrated his leadership ability by serving as president of Burrall, the largest student Sunday-school class in the world.

By the end of the thirties the state was beginning to recover from

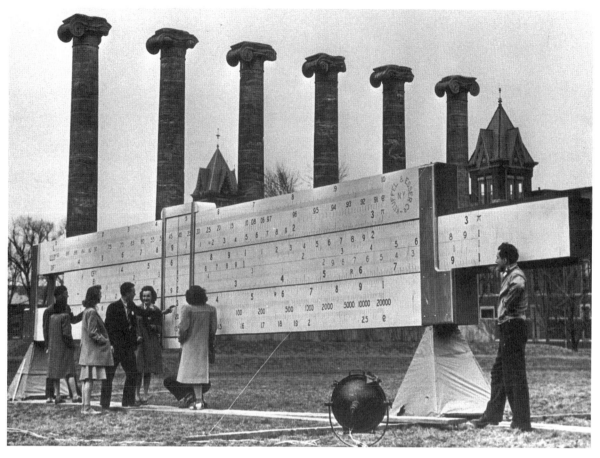

Engineers Week in 1940 featured a slide rule forty feet long and six feet high, weighing more than a ton. It worked accurately and could be manipulated by one student.

An anti-war parade, ca. 1940.

Tap Day, 1941. The day on which members of the Mystical Seven and Mortar Board are chosen is always a highlight of the spring season.

the Depression, and the university could celebrate its centennial with a renewed spirit of hope for the future. Centennial events throughout 1939 reflected the state's pride in the oldest public university west of the Mississippi, and one that, despite difficulties, had in a century developed a secure place for itself as one of the major universities in the country.

Academically, the highlight of the year came in the fall when the prestigious American Association of Universities held its annual meeting in Columbia to help Missouri celebrate its centennial. Twenty-two of the nation's leading university presidents were in attendance to honor their colleague Frederick Middlebush and the institution he led.

The clouds of war hung heavily over the centennial celebration. The Nazis had invaded Poland on 1 September, engulfing Europe in War. In the beginning, most Americans hoped that the United States could stay out of the conflict, but as the months wore on it became increasingly clear that it was neither possible nor desirable for the United States to remain aloof.

Welding students in the National Defense Training Program make a metal flag, 1941.

Even before the Japanese attack on Pearl Harbor, enrollment in ROTC had steadily increased, and the only new building constructed during the late 1930s was Crowder Hall—named for the university's most distinguished military alumnus—as headquarters for all military activity on the campus.

The war itself had a profound effect on the university. Enrollment, which had been over 5,000 in 1938, dropped to 1,500 in 1943. Most of the regular students were women, men under the age of eighteen, 4-Fs, and inductees deferred for educational reasons. Many members of the faculty entered the service or were involved in defense work away from the campus. Head of all war production was Donald Marr Nelson, an engineering graduate of 1911.

The university conducted a substantial amount of military training through a large Army Specialized Training Program (ASTP) and through intensified ROTC activity. A Naval ROTC unit was established in 1940. Military training programs did not follow the regular academic calendars and there was a great deal of movement on and off the campus as units came and went. There was some pressure on housing, and Gentry Hall was used as a barracks.

Student activities in general were curtailed, but intercollegiate athletics continued as part of a national policy encouraging athletics as a morale builder. The NCAA permitted freshmen to play in intercollegiate games, and enrollees in the specialized training units also were encouraged to participate. Don Faurot was absent—he was coaching the Iowa Seahawks for the Navy—but Chauncey Simpson, who substituted for him, won the Big Six in 1945.

The impact of the war was far greater than any rendition of campus activities can describe. It was felt most in the steady arrival of news from the far-flung battlefields that yet another gallant student had lost

Men's calisthenics in Rothwell Gymnasium, 1940s.

President Middlebush and General Omar N. Bradley descend the steps of Jesse Hall, Commencement Day, 6 June 1946. At the end of World War I the university had awarded an honorary degree to General Pershing, and now at the end of World War II, in similarly honoring General Bradley, the university once again called attention to the important role played by native Missourians in the nation's military history.

his or her life in the cause of freedom. Altogether, 328 University of Missouri students gave their lives in World War II.

The end of the war brought untold relief to the university as well as to the country at large. Missourians, with a native son as president of the United States, took great pride in the accomplishments of the state's citizens in the great struggle. The university was to express that pride frequently. At Commencement 1946 they did so by conferring an honorary degree on General Omar Bradley, native of Moberly, who had led the Twelfth Army Group in Europe, the largest single field command in American history.

Yet even as they were honoring the past, the men and women of the university were in the throes of beginning a new era in American life and American higher education—an era that in a few years would see a profound transformation in both.

# 4 A TIME
## OF GROWTH

At the end of the war campuses across the country were inundated with students as returning veterans sought to take advantage of wartime legislation—popularly known as the "GI Bill of Rights"—that provided educational benefits for all honorably discharged servicemen. The federal government not only paid for tuition and books but also provided subsistence allowances. College, instead of being reserved for the privileged few, became a realistic possibility for almost everyone.

The university felt the impact immediately. By the second semester of the 1944–1945 school year, enrollment, which had fallen to 1,500 during the war, jumped to 5,000. A year later there were more than 11,000, and during the 1947–1948 school year—the peak year of the immediate postwar boom—the number reached 11,452.

As was true of educational institutions everywhere, the university was poorly equipped to meet the demands of its swollen enrollment. The years of depression and war had decimated the faculty, and the state had not provided buildings sufficient for the needs of the institution. Board and administration had to scramble to keep the university from being swept away by the flood.

New faculty were hired wherever possible, but many of the additional classes were taught by graduate assistants and temporary, part-time instructors. Dining and dormitory space was provided by 224 surplus barracks and other buildings from nearby military posts and by 150 government-owned trailers. The opening of school even had to

As enrollment increased so did the length of the lines at registration. These students await their turn at a window in Jesse Hall during second semester registration in 1946.

Veterans wait in line for assignment of emergency housing, 30 September 1946.

"Pneumonia Gulch," temporary student housing built to accommodate the influx of students after World War II. Spreading out over the golf course, the war surplus buildings occupied the site of the current medical complex. This photograph was taken from the southwest. Bordering the temporaries on the east were Stafford, Cramer, Graham, and Defoe dormitories. Brewer Field House and Rothwell Gymnasium are visible at the northeast corner of the tract.

A resident meets the milkman at the door of her trailer in Dairy Lawn, one of two trailer communities set up to provide low-cost housing for married veterans.

A dormitory room all spruced up for the photographer.

be postponed two weeks in the fall of 1946 to enable workmen to finish the temporary housing.

Ramshackle and unsightly temporary buildings were everywhere on campus, spreading out over the golf course north of the stadium. While the crush of veterans would subside, it was realized that the university would never again be its prewar size. The need for additional permanent housing was obvious. At the same time it was obvious that the legislature would never appropriate sufficient funds on an annual basis to meet the need. To solve the problem, the board of curators, with legislative encouragement, began a program in 1950 of paying for dormitories with bonds to be amortized through dormitory fees assessed against the student residents.

A massive building program began in the 1950s. New instructional buildings completed in the early 1950s were a chemistry laboratory and an agricultural laboratory. By 1960 there were 16 residence halls for single men and women and 32 apartments for married students, housing 3,564 single and 360 married students. This was about 36 percent of the total student population—although more than three-fourths of the highest enrollment of prewar years. As the new buildings were completed, the temporaries came down, but the university would find it necessary to continue to build dormitories throughout the 1960s and into the 1970s.

In naming the new dormitories the board sought to honor a variety of persons who had made important contributions to the university and to society. The first women's dormitories were named for Sarah Gentry, the second woman to graduate from the university and a teacher in the Kansas City schools for nearly forty years; and for Eva Johnston, an 1892 graduate who devoted her life to the university as professor of Latin. Later women's dormitories were named for former presidents Lathrop, Laws, and Jones; a residence for nurses was named for Powell McHaney of St. Louis, a recently deceased member of the board who had been active in securing the four-year medical school.

The names of the first new men's dormitories honored three students who had been killed in the nation's wars: Bruce Cramer, Spanish-American war; Robert Graham, World War I; and Richard Stafford, World War II. Another group was named for former governors, with each building honoring two: Dockery-Folk, Hadley-Major, Gardner-Hyde, and Baker-Park. In the Loeb Group, honoring Isidor Loeb, were buildings named for former curators Frank McDavid and Allen McReynolds.

To meet the administrative needs of the greatly expanded enrollment, and particularly of the veterans, the curators created a Veterans Service Committee and appointed Thomas A. Brady of the Department of History as its director. Brady, a graduate of the university with a Ph.D. from Harvard, had developed curricula for the area and language studies of the ASTP during the war. In 1946 he became vice president of the university. A second vice presidency was created for business operations, and Leslie Cowan, who had been on the staff since 1913 as purchasing agent, business manager, and secretary to the board, was named to the post.

There were important developments in the College of Agriculture during the postwar years. John H. Longwell, an alumnus who had become president of North Dakota State Agricultural College in Fargo, was brought back to the campus as dean in 1948 following the death of Edwin A. Trowbridge, who had been appointed in 1945 to succeed Merritt F. Miller. The Department of Veterinary Medicine was enlarged, first to a school in 1949 and then to an independent division in 1958, with Aaron Groth as its dean. Forestry, originally part of the Department of Horticulture, became a separate department in 1947, and a school in 1957, with R. H. Westveld as its director. Instruction and research in wildlife conservation, established in the thirties, grew substantially with support from a 2,200-acre research

Thomas A. Brady, appointed assistant professor of history in 1930, remained on the faculty until his death in 1964, serving as vice president and as dean of extra-divisional administration. Brady Commons is named in his honor.

area in southern Boone County.

The dairy department received a major boost in 1952 when J. C. Penney gave the university his world-famous herd of 270 blooded Guernsey cattle. Penney, who began his spectacular merchandising career in his hometown of Hamilton, Missouri, became one of the university's major benefactors. The Penney awards in the School of Journalism are nationally significant.

Another significant acquisition was Tucker Prairie, 160 acres of unbroken land on Interstate 70, eighteen miles east of Columbia. This tract came to the university through a grant from the National Science Foundation and through numerous individual gifts, including those of members of the R. J. Tucker family.

The postwar years saw the full flowering of profoundly significant agricultural research that had been going on for more than half a century under the auspices of the College of Agriculture and the Agricultural Experiment Station. University scientists became well-known nationally and among Missouri farmers for their pioneering work in a number of important areas: William A. Albrecht identified the soil sample in Sanborn Field from which aureomycin was produced; Leonard Haseman and L. F. Childers found a way to eradicate a disease that was threatening to wipe out the nation's bee colonies; W. C. Etheridge brought about the introduction of Korean lespedeza and the soybean to Missouri; J. M. Poehlman worked to improve barley and oats; Marcus Zuber produced hybrid corn with a cob from which the "Missouri Meerschaum" could be manufactured; Ernest Sears conducted pioneering research in wheat genetics, becoming the first Missouri faculty member elected to the National Academy of Sciences. These individuals and others contributed mightily to the state's economy and the university's reputation.

There were important developments in the College of Engineering. In 1948, Harry A. Curtis, who had been serving as dean for a decade, resigned to accept the post of vice chair of the Tennessee Valley Authority. He was succeeded by Huber O. Croft of the University of Iowa. The college still headquartered in ancient Switzler Hall, but a new building for electrical engineering opened in 1960.

In the School of Journalism, the creative spirit was nurtured through "Ye Tabard Inn," an all-male writers group, brought to the university by Winston Allard, a member of the faculty. The title came from Chaucer's *Canterbury Tales,* with each member being given a nickname from a character in the work. Among the members was William Manchester (M.A., 1947), who achieved fame as a journalist and as the author of such books as *The Death of a President* and *American Caesar.* He was "The Reve." Dr. Earl English, Mott's successor as dean and famous as the author of the country's most widely used journalism text, was known as "The Sergeant of the Lawe." Another member, "The Wit of Bathe," was Professor Edward C. Lambert, who became director of the university's television station, KOMU-TV, established in 1953 as a laboratory for television students. As a commercial station, KOMU-TV gave Missouri journalism students the advantage of "real time" experience, although the decision to go com-

Among the significant research efforts in the College of Agriculture was that of Earnest Sears, whose work in wheat genetics would make him the first Missouri faculty member elected to the National Academy of Sciences.

A class in journalism—the excitement of learning in one of the nation's most prestigious schools is evident.

"The Class of '49." In the postwar years going to college frequently was a family affair.

mercial did prevent the university from participating in the public television experience that has been so much a part of higher education in America.

The School of Journalism celebrated its fiftieth anniversary in 1959 with the establishment of the Freedom of Information Center. Professor Paul Fisher—"The Clerke" in "Ye Tabard Inn"—was named the first director of the center that was to bring distinction to the university for its efforts to breach the barriers of official secrecy. The United States Post Office issued a stamp to commemorate the event, and a world press conference brought dignitaries from all over the globe to Columbia. In 1962 the *Missourian* got a home of its own with the construction of an annex to Neff Hall.

Graduates of the School of Journalism continued to make names for themselves in the field of communications. Among the best known from this period are Helen Delich-Bentley, maritime editor of the *Baltimore Sun* and later member of Congress from Maryland; James Lehrer, co-anchor of the MacNeil-Lehrer Report; Marshall R. Loeb, editor of *Fortune;* and Seymour Topping, managing editor of the *New York Times.* Journalism was by no means the only division to produce graduates who would go on to become well known in their fields. The College of Arts and Science, to name another, counts numerous well-known persons among its graduates and former students of the forties and the fifties. Among them are Robert A. Burnett, president and CEO of the Meredith Corporation; Martha Wright Griffiths, lieutenant governor of Michigan and former congresswoman; R. Crosby Kemper, Jr., Kansas City banker and philanthropist; Charles H. Price, II, ambassador to Great Britain; and Beryl W. Sprinkel, chair of the Council of Economic Advisors.

During these postwar years of growth, when an increasing number of young Missourians had the opportunity to attend the university, one group was systematically excluded. Since the Civil War, Missouri had enforced the policy of "separate but equal" education for whites and blacks. During this time the policy of the state was to pay tuition and fees to institutions outside the state for black citizens pursuing courses not offered at Lincoln University, the land-grant school for blacks in Jefferson City.

In 1939 Lucile Bluford, a graduate of the University of Kansas and managing editor of the *Kansas City Call*, applied for admission to the School of Journalism. She was denied admission, and when she appealed the matter to the courts, she was told by both the State Supreme Court and the Federal District Court that she needed to apply to Lincoln University. This she had no interest in doing— she doubted that the struggling program at Lincoln could teach her much about journalism that she did not already know. In 1981 Miss Bluford was invited to the campus as one of the School of Journalism's Missouri Medalists.

For example, Marion Oldham, a St. Louis leader who served on the board of curators from 1978 to 1984, had her tuition paid by the state of Missouri to attend the University of Michigan. Black leaders in the state, particularly in Kansas City and St. Louis, became increasingly resentful of a policy that provided their children with educational opportunities that were definitely separate but very far from equal.

The university at times even refused to let its athletic teams compete against teams that included blacks. In 1935 the university's admission policies were officially challenged by Lloyd Gaines, an honor graduate of Lincoln University from St. Louis who was seeking admission to the School of Law. The curators were upheld by the State Supreme Court in their refusal to grant admission, but the decision was reversed by the Supreme Court of the United States. Gaines, however, left the state and did not pursue the matter.

Even after World War II, when Missourian Harry Truman had desegregated the armed forces, the University of Missouri continued to enforce a narrow interpretation of Missouri law. Although the board of curators, in testimony before the Civil Rights Commission in 1948, advocated legislation permitting blacks to enroll in programs at the university that were not available at Lincoln University, neither Middlebush nor the board provided any leadership in the matter of trying to change the law. A student referendum in 1949 showed two-to-one support for the admission of blacks to the university—but only to those students seeking programs not offered at Lincoln University.

In 1950, the St. Louis chapter of the National Association for the Advancement of Colored People decided to test the law once again,

Marion Oldham, who served on the board of curators from 1978 to 1984, was not permitted to enroll at the University of Missouri as a student, but she had her tuition paid by the state to attend the University of Michigan.

Although the weather usually cooperated, occasionally, as in 1950, umbrellas were a necessary part of Commencement in the stadium.

and three blacks applied for admission to engineering and graduate programs not available at Lincoln University. The board asked for a ruling from the Cole County Circuit Court; when Judge Sam Blair ruled that the applicants must be admitted, the board decided not to appeal and granted admission. The board adopted a policy providing for admission of blacks who were residents of Missouri to programs not available at Lincoln, but there were very few admissions until after the Supreme Court decision of 1954 in *Brown* v. *Topeka* overturned the Missouri law. Even then, progress for blacks at the university was slow—for example, it was not until 1958 that the Tiger football roster included a black.

In common with their counterparts everywhere, most Missouri students in the fifties showed little concern for the struggle of blacks or for any events beyond the campus. The veterans, many with family responsibilities, were anxious to get through school as soon as possible; the younger students were busy coping with university life. During a panel discussion on "student purposes," one participant remarked, "We need a purpose. I mean a purpose other than a search

*Dark of the Moon,* a 1961 Workshop production directed by Donald Rhynsburger.

In the 1950s "panty raids" were something of an annual rite of spring.

for security, or getting that $18,000-a-year job and being content for the rest of your life."

The university relaxed its social regulations somewhat, but it still behaved very much in loco parentis. The board in 1950 created a new position of dean of students, and selected Jack Matthews, a member of the physical education faculty, to fill it. Matthews, known affectionately as "Black Jack," held the position for twenty years and was the point man for the board and the administration in everything from the panty raids of the fifties to the student troubles of the late sixties and the early seventies.

Working one's way through college became less and less practical as increased academic pressures and stiffer degree requirements reduced the amount of time available to students taking a full load of courses. To be sure, many students secured part-time jobs, but increasing numbers had to depend on financial aid in one form or another—much of it coming from the federal government. Allan Purdy administered the program for more than twenty-five years, helping thousands of students obtain funding to attend college and becoming nationally recognized as an authority on student financial aid.

Students began to be a little more self-conscious about their rights. In 1959 the Missouri Students Association replaced what was known as the Student Government Association. Through the administration of student activities money, MSA developed considerable clout, occasionally taking positions on issues independent of decisions made by the administration and the board of curators. Among those elected to the first MSA student council was Jerry Litton, a farm boy from Chillicothe who moved from student politics to a meteoric career in state politics, cut short by his tragic death in a plane crash on the night of his nomination as Democratic candidate for the United States Senate in 1976.

In 1955, the old *Missouri Student*, a paper with a pallid personality and minimal influence, became the *Maneater*, with a "new staff, new format, new ideas, new freedom, new enemies." The Board of Publications concluded that a student newspaper, in order to be effective, had to possess the freedom to be controversial. Even more controversial was *Showme*, a humor magazine that had a checkered existence for more than forty years. It finally ceased publication altogether in 1964.

Although the library remained the central resource for most courses, many programs, particularly in the professional schools, combined theoretical instruction with practical or clinical experience using the latest methods and the most sophisticated equipment.

Lectures by famous people and performances by well-known artists became a regular feature of campus life. To be sure, the university and student organizations had for years provided students, faculty, and townspeople with opportunities to enjoy outside lecturers and performers, but with the improvement of transportation, the lecture and performance circuits became much more heavily traveled.

The university, well into its second century, was rich in tradition. The honor societies—Mortar Board, QEBH, and Mystical 7—did

Dean Jack Matthews makes a point, probably from the rule book.

*Showme* seems relatively tame in the 1980s, but it was frequently banned for editorial indiscretions.

*Showme* provided training for a number of well-known cartoonists, including Mort Walker, creator of "Beatle Bailey."

With the first issue of the *Maneater*, 18 February 1955, a new era in student journalism began. From the beginning the *Maneater* consistently exercised its freedom to be controversial, and in the process it usually provided high quality, independent coverage of campus life and concerns.

much to perpetuate a sense of continuity in a rapidly changing world. Tap Day, occurring each spring, was second only to Commencement in pageantry and significance. The military tradition remained strong. After the war, all three branches of the service had ROTC units on the campus. All males were required to take basic ROTC and a substantial number of men continued into advanced work.

Going to school at Mizzou was not all work. As a matter of fact, Missouri in the 1950s had the reputation of being a great party school.

William B. Trogden, who as William Least Heat Moon is famed as the author of *Blue Highways*, once wrote, "We drank beer there and we talked there. . . . We also drank in legend and touched fame in that strangest of all Columbia beerhalls. Mort Walker, we knew, invented Beatle Bailey there as he drew cartoons for *Showme* . . . on those rickety, initials-upon-initials incized tables . . . Tennessee Williams, before he had pulled out of the University in disgust with the English department, had supped over those carvings. Never mind that Mark Twain had stood on the steps of Jesse Hall. History was at the Shack."

As is true of most academic reputations, this one was only partially justified. But it is difficult to imagine a more attractive setting for lively gatherings than the lovely wooded banks of Hinkson Creek, rendezvous site for generations of Missouri students. Andy's Corners, a one-room roadhouse at the corner of old Route K and Rock Quarry Road, was a favorite roistering spot, but nothing compared with The Shack, a legendary tumble-down tavern on Conley Avenue, south of Jesse Hall.

Organized annual events—some of them dating from the turn of the century—could rival the spirit on any American campus. The Savitar Frolics, a highlight of every year, provided fraternities, sororities, and other groups an opportunity to strut their stuff in original skits. As a sign of changing times, men and women came together in 1957 for the first time in putting on the skits. "Aggies" contributed hilarity to the fall schedule with their annual barnwarming. Engineer high jinks around the throne of Saint Patrick did the same for the spring semester.

Despite the fact that increasing numbers of students lived in dormitories, the fraternities and sororities continued to serve as centers and arbiters of campus social life and havens from the stresses of the big, impersonal campus. The Greek system, always strong at Missouri, particularly flourished during the fifties. Freshmen electing to go through "rush" came to the campus early each fall for a hectic,

For years it was assumed that the homecoming queen would come from a sorority, but in 1958 Carol Earls of Gentry Hall, an Independent, won the honor.

fun-filled week climaxed by the drama of pledging.

The grandest event of the year was homecoming. From the beginning, the Greek-letter organizations had participated in the parade, vying with each other for the "best float" award. In 1935 decorations began to appear in front of the houses. Each year they became more elaborate, and, on the eve of homecoming, traffic in Greek Town came to a standstill as thousands thronged the streets to see the decorations.

Marching Mizzou, the university's 200-piece band, added to the excitement of homecoming by leading the parade and performing at half time. For many an old grad the Gates of Heaven flew open when the band ran onto the football field led by high-stepping drum majors and flanked by the baton twirlers and the cheerleaders.

As had been the case from the beginning, homecoming was built around football, and football continued to dominate athletics at Missouri. Don Faurot returned from the war to pick up the reins he had held so successfully in the thirties. To help pay off the stadium debt and to finance piecemeal expansion, Faurot filled the nonconference schedule with powerhouses like Ohio State, Southern Methodist, Texas, and Maryland. Although the Tigers seldom won, occasional victories against these leviathans added excitement to seasons that on the whole were fairly drab.

There were some very good years—1948 and 1949, for example, when Missouri went to the Gator Bowl (only to lose in both games)—but in Faurot's last seven years, his teams broke .500 only once. He was never out-coached, but there were times when he seemed to be out-recruited. He announced that the 1956 season would be his last, and after his last game his devoted players carried him off the field on their shoulders.

Faurot—now full-time athletic director—chose as his successor Frank Broyles, an assistant coach from Georgia Tech. Broyles was highly popular and moderately successful, but at the end of his first year he was lured away by the University of Arkansas. Broyles, frustrated by the home-state recruiting policy, managed to give scholarships to two blacks—the first in Missouri's football history.

Faurot this time persuaded Dan Divine, a 33-year-old former assistant coach at Michigan State who had just finished three successful seasons as head coach at Arizona State, to come back to the Midwest. In his thirteen years at Missouri, Divine compiled one of the nation's most successful coaching records, winning seventy-seven games, losing twenty-two and tying six. He won two conference championships and took the Tigers to six bowl games.

As Memorial Stadium expanded to meet the needs of ever-increasing crowds, aging Brewer Field House deteriorated into one of the poorest facilities in the conference. The Tigers were tough there during Sparky Stalcup's fifteen years as head coach. Stalcup, who succeeded George Edwards in 1946, served as head basketball coach until 1962 when he retired to become an assistant athletic director. He won a total of 186 games and lost 153, producing such outstanding players as All-Americans Bill Stauffer and Norm Stewart. His record

Don Faurot, one of college football's
legendary figures, coached the Tigers
from 1934 to 1956, with time out during
World War II as coach of the Navy
pre-flight team at the University of
Iowa. Here he is being carried off the
field after his last game as coach—a
15 to 13 win over Kansas.

A capacity crowd at Memorial Stadium, ca. 1947, before the new press box and the south addition. The big rock "M" at
the north end, built by the freshman class in 1927, remained —and remains—the stadium's distinguishing feature.

John "Hi" Simmons coached baseball for thirty-five years, producing four straight conference titles and a national championship. Simmons Field is named in his honor.

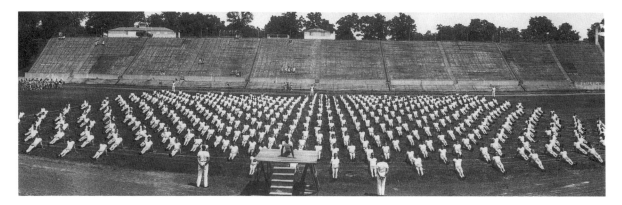

Tom Botts did more than coach track. Here he directs aviation cadets in calisthenics at Memorial Stadium, 3 June 1944.

at home was 97 won and 52 lost.

Baseball provided Missouri with more victories than any other sport. Under John "Hi" Simmons, baseball coach for thirty-five years, Missouri established something of a baseball dynasty, winning four straight conference titles in the early sixties and one national championship.

Track, a poorly supported sport, provided Missouri with consistent winners. Tom Botts, head track coach from 1944 to 1972, won eight conference championships, and at one time enjoyed a winning streak

Jesse Hall Auditorium under construction, June 1953. Completed in 1954, the new auditorium could seat about two thousand people and provided a handsome, acoustically well-tuned facility for concerts, lectures, plays, and other functions.

of twenty-two consecutive meets. A new track, encircling the field at Memorial Stadium, completed in 1958, provided adequate facilities for a time, but new tracks at other Big Eight schools soon pushed Missouri into a disadvantaged position from which it has not recovered.

Golf became a competitive sport, and with a private donation from A. L. Gustin, Jr., a former student from Kansas City, the university created a new eighteen-hole golf course and club house on the Rollins farm west of the stadium, which the university purchased in 1955.

Although Memorial Stadium was built on schedule, the Student Union Building, begun at the same time, languished. Memorial Tower, completed in 1926, stood for twenty-five years as a monument to unfulfilled aspirations. In the early fifties, however, the project revived. The north wing of the proposed student union was opened in 1952, and for the first time in its history the university had a student union worthy of the name. Carrying on the tradition of being a memorial, the walls of the north wing bear the names of 328 students who gave their lives in World War II. It was another decade before the south wing came into being, but in 1963 the building as originally envisioned was finally completed.

The A. P. Green Chapel, built in 1959 with funds given by the A. P. Green family of Mexico, Missouri, was later attached to the Memorial Union. It provides a quiet place for meditation and remains a popular spot for student weddings.

Also during the early 1950s, a new auditorium in Jesse Hall replaced the old chapel built in the 1890s. A new chapel attached later to the Memorial Union, donated to the university by the A. P. Green family of Mexico, continues to be a popular spot for student weddings.

Both Presidents Middlebush and Ellis were conscious of the importance of relating the university to the state, and of using the university as a platform to call attention to the achievements of prominent Missourians, whether they had attended the university or not. Commencements, held in the stadium, were gala affairs, and honorary degrees provided a good way for the university to recognize important people.

In 1948 Thomas Hart Benton, Missouri's famed regional artist, received an honorary doctorate of fine arts. Benton had never been a

General Maxwell Taylor, another distinguished native son, speaking at the 1951 Commencement, where he also received an honorary degree.

President Truman seems to be the only person undismayed by the rain as he attends the 1950 Commencement exercises where he received an honorary degree.

student at the university, but, as already noted, a number of his drawings were published in the 1908 *Savitar.* Benton's relationship to the university remained close. In 1968 the University of Missouri Press published his new book, *Tom Benton and His Drawings,* and in the same year issued a third, revised edition of his autobiography, *An Artist in America.* In 1974 Benton, as an old man, full of international acclaim, made a memorable appearance before the Jefferson Club, the organization that recognizes the university's major donors.

In 1950 Middlebush conferred an honorary degree on the most famous Missourian of them all, the President of the United States. Truman, like Benton, remained close to the university, returning to the campus several times in the ensuing years. General Maxwell Taylor, a native of Keytesville, received honors at the 1951 Commencement, and Homer Croy, who had written extensively for the *Savitar* but who had flunked English during his senior year, returned in 1956 to be honored as a leading novelist and playwright.

In 1957, the university honored the heads of Missouri's two private universities, Ethan Shepley and Paul Reinert. The 1960 honorary degree recipients were Carl C. Taylor, Roy Ellis, the University of Chicago president Lawrence Kimpton, and the *Kansas City Star* publisher Roy Roberts. In 1963, Joyce C. Hall, founder of Hallmark Cards, and Missouri Governor John Dalton received honorary degrees, along with Fred N. Briggs, Charles W. Singleton, and James W. Mc-

Homer Croy, well-known novelist and playwright, receives congratulations from President Ellis on his honorary degree during the 6 June 1956 Commencement. Croy as a student wrote extensively for the *Savitar*—although he flunked English as a senior.

Gloria Behrens, president of Theta Sigma Phi, honorary women's journalism society, greets campus visitor Eleanor Roosevelt, 1959.

As a reminder that graduates of the College of Engineering frequently distinguished themselves in business and in industry, four graduates who had risen to become presidents of Bell Telephone Companies were asked back to help celebrate the college's 110th anniversary in 1952: W. W. Kahler, Illinois Bell; E. J. McNeely, Northwestern Bell; N. J. Kelly, Bell Laboratories; and Cleo Craig, AT&T.

Afee. McAfee was but one of a number of prominent St. Louisans of the 1950s who had graduated from Missouri. Tom Smith, for example, a Phi Beta Kappa graduate of 1904, had received an honorary degree in 1935, and had served as president of the board of curators; Powell McHaney, president of General American Life Insurance Company, had been president of the board of curators; Sidney Maestre, a Phi Beta Kappa, served as chairman of Mercantile Trust.

During these years, on many occasions other than Commencement, the university played host to notable visitors. None was more memorable than Eleanor Roosevelt, whom the Student Union Board brought to campus in 1957 to speak on the United Nations.

Middlebush expected, and everyone connected with the university hoped, that he would remain as president until he reached retirement

age of sixty-five. In 1953, however, his health became so undermined
that the next year he found it necessary to resign. He had served in
the office longer than any other person in the history of the university, and he had served with distinction, leading the institution
through the Great Depression, World War II, and the great postwar
transformation.

The board, unable to find a president before Middlebush's resignation became effective, asked Elmer Ellis, who had been dean of the
College of Arts and Science since 1945, to serve as acting president. It
became clear as the search wore on that among the individuals being
considered for the job Ellis was the best qualified. In April 1955 he was
appointed president. It was a popular appointment. Ellis had been a
member of the faculty since 1930, he had developed a solid scholarly
reputation in history, and he was known for his good humor and
sound judgment.

Ellis continued and expanded the program of growth begun under
Middlebush. He had strong support from an able board, and particularly from James A. Finch, Jr., who served as president of the board
during most of Ellis' years as president. This was a time of general
progress for the entire university. An important element in that progress was approval of a $75 million bond issue in 1956 to provide facil-
ities for state institutions. Ellis headed the campaign committee, and
his successful leadership in this role did much to get his presidency
off to a good start. The university received $18.5 million in bond mon-
ey, and its use over the next five years provided the campus with a
number of badly needed new buildings.

Ruth and Elmer Ellis on the staircase
at the president's house. Ellis joined
the faculty in 1930 as assistant professor of history. After serving for a
decade as dean of the College of Arts
and Science, he was appointed acting
president in 1954 and president in 1955,
a position he held until his retirement
in 1966.

John G. Neihardt, one of the nation's
major regional poets, who had been
appointed Poet in Residence in 1948,
gave the library his personal collection
of some five thousand volumes in 1961.
Neihardt's great epic, *A Cycle of the
West*, was particularly popular with
students in the sixties, and he inspired
Missouri students during two decades
of teaching. The library contains a
bronze cast of a bust of Neihardt made
by his wife, who was a student of
Rodin.

The Fine Arts Building, completed in 1961, provided the first adequate facility for music, drama, painting, and sculpture on the UMC campus.

Making up the cast for *Die Fledermaus*, produced jointly by the theater and music departments to celebrate the opening of the Fine Arts Building in 1961.

Ellis chose as his successor in the deanship of Arts and Science his assistant dean, Francis W. English, also a member of the Department of History. It was a fortunate choice; the College of Arts and Science made great progress under English's leadership. A new facility for history, English, and modern foreign languages was built to accommodate expansion, and when the Fine Arts Building was completed in 1961, the university for the first time acquired an adequate facility

Two deans of agriculture and a future
president of the university absorbed
in a newspaper—Elmer Kiehl,
C. Brice Ratchford, and John Longwell.

for music, drama, painting, and sculpture. The music and theater
departments celebrated the new building by joining together for the
first time to produce Mozart's *Die Fledermaus*.

Also during this period the library accessioned its millionth volume, and the east wing of the building was completed. Part of the
east wing was given over to the State Historical Society of Missouri,
which had been housed on the campus since its founding in 1898,
although never in adequate quarters. When Floyd Shoemaker retired
as director of the society in 1972 after forty-five years of service, Richard Brownlee, a native Missourian with a Ph.D. in history from the
university, succeeded him and filled the post with distinction until
his retirement in 1985, when he was succeeded by James W. Goodrich.

Also housed in the library, and administered jointly by the university and the State Historical Society, was the Western Historical Manuscripts Collection, established in 1943 with a grant from the Rockefeller Foundation. Under the leadership first of W. Francis English and
then of Lewis W. Atherton, both professors of history, the collection
developed into a major repository of personal, corporate, and public
papers relating to the history of Missouri and the West.

The university moved forward in another area of the humanities in
the 1950s as Saul Weinberg, professor of classical languages and archaeology, together with his wife, Gladys Davidson Weinberg, conducted the first Missouri-Cyprus expedition in 1954. This was followed by expeditions to other Mediterranean areas that resulted in a
museum collection of national repute. Indeed, through its museum,
library, and faculty, Missouri became an important center for the
study of classical archaeology and art history.

As further indication of the university's commitment to scholarship,
the University Press was established in 1958, with William H. Peden of

the Department of English as director. The first volume, *Seventeenth Century Songs and Lyrics*, presaged a distinguished output of award-winning literary, historical, and artistic works.

The Medical Center, renamed the University Hospital and Clinics, grew out of a 1951 decision to transform the two-year medical school into a full four-year program with a hospital. It was completed in 1960, thus providing the university with an impressive facility for patient care and clinical instruction. Adding to the clinical facilities available to medical students was a veterans hospital, constructed adjacent to the university hospital. Roscoe Pullen of the University of Texas was brought in to organize the new school, but he resigned in 1959, and the principal developmental work was continued by his successor, Vernon Wilson from the University of Kansas.

In the College of Agriculture, John H. Longwell retired as dean in 1960 and was replaced by Elmer R. Kiehl, chair of the Department of Agricultural Economics, who had been a member of the faculty since 1941. Dean Kiehl, an alumnus and a native Missourian, was an expert on world food problems; in addition to providing leadership for the College of Agriculture for more than twenty years he served as an adviser to Presidents Kennedy, Johnson, and Ford. During his years as dean, the college began its extensive involvement in agricultural technology transfer to underdeveloped countries—an involvement that continues to the present and in which the university has provided national leadership. Agriculture established an imposing presence on the campus with the completion in 1960 of a classroom and administrative building just south of McKee Gymnasium on Hitt Street. Also in 1960, the Department of Home Economics became a separate school, with Margaret Mangel as director.

Cooperative Extension, an important part of the College of Agriculture, was transformed in 1960 when C. Brice Ratchford, appointed director of Cooperative Extension in 1959, was named director of the Extension Division, which embraced general as well as agricultural extension. Ratchford, a national leader in the field, saw that to be truly effective in the mid-twentieth century extension must serve all segments of the population and not confine its services to agriculture. Despite substantial opposition he succeeded in putting extension together and made Missouri a model for the nation.

In the School of Law, Glenn A. McCleary, who had served as dean for twenty years, resigned in 1958 to give his full time to teaching. He was succeeded by Joe E. Covington of the University of Arkansas. Bond money made possible the enlargement of Tate Hall to accommodate the addition of nearly 40,000 volumes acquired from Lincoln University when at the end of segregation Lincoln closed its law school and law library. With this increment, the university law library became one of the fifteen largest in the country. In addition, the expansion of the building also provided the law school with a court room for the first time in its history. The law school also began to benefit from the Law School Foundation, established in 1928 by Earl F. Nelson, an alumnus. Law Day, the annual spring gathering of alumni, increasingly became a celebration of progress for one of the uni-

Law Day, 1950s.

versity's most prestigious schools, as prominent alumni returned to
the campus to renew friendships and to receive honors.

Another beneficiary of the state bond issue was the School of Business and Public Administration, which dedicated a new building in
1960. As a precursor of things to come, the new building contained
"an electronic computing machine" that was expected to be used by
the entire university. The School of Business and Public Administration enhanced both its services and its reputation through the establishment of a Bureau of Business and Economic Research directed by
Robert W. Paterson and a Bureau of Government Research directed
by Martin L. Faust. Paterson became dean of the school in 1971. Pinkney C. Walker, dean since 1964, had resigned to become a member of
the Federal Power Commission.

The College of Education, which had earlier benefited from the
construction of Hill Hall, completed in 1951, continued to grow apace,
as increasing numbers of students prepared themselves to meet the
needs of the exploding populations in the elementary and secondary
schools. Increasingly, they went on to graduate school—in the fifties
an average of nearly two hundred students received masters' and
doctors' degrees each year. A. Sterl Artley, an authority on teaching
children to read, achieved national fame for his "Dick and Jane"
books.

The Ellis years, then, were years of growth and improvement. It
was during this time that the character and structure of the university
was transformed—a change greater than any development in the
institution's long history. Ellis was convinced that for the university to
serve adequately the needs of the state it must have a presence in the

Lathrop, Laws, and Jones, 1960. Situated across from the Memorial Stadium, the Dobbs Group buildings are often draped with cheering words for the Tigers during the fall football season.

two large cities. Neither Kansas City nor St. Louis had a public institution of higher learning, and the university simply would not be able to take care of their growing needs for higher education from its campus in Columbia.

Thus, the University of Missouri became a four-campus institution, and the continuing story of the original campus at Columbia—Old Mizzou—goes forward under the name University of Missouri–Columbia.

# 5 UNIVERSITY OF
## MISSOURI–COLUMBIA

When the students returned to the campus in the fall of 1963—all 14,263 of them, more than in any earlier year—they found little evidence of the changes that had taken place over the summer. The lines at registration were just as long, the hassle over housing was just as intense. For those who went through rush, the excitement was just as great. The sights and sounds of the campus were about the same as they had always been.

For the students and faculty the most important and visible change was the completion of the south wing of Memorial Union. The new wing contained a small auditorium, an elegantly furnished alumni-faculty lounge, and meeting rooms of various sizes, including one set

Lines continued to be a feature of registration.

Completing a schedule was serious business.

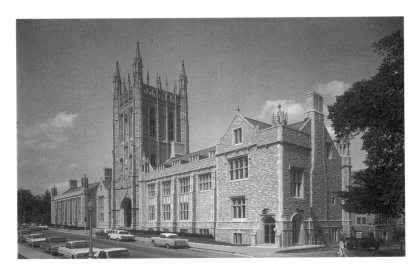

With the opening of the south wing of Memorial Union in 1963, a project that had begun just after World War I was finally completed.

aside for the board of curators. Adding to facilities available for students was the student commons—soon to be known as Brady Commons—on the mall between Conley Avenue and the medical complex.

Inside Jesse Hall, less visible but considerably more dramatic changes were taking place as President Ellis worked to enlarge the university from a main campus with a subordinate school of mines to a four-campus university system. The summer Commencement, held as usual on Francis Quadrangle between Jesse Hall and the columns, provided a hint of the changes that were taking place: the speaker was Carleton F. Scofield, formerly president of the University of Kan-

John W. Schwada, the first chancellor of the Columbia campus, confers with President Elmer Ellis. Schwada served as chancellor from 1964 to 1971, when he resigned to become president of Arizona State University at Tempe.

sas City, but now chancellor of the University of Missouri at Kansas City.

Although Ellis remained close to the campus, he separated himself somewhat by appointing a chancellor, John W. Schwada, dean of faculties. Schwada, a forty-three-year-old political scientist, had been a member of the faculty since 1951 and had served as dean of the School of Business and Public Administration. He was well known in Jefferson City, having served as state comptroller and director of the budget. His wife Wilma had grown up in Columbia.

The system was barely in place when the university paused to celebrate its 125th anniversary. The festivities involved alumni from around the country. Altogether there were sixty-nine alumni dinners, with thirteen of them occurring on 13 April when diners in twelve cities from coast to coast were connected by telephone to the celebration in Columbia. The connections were not very good, but nobody seemed to mind.

Governor John Dalton, himself an alumnus and one of the architects of the four-campus system, spoke glowingly of the university's service to the state but voiced a warning about the future. He did not see much hope for changing Missouri's low per capita support of higher education; private and corporate gifts would have to play an increasingly important role in university growth.

The university had not been particularly aggressive in seeking private funds, but earlier in the year the board had established a development council that became the basis for a greatly expanded effort to seek private funds in support of university activities. The result was slow but steady growth in private funds received. In 1970–1971 the annual total exceeded $1 million for the first time; in 1978–1979, it exceeded $5 million; in 1981–1982, $10 million (actually the total that year was over $14 million); and in 1986–1987, $15 million. Most of the gifts were small, but some, principally in the form of estates, exceeded $1 million, with the largest being from the estates of Henry and Alberta Ponder, which amounted to more than $8 million designated primarily for athletic scholarships and the School of Business and Public Administration. The G. Ellsworth Huggins estate provided $2.5 million for general scholarships; other gifts in excess of $1 million came from the estates of Olive G. McLorn, Elyzabeth Schell, Maybelle H.

Hillda (left) and Louise, mascots of the College of Veterinary Medicine, continue the long tradition of Missouri mules. Because of their many public appearances, they are becoming one of the most recognizable symbols of the university.

McIntyre, and Fred Miller. Jean Deal gave over $1 million through a life income trust, and J. Otto Lottes gave land valued at more than $1 million to assist in the construction of a health sciences library. In 1988 Donald W. Reynolds gave $9 million for a new alumni center, the largest single gift ever received.

The anniversary year brought visible signs of continued progress. Schurz and Hatch halls in the Bingham group, a new high-rise dormitory complex housing 1,164 students, consisted of two eight-story buildings, one for men and one for women, with central dining and lounge facilities. Wolpers Hall provided additional quarters for 351 women. A new swimming pool gave the university its first facility suitable for intercollegiate swimming meets.

The School of Veterinary Medicine was able to double the size of its entering class from thirty to sixty because of additions to Connaway Hall and completion of a new clinic. Adding to the research potential in veterinary medicine and other fields was a 500-acre farm given by Charles and Josie Sinclair. The Sinclair farm, under the direction of Charles C. Middleton, would develop a world-renowned herd of miniature pigs that would be used for significant research in such areas as aging and alcoholism.

Not as visible as the new buildings, but in some respects more pervasive, were the computers that seemed to be showing up every-

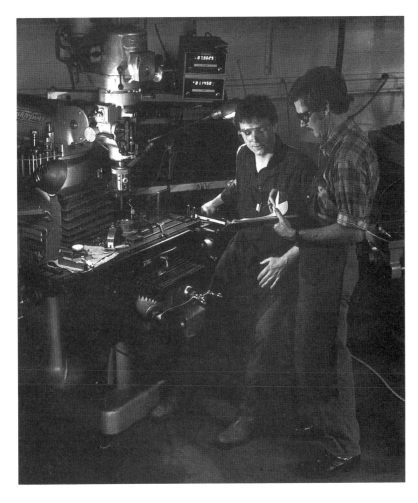

Research experience is offered to engineering students at every level. Here students receive supervised hands-on laboratory experience through a graduate program offered by the College of Engineering.

where as the university developed an international reputation for its pioneering work in the utilization of computers. In the medical center, Vernon Wilson, with the aid of federal grants in excess of $5 million, pioneered in the development of a regional medical program that brought the benefits of the university's advanced scientific and technological capacity to communities in all parts of the state. As part of that program Donald Lindberg directed a national pilot program in the use of computers as an aid to physician diagnosis. Gwilym S. Lodwick and Sam Dwyer gained international acclaim for their work in radiological computer research.

Further recognition of the university's leadership came in the seventies with a grant of $3.5 million to establish a health services research center with a national special emphasis program in health care technology. In the College of Arts and Science the National Science Foundation provided grants in excess of $4.5 million to aid in the further development of the mathematical sciences. An NSF grant also helped to construct a new building for physics. The library, under the leadership of Ralph Parker, acquired an international reputation as a world leader in the development of automated library systems. The university continued to maintain state-of-the-art computing capacity and to make it broadly available—by 1988, for example, every faculty

The Research Reactor dominates Research Park southwest of Memorial Stadium. The most powerful university reactor in the country, it is of particular importance to researchers in engineering and physics.

Just before a test in the physics building auditorium.

member in the College of Arts and Science would be equipped with a personal computer.

As computers were revolutionizing teaching and research, a $3.25 million research reactor was rising in the Hinkson Valley. Built under the supervision of Ardath Emmons, it was five times more powerful than any other university reactor in the country.

In addition to adding facilities at Columbia and moving the university into St. Louis and Kansas City, Ellis also encouraged the extension division to expand its program of carrying courses to all parts of the state. Brice Ratchford, dean of extension and an ardent proponent of off-campus instruction, used the university's newly acquired DC-3 aircraft to fly groups of faculty members around the state to conduct intensive short courses in a wide variety of subjects—under Ratchford extension expanded well beyond agriculture.

As the university grew it also developed a degree of faculty stability that had been quite unknown during most of its history. Illustrative of that stability were the number of faculty on whom the emeritus title was conferred and the years of service each of them had given. For example, at Commencement 1964, Ellis conferred the emeritus title on seven veteran teachers, with service ranging from fifteen to forty-five years: William H. Reid, dairy husbandry; Earnest T. Itschner, dairy husbandry; Arnold W. Klemme, soils; Horace W. Wood, Jr., civil engineering; Darwin A. Hindman, physical education; Chauncey D. Holmes, geology; and Frank Miller, agricultural economics.

In 1965 there were seven more emeriti, including some who had been legendary figures on the campus: Harold Swartout, horticulture; Bredelle Jesse, French; Herbert Bunker, physical education; Anton Stankowski, physical education; Glenn McCleary, former dean of law; Louis Eubank, education; and John Longwell, former dean of agriculture.

Alpha Pi Alpha, 1966, left to right: Charlie Brown, Alonzo Ledman, Cecil Webb, Mike Middleton, Charlie Rudd, Tom Polk.

The class of 1966 was even larger and their service ranged from eleven to forty-three years: Eleanor Taylor, education; Thomas Morelock, journalism; Elsa Nagel, German; Adella Ginter, home economics; J. U. Morris, extension education; W. R. Martin, Jr., horticulture; Lee Jenkins, entomology; Douglas Hansen, art; A. Cornelius Benjamin, philosophy; and Clyde Duncan, extension education.

The 1966 Commencement was the last over which Ellis presided. Although his appearance belied the fact, he had reached the statutory retirement age of sixty-five. He had spent thirty-six years at the university, and his twelve years as president had brought profound changes. The university not only had grown in size but also had changed in character.

For many Missourians, the Columbia campus remained *the* University of Missouri, and Ellis himself continued in many respects to function as Columbia's chief executive. He retained his office in Jesse Hall, and the Ellises continued to live in the president's house on Francis Quadrangle. With Ellis's retirement, the chancellor became the chief campus officer in fact as well as in name. The Schwadas moved into the president's house—which became the chancellor's residence—and as soon as University Hall was completed, Schwada occupied what had been the president's office in Jesse Hall. For most of the faculty, however, and for virtually all the students, the new

The Columns provide a favorite study hall.

It's hard to distinguish from the real thing—campus Republicans hold a mock political convention in 1968.

administrative relationships had little impact on their day-to-day activities.

Although students were touched by the idealism of the Kennedy years, Missouri seemed little affected by the convulsions that were rocking campuses on both coasts in the mid-sixties. While some would have agreed with John Kuhlman, popular professor of economics, who denounced the Greek houses as "increasingly irrelevant," the Greek system remained strong. Almost a fifth of the students were married, and the young couples living in the university-owned apartment complexes—the Village, the Heights, and the Terrace—were primarily concerned with grades and with making ends meet.

A study of student self-perceptions found that the students at Missouri saw themselves as being "work-oriented, or willing to work,

Students for a Democratic Society (SDS) designated the day of President Weaver's inauguration as "Gentle Tuesday," which they billed as a kind of "non-demonstration" against a "non-student event which characterizes undemocratic administration." Converging on Francis Quadrangle, the crowd was a mixture of long-haired students in colorful clothes and those in customary weejuns and Oxford shirts who had come to have a curious look at the campus's first "happening." The police were concerned, but nothing happened as "animals, picnic lunches, small children and floating balloons lent themselves to the pervading air of love for all in the sunny springtime."

mildly self-assertive, not very intellectual, somewhat constrained rather than self-expressive, deferent, and not very close to other students." Another survey concluded, "There is a wide range of student characteristics at the University, both in ability and personality. There are enough radical students to be noticed, as well as some extreme conservatives."

Increasingly, the radical students came to be noticed. Their vehicle was Students for a Democratic Society (SDS), a small but highly vocal and inventive group that carried on a constant battle with the campus administration concerning student rights and antiwar protests. A particularly celebrated case involved Barbara Susan Papish, a graduate student in journalism who was expelled for distributing a newspaper "containing forms of indecent speech." Miss Papish took her case all the way to the United States Supreme Court, which overturned the expulsion.

The most serious difficulty of the period grew out of the tragedy at Kent State University in the spring of 1970, when six students were killed during a peace demonstration. In reaction to the Kent State killings some faculty dismissed their classes, students (and some faculty) stormed Schwada's office, and mass meetings, attracting as many as 3,000, provided forums for airing student grievances and criticizing the war in Vietnam. In what hindsight would describe as overreaction, the curators dismissed one professor and suspended another without pay. The action resulted in censure by the American Association of University Professors that was not lifted until 1981.

In the long run, the students won some important points. Increasingly, students were appointed to campus committees and the

An SDS rally, 1967. Essentially SDS was carrying on the California-inspired crusade for "student power" and free speech, with "free speech" frequently being realized through the utterance of obscenities either vocally or in print.

Dean of Students Jack Matthews, beloved and respected by generations of students, was anathema to the members of SDS who expressed their views during a 1969 rally.

SDS represented a small minority of students. The vast majority were indifferent, but occasionally there was a counter rally.

curators began to meet regularly with student leaders. Intervisitation hours were gradually introduced and extended, and in 1977 some dormitories were made co-educational. By that time, the issue created hardly a ripple.

Responding to the demands of black students, the university created a minor in black studies in the College of Arts and Science. Arvarh Strickland, professor of history, was appointed head of an effort to recruit more black faculty, and George C. Brooks, a graduate of Lincoln University, succeeded Allan Purdy (who was transferred to a system responsibility) as director of Student Financial Aids.

Schwada resigned in 1971 to become president of Arizona State University at Tempe, being succeeded by Herbert W. Schooling, first as interim chancellor and then as chancellor. Schooling, sixty years old, was a seasoned administrator with extensive Missouri experience. He was Missouri born and educated, and except for a couple of years on the faculty of the University of Chicago, his entire professional career had been spent in Missouri. He had served as superintendent of schools in Webster Groves and North Kansas City, and since 1963 at the university as dean of the College of Education, dean of faculties, and provost.

Army ROTC training includes float trips in Missouri and skiing in Colorado.

While still interim chancellor, Schooling faced serious problems growing out of President Ratchford's efforts to reorganize the university under a plan that would avoid duplication by assigning each campus a specific role and scope within the overall mission of the university. A preliminary draft of the plan created an uproar on the Columbia campus as faculty members and administrators perceived a diminution in programs, particularly at the graduate level, in favor of developments on the other campuses. Schooling took the lead both in dampening the uproar and pressing for revisions in the plan. The plan went through several revisions, and when the curators finally approved it in the summer of 1974, little was changed at UMC. At the same time, opportunities for program expansion were severely curtailed.

There was change, to be sure—particularly in the development of an impressive array of interdisciplinary programs, made possible by the presence of a unique set of specialties in agriculture, engineering, and the health sciences. For freshmen and sophomores, an interdisciplinary honors program, dating from the 1960s, continued to flourish. This program was expanded to include all four undergraduate years, and, under a series of directors whose reputations as good teachers spread across the campus—W. "Mack" Jones, Richard Renner, William Bondeson, George Fasel, Theodore Tarkow, and Edward Kaiser—remained an exemplar of the strong interdisciplinary focus that was becoming the hallmark of a Missouri education.

There were changes in some senior administrative positions on campus. Jack Matthews retired in the summer of 1970 and was replaced by Ed Hutchins, assistant for student affairs to the president of Iowa State University. Hutchins, a low-key administrator with a reputation as a good listener, got on well with the students, but he was perceived as too permissive by a number of curators. After he

Herbert and Bess Schooling pose for a Christmas portrait at the front door of the chancellor's residence. Schooling, a veteran public school administrator, former dean of the Teachers College and dean of faculties, served as chancellor from 1971 until his retirement in 1978.

Chancellor Schooling presides over
Tap Day ceremonies held each spring
at the base of the columns.

A number of campus spots are enhanced by the "impact sculpture"
of Joseph Falsetti, professor of interior design.

Workmen placing the Jefferson Tombstone on Francis Quadrangle just west
of the chancellor's residence. The
tombstone, acquired by President
Laws, was first placed near the north
entrance of Academic Hall, where it
was unveiled during Commencement
in 1885. It was moved to its present
location during the bicentennial ceremonies in 1976.

resigned in 1972 to return to teaching, Hutchins was replaced by
James H. Banning from the University of Colorado in 1973. In many
respects, Banning's views and approaches to the students were similar to Hutchins's, but by the late seventies the student activism of the
early years of the decade had played itself out considerably.

Some student activism remained, but campus issues, which had
always tended to overshadow such global issues as racism and the
war in Vietnam, replaced the more universal questions on the student
agenda. Students continued to fight for more participation in university governance, and they gained membership on virtually all university committees. They established a student lobby in Jefferson City to
press student issues in the legislature. The issue that interested them
most was gaining a seat on the board of curators, and they finally
succeeded in 1984.

Schooling completely reorganized campus administration by creating provosts for academic affairs, administration, and health affairs.
Another new post, that of vice chancellor, went to Walter Daniel,
president of Lincoln University, who became the first black administrator on the campus.

Schooling appointed a substantial number of deans during his
five years as chancellor, including Armon Yanders, arts and science;
S. Watson Dunn, business and public administration; William Kimel,
engineering; Lloyd Berry, graduate school; Roy F. Fisher, journalism;
Allen Smith, law; Edward Miller, library science; Charles Lobeck,
medicine; Gladys Courtney, nursing; George Nicholas, social and

community services; and Kenneth Weide, veterinary medicine. Margaret Mangel, the first dean of home economics, was succeeded on her retirement by Bea Litherland.

Schooling also dedicated a number of new buildings: an alumni center built entirely with private funds, a general classroom building, a veterinary clinic, and a mathematics building. Of particular interest was Pickard Hall, the new museum opened in 1976. The old chemistry building on Francis Quadrangle was rehabilitated as a creative means of preserving one of the nineteenth-century buildings that formed the heart of the campus—one that in 1973 had been included on the National Register of Historic Places. This restoration gave the university an adequate place to exhibit the substantial collection that had been built over the years by the Department of Art History and Archaeology. The museum under the leadership of Saul Weinberg, and later of Osmond Overby, developed a central role in the cultural life of the campus.

Overshadowing all construction, however, was the Hearnes Multipurpose Building, opened in 1972. The huge structure covered 4.4 acres just east of Memorial Stadium. Although primarily an athletic facility, the building, as the name implies, was used for everything from commencements to rock concerts, from huge conventions to small conferences. The board named the building for Governor Warren Hearnes who had been one of its strongest proponents and who had been responsible for pushing it ahead of buildings to which the university had assigned higher priorities.

Meanwhile, change was imminent in the chancellor's office at Columbia. Schooling announced in 1977 that he would be sixty-five in 1978 and would retire no later than 31 August of that year. The board, on recommendation of the president, selected Barbara S. Uehling, provost of the University of Oklahoma, as UMC's third chancellor. It was a revolutionary appointment. Uehling, whose meteoric career had been a series of firsts, became the first woman to head a major land-grant campus. She was soon a national celebrity.

On the campus she confirmed her reputation as a decisive, nononsense administrator, standing in marked contrast to her easygoing, much-beloved predecessor. Early in her tenure, she abolished the position of provost of health sciences and provided that the head of the hospital should report directly to her. To manage the hospital she brought in Robert Smith, an experienced administrator from California, who in a short time revitalized the institution, turning a fiscal and physical embarrassment into an enterprise that could fund parts of its renovation and expansion from self-generated income. In addition, a combination of private gifts and state appropriations made possible such improvements as the John O. Lottes Health Sciences Library, the Eye Clinic, and the Diabetes Center. A new building for the School of Nursing provided badly needed teaching facilities. A neonatal clinic became one of the best in the nation. Helicopters, poised for flight around the clock, helped to extend the medical center's emergency service throughout central Missouri.

Initially, Uehling turned to former associates from Oklahoma for

The Museum of Art and Archaeology adds to its collections through gifts from organizations and individuals. This carrera marble sculpture, *Bathing Nymphs* by Johann von Halbig, 1867, was a gift of the Unrestricted Development Fund.

Chancellor Barbara Uehling about to serve a product of the dairy department. Uehling, the first woman to head a major public university, was chancellor from 1978 to 1986.

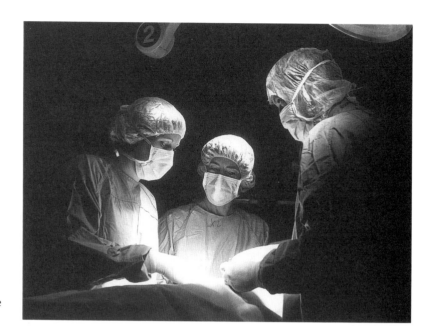

The University Hospitals and Clinics provide patients throughout the state with a variety of medical facilities.

To extend the services of the University Hospitals and Clinics, helicopters are used to bring accident victims and critically ill patients in from a wide area in mid-Missouri. Here one of them hovers over Francis Quadrangle.

her central staff. Shaila Aery, appointed assistant to the chancellor, later became Missouri's commissioner of higher education. Norman Moore became vice chancellor for student life. Duane Stucky, first appointed as a planner, became vice chancellor for administrative

Haskell and Jo Monroe enjoy a freshman picnic on Francis Quadrangle. Monroe, appointed chancellor in 1987, came to the university from the University of Texas–El Paso, where he had been president. Prior to that he taught history and served as dean of faculties at Texas A&M University. During their first summer in Missouri the Monroes toured the state in a van. During his first semester on campus, Monroe taught an early morning class in American history.

A piece of university history was rediscovered in 1981 when the bones of the notorious "Emperor" were found in the attic of Lefevre Hall. The carcass of the elephant was brought to the university and displayed in the Academic Hall museum by President Laws in 1887, although the financial scandal caused by his purchase of the elephant played a part in his resignation. The carcass was destroyed—although not the bones—when the elephant was dragged from the burning Academic Hall and abandoned in the snow.

affairs and, after Uehling's resignation in 1986, served as interim chancellor until Haskell Monroe, president of the University of Texas at El Paso, became chancellor.

During Uehling's early years Owen Koeppe filled the key position of provost. When he resigned, Uehling appointed Ronald Bunn of the State University of New York at Buffalo to the post. When Bunn left the position to return to teaching, Lois Defleur of the University of Oregon became the first woman to serve as provost.

Uehling appointed a substantial number of deans. In agriculture, Max Lennon of North Carolina succeeded Elmer Kiehl, who retired.

The university chorus and orchestra in one of the great oratorios that have become a highlight of the musical year.

When Lennon left to become a vice president at Ohio State University, Roger Mitchell, a former staff member, returned from Kansas State University, where he was vice president, to become dean. Other new deans included Milton Glick, arts and science; Stanley Hille, business and public adminstration; Will Miller, education, succeeding Bob G. Woods, who had served since 1970; Anthony Hines, engineering; James Atwater, journalism; Dale Whitman, law; Mary Lenox, library science; Michael Whitcomb, medicine; Phyllis Drennan, nursing; Robert Kahrs, veterinary medicine; and Don Blount, graduate school.

In a far-reaching change, the Missouri School of Religion, which had existed on the campus as an independent institution since 1896, closed its doors. The university created the Department of Religious Studies, with Jill Raitt, from Duke University, as chair.

Uehling continued the support of the performing arts that had been emphasized by her predecessor, and the Chancellor's Festival of Music, begun by Schooling, continued to be a major series of outstanding events, under the leadership of William Bondeson and Don McGlothlin. At the same time, campus groups—the Esterhazy Quartet and the University Singers, to name but two—improved in quality

Members of the Esterhazy Quartet, from left, artists-in-residence Eva Szekely, violin; John McLeod, violin; Carleton Spotts, cello; and Carolyn Kenneson, viola. The Esterhazy Quartet divides its time between performing and teaching. Founded in 1964, the quartet tours regularly throughout the United States and South America and records for the Spectrum and CRI labels.

and reputation. Collegium Musicum, founded by Andrew Minor, delighted audiences on campus and around the state with medieval music. Student theater, led by Larry Clark, continued its fine tradition; "11 Zulu," an original student production, was performed in the Kennedy Center in Washington as one of the 1984 winners in the American College Theater Festival. In 1978 an extraordinarily creative group in the Department of English started *The Missouri Review,* a literary journal with a contemporary orientation, which in a decade, under the editorship of Larry Levis, Martha Southwick, and Speer Morgan, developed a secure place for itself.

Schools and colleges continued to provide outstanding lecturers, with Journalism Week in the spring furnishing the campus community with particular opportunities to hear noted personages in the field of communications. A lecturership established by R. Crosby

During its first ten years, *The Missouri Review* established its reputation as one of the finest literary magazines in the country.

One of two Ming Dynasty stone lions standing guard at the northeast entrance to Francis Quadrangle. The lions, given by Chinese friends in 1931, symbolize the strong ties between the university and the people of China.

Kemper, Jr., of Kansas City, in memory of his mother, Enid Kemper, and inaugurated by Moshe Dayan, brought world figures to the campus each year. The Maxine Shutz Good Teaching Award, established by Byron Shutz in memory of his wife, who had served on the board of curators, gave the campus a special opportunity to recognize its outstanding teachers, with the first award being given to John Kuhlman in 1983. The Byler awards, established by Wiliam H. Byler, annually recognized faculty members for outstanding research.

The campus became rich in endowed scholarships as grateful alumni, many of whom had worked their way through school, used their resources to help make it possible for increasing numbers of young Missourians to attend the university. The private grants and the curators scholarships, continued from the nineteenth century, attracted increasing numbers of the state's brightest young people to Old Mizzou.

The Alumni Association, traditionally concerned almost solely with athletics, began to turn its attention to other aspects of campus life, in particular to providing funds with which the university could actively recruit outstanding students. As a result UMC became a national leader in the number of merit scholars on campus. Appropriately, UMC is chosen regularly by students winning the coveted Truman scholarships.

These bright students found good teachers in every department—dedicated scholars who had enthusiasm for teaching students at all levels. There are too many even to list. The *Missouri Alumnus* paid particular attention from time to time to some of the teachers judged by students to be among the campus's best. In 1970, for example, the magazine featured ten outstanding teachers from a broad range of disciplines: William D. Klapp, art; Karl Evans, civil engineering; Richard S. Kirkendall, history; Joseph Falsetti, interior design; Fred Davis, law; Betty Crim, nursing; William B. Bondeson, philosophy; Alfred S. Illingworth, religion; A. A. Case, veterinary medicine; and John Farmer, zoology. Again, in 1983, the magazine featured another group of outstanding teachers. They, like the earlier ones, came from all parts of the campus: Vera Townsend, art and art history; John Bauman, chemistry; John Kuhlman, economics; W. "Mack" Jones, English; Ira Papick, mathematics; Roland Hultsch, physics; and Greg Casey, political science.

The products of the university's classrooms, as in earlier years, built enviable reputations in a wide variety of activities. As with the good teachers, there are too many even to list, but among the more outstanding are Bruce Barkelow and Thomas R. Smith, computer experts who developed Procomm; Tom Berenger, actor; Linda Bloodworth-Thompson, television writer; Kate Capshaw, actress; Dan Coffey, San Francisco radio personality known as "Dr. Science"; Linda Gorman, producer of the television show "NOVA"; Linda Godwin, astronaut; Francis Peay, Northwestern University football coach; Richard Richards, astronaut; and Larry Smarr, director of the supercomputing research center at the University of Illinois.

When Lowry Street was closed and transformed into Lowry Mall the campus acquired a much used walkway and meeting place.

The Conley House was restored and rehabilitated in 1986 for use by the Missouri Cultural Heritage Center and the Honors College.

One of Uehling's major accomplishments was the beautification and general improvement of the campus. Most notable was the creation of Lowry Mall north of Ellis Library, a pedestrian area in the heart of the campus. The handsome old Conley House was restored

Johnny Roland, All-American 1965, a highly respected student who was described as "the finest all-around back in the United States."

Dan Devine visits with Alabama coach Paul "Bear" Bryant before the Gator Bowl game at the end of the 1968 football season. The Tigers upset Alabama 35 to 10.

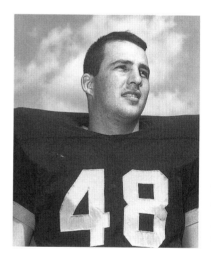

Woody Widenhofer, appointed head football coach in 1985, as a member of the 1964 Tiger football team.

for use by the Missouri Cultural Heritage Center and the Honors College.

Some specific appropriations and the university's share of a $600 million bond issue approved in 1980 made possible the construction of a number of badly needed new buildings: an animal science center, an agricultural engineering building, an engineering laboratory, a new law school, and an addition to Ellis Library.

Essentially, though, the late seventies and the early eighties were difficult years at Mizzou. State appropriations were never equal to the needs of the university, and for several years the governor was forced to withhold part of the money appropriated because of inadequate revenue. Repeatedly Uehling had to make hard decisions as she struggled to maintain quality in the face of fiscal stringency, and those decisions often were controversial.

Nothing, it seemed, created more controversy than intercollegiate athletics, and particularly football. Dan Devine, who gave Missouri more championship seasons than any coach in history, scored less than .500 in his last year at the Tiger helm. Al Onofrio, Devine's assistant, became head coach when Devine went to the Green Bay Packers, and took the Tigers to three bowl games, as well as scoring some record-shattering upsets—such as in 1974 when the Tigers defeated Alabama and in 1976 when Missouri defeated Southern California, Ohio State, and Nebraska—but he was never able to win a conference championship. When the Tigers lost ignominiously to Kansas, at the end of a 4 to 7 season, Schooling bowed to alumni pressure and let him go.

To rebuild the program, Schooling hired Warren Powers of Wash-

Tony Galbreath (30), Morris Townes (75), and Bill Marx (33) "in the thick of it" during the 1974 Missouri–Kansas game, final score 27 to 3 Missouri.

ington State, a former Nebraska and Oakland Raiders' star whose one season as head coach had produced a winning record, including a victory over Nebraska. In seven years Powers took the Tigers to five bowl games, but he was never popular, and at the end of a losing season in 1984 he suffered the fate of Onofrio.

The controversy surrounding football was by no means confined to the win-loss record. Indeed, it was focused on a controversial ticket policy developed by athletic director Dave Hart. Faced with the need to pay for an addition to the stadium and to meet rising costs everywhere, Hart developed a plan that required fans to contribute to the athletic scholarship fund for the privilege of buying season tickets in the prime locations. Although the plan was similar to those in use at almost every major football school, alumni and others rose up in arms. There was even a legislative investigation! Hart, with Uehling's backing, stuck by his guns. The policy continued to be a problem for alumni, and Hart, despite substantial achievements in the management of the athletic program, remained unpopular with many alumni during his career at Missouri. He resigned in 1985 to become commissioner of the Southern Athletic Conference, being replaced by Jack Lengyel.

Uehling's problems with athletics were further compounded by her insistence on following affirmative action procedures in hiring a replacement for Powers, rather than letting Hart negotiate freely. The fact that Woody Widenhofer, hired as a result of the process, won

Workmen repairing the sod on Faurot Field. Missouri was one of the last major football powers to convert from grass to artificial turf.

Marching Mizzou, the pride of all Missouri, struts its stuff at a home football game.

Fans enjoy a little diversion during a dull moment in a game against Kansas State.

The Golden Girls add to the excitement at Faurot Field.

only three games in his first two seasons and suffered the most lopsided defeat in Missouri's history—a 70 to 0 drubbing at the hands of Oklahoma—did not help matters. Memorial Stadium was seldom more than half full.

Basketball was a different story. Norm Stewart, former Mizzou All-American, produced one championship team after another, including a spectacular four-in-a-row, when the Tigers, sparked by Steve Stipanovich and Jon Sundvold, won the Big Eight Conference and the Big Eight Tournament every year between 1978 and 1983.

In baseball the Tigers continued to do well, frequently winning the Big Eight title and almost always finishing in the first division. A new, lighted diamond, named for Hi Simmons, provided the team with adequate facilities for the first time in history. The Tiger thinclads, coached by Tom Botts and then Bob Teel, maintained respectable records both in the Big Eight and nationally, despite the fact that their facilities remained the poorest in the conference.

As a result of the growing emphasis on equal opportunity for women in all phases of university life, women's teams began to compete in the full spectrum of intercollegiate sports, with basketball

The goal posts become a casualty of the 48 to 0 victory over arch-rival Kansas in the last game of the 1986 season.

Athletic Director Dave Hart makes a valiant effort to join in the high jinks of the Antlers, whose unrestrained exuberance is a feature of all Tiger home basketball games. Hart served as athletic director from 1978 to 1985, being succeeded by Jack Lengyel.

being the most popular and the most highly publicized. And even though athletics continued to be important, they were kept in perspective. If Missourians could not boast of spectacular winning streaks in any sport (except in men's basketball) they could take pride in the fact that their programs had never been tainted by even the hint of scandal. There were many reasons for this: the Faurot tradition remained strong; the program was closely watched by faculty members who understood the role of intercollegiate athletics in a university—typical was Henry Lowe of the law school, for many years

Norm Stewart in a characteristic "con-
versation" with an official. Stewart, a
former Mizzou All-American, was appointed head basketball coach in 1967.

Steve Stipanovich dominates the Irish of Notre Dame. Stipanovich and Jon
Sundvold provided the spark that produced four consecutive Big Eight
championships.

As intercollegiate competition opened
up for women, Missouri soon developed winning teams. Joni Davis, with
2,126 points in her four-year career
and whose jersey number was retired
when she graduated, holds the distinction of being the most prolific
scorer in Mizzou basketball history.

Missouri's faculty representative to the Big Eight Conference, whose enthusiasm for athletics was equaled by his enthusiasm for and knowledge of classical music.

Although details changed with the times, traditions continued. Homecoming remained the year's most elaborate event, but much of the old hurrah was replaced by serious efforts on the part of students to become better acquainted with alumni. Some houses donated to charity the funds they would have spent on decorations. An alumni-student lunch, first held in the Hearnes Multipurpose Building in 1973, became a major event. The homecoming queen was replaced in 1977 by a king and queen (Dan Downing and Mary Barnes), and in 1985 a black couple was chosen (Jill Young of St. Louis had been the first black queen in 1971; Marvin Cobbs of University City and Vivian King of St. Louis were the first black couple).

Perhaps nothing symbolized the changing campus more than the changes that took place in Commencement. For years Commencement had been held in Memorial Stadium, but with the completion of Hearnes the exercises were moved inside. They were never the same—air-conditioned comfort could not replace the magic of the outdoor ceremony. Moreover, as enrollment reached 25,081 in 1981, convocations sponsored by the individual schools replaced the general Commencement in importance. In 1972, during the last year of com-

"Oozeball," during the 1986 annual free-for-all tournament sponsored by the Alumni Association Student Board.

Sorority Rush may have been serious for some, but not for all.

The dome on Jesse Hall, lighted 1 October 1987 as the symbol of the sesquicentennial.

mencements in the stadium, fewer than half the eligible seniors attended.

The individual schools, under the leadership of a very competent cadre of deans, continued to improve their programs of teaching, research, and service. Virtually every department included faculty members with national reputations in their fields. Some had received extraordinary recognition, as was the case with Earnest Sears in agronomy and James Davis in physiology, who were elected to the National Academy of Sciences.

There was never enough money, and budgetary problems tended to cast a shadow over underlying accomplishments, but as the university approached its sesquicentennial, its oldest and largest campus stood in the center of the state as a living monument to the efficacy of the idea of a public university. The lighted dome on Jesse Hall—symbol of the sesquicentennial—shines across the land as Missouri's enduring lamp of learning.

# Rolla

# 6 BEGINNINGS

## AT ROLLA

Long before Missouri became a state, adventuresome entrepreneurs had arrived to exploit the rich mineral deposits known to Europeans since the early eighteenth century. As early as 1819, Henry Rowe Schoolcraft suggested the establishment of a school of mines in the Missouri mineral area, observing that the greatest drawback to the development of a mining industry throughout the nation was the lack of scientific knowledge. When the Morrill Act of 1862 provided for federal land grants to support at least one "college of agriculture and mechanic arts" in each state, the proposal was seriously considered.

The legislature almost lost the state's land grant because of a disagreement about location, but Senator James S. Rollins of Columbia and Representative William N. Nalle of Fredericktown finally worked out a compromise. The land-grant college was to be incorporated into the university, with the understanding that the board of curators was to establish a school of mines and metallurgy in the mining district of southeast Missouri.

The curators asked five eligible counties to bid for the school, but only Iron and Phelps counties did so. Although both bids were in bonds and land, the board was particularly impressed with the Phelps County inclusion of a 130-acre tract known as Fort Wyman at the edge of the village of Rolla. On 10 March 1871, the General Assembly confirmed the curators' decision to locate the Missouri School of

Henry Rowe Schoolcraft, the noted scientist and explorer, surveyed the mineral resources of southeastern Missouri in the 1820s. He suggested the establishment of a school of mines in the area for the benefit of the entire nation.

Map of Missouri, 1869, showing the mineral area of southeast Missouri.

Charles P. Williams, the first director, served from 1871 to 1877. Age thirty-three when appointed, he was married, with two small children. He had two degrees from Polytechnic College of Pennsylvania. At the time of his appointment he was professor of chemistry at Delaware State College. Prior to teaching at Delaware he had acquired considerable experience as a geologist and metallurgist in various western states, Mexico, and around Lake Superior.

Mrs. Charles P. Williams. Of her, an early historian wrote, "She was a highly educated, refined and cultured woman, of unusual practical good sense and social charm."

Mines and Metallurgy at Rolla. Even before receiving legislative approval, the board began making plans to construct a building and to hire a director. They appointed Charles P. Williams, professor of chemistry at Delaware College and chemist for the state of Delaware, as director.

The town of Rolla, while beautifully situated, did not provide a particularly auspicious site for a new school. It had a population of about 1,300 and no improved streets. There were four churches and nine saloons. Its most impressive building was a four-story brick school. The building provided more space than could be used by the public schools, so Williams arranged to rent the top two floors for the School of Mines for $1,300 a year, pending completion of a building on the Fort Wyman site.

With quarters assured, Williams announced in the two local newspapers that the Missouri School of Mines would begin classes 6 November 1871. Advertisements offered a broad curriculum in engineering, promising that "Students of the full course, on satisfactory examinations, will be entitled to the degree of Mining Engineer; though certificates of proficiency will be issued, on satisfactory evidence, to those pursuing studies in any of the branches of instruction."

Although classes began 6 November with an enrollment of thirteen, the formal dedication took place 23 November. Prominent persons from all parts of the state converged on Rolla for the ceremonies. As a strong supporter of practical education, President Read, who had come from Columbia, spoke of his high hopes for the new school. Director Williams expanded on these themes, stating, "It must always be borne in mind that our school is necessary to the integrity of the university system of the State—not incompatible with its objects and designs, but on the contrary making these fuller, nobler and grander,

The Rolla Building, acquired from the Rolla Board of Education, was the only building on the campus during the school's first fifteen years. It is still in use.

A drawing class in the Rolla Building. Only an occasional student worked in vest and shirtsleeves.

bringing them in more intimate relations with the technical wants of the age."

In the months following the dedication Williams struggled to develop a curriculum and to find a faculty to teach it. He had few precedents to guide him. The Polytechnic College of Pennsylvania, where he had been educated, conferred the first American degree in mining engineering. Columbia University in New York awarded the first degree from its School of Mines in 1867, and the Massachusetts Institute of Technology granted its first mining degree in 1868. Following the examples of these schools, Williams devised a program in which students first studied pure sciences and mathematics and then applied their learning to practical problems, a combination that is still the hallmark of a Rolla education.

Initially Williams was assisted by Nelson Allen, who was studying for a degree in mathematics at Columbia, and William Cooch, who had been a student of Williams at Delaware College. As enrollment increased and the curriculum developed, Williams added faculty. Colonel James W. Abert, professor of English at the University in Columbia, was appointed in 1872 as professor of applied mathematics and civil engineering and served until 1877. A seasoned army officer, he was placed in charge of military training.

James W. Abert with students, ca. 1873. Abert, a graduate of Princeton and West Point, had accompanied General Frémont on his expedition of 1845 and had developed a considerable reputation as a cartographer. He had fought in the Seminole and Mexican wars as well as the Civil War.

Captain R. W. Douthat, a Confederate veteran of the Battle of Gettysburg, served as professor of English from 1873 to 1884. In an effort to increase enrollment, he established on his own authority a "Girls Course in the Arts." He also founded the short-lived Western Musical Conservatory.

Captain R. W. Douthat joined the faculty in 1873 as professor of English. Although he called himself "Doctor," he did not have a college degree. He was adept at languages, however, and at various times taught Latin, Spanish, and German. George D. Emerson, who held a degree from Cincinnati Law College and had served in the Union Army as a military engineer, also joined the faculty in 1873 as professor of mining engineering and graphics. Rounding out the early faculty was Dr. William Ellis Glenn, a Rolla physician who was appointed lecturer in anatomy, physiology, and hygiene. He became a member of the board of curators in 1875 but continued to lecture at the school without salary.

Almost from the beginning Williams recognized the need for a "preparatory" curriculum (only two percent of the nation's seventeen-year-olds were high school graduates), and in 1872 the school added a preparatory department, which was met with enthusiasm by local residents. By 1874, three-fourths of the more than one hundred students were enrolled in the preparatory department.

Interestingly, in a school that for most of its history has been a male bastion, approximately one-fourth of the students were women, all of them in the preparatory department. There was, of course, much concern that the women students be sufficiently segregated. They were allowed to attend classes with the men, but they came and went by different stairways, and a room was set aside on the third floor "exclusively for the ladies." Communication between the sexes in the building or on the grounds surrounding it was not allowed. However, Gustavus Duncan, a member of the first graduating class, remembered that "co-eds enlivened the old Rolla building . . . and . . . romance was not wanting."

All students were governed by strict regulations imposed by the board of curators. They were expected to attend church services once a week and could hold meetings only with the consent of the president of the university. Under no circumstances were they to submit petitions or to criticize the operations of the university.

The first three graduates—Duncan, Gill, and Pack—started their working lives together in Colorado. Shortly after they began, Gill called them to order for "the first Meeting of the Alumni of the Missouri School of Mines and Metallurgy." Although the Alumni Association was not formally organized until 1921, meetings were held occasionally. Duncan recalled a meeting in Denver in 1882, with Professor Emerson serving as toastmaster.

Literary and debating societies, organized soon after the school opened, provided entertainment for students, faculty, and townspeople. Dr. Glenn served as president of the Shakespearean Club. The Emersonian Club, with twelve members, took its name from Professor Emerson, whose book reviews were particularly popular. The Irving Literary Society sponsored the reading of original poetry and presented such performances as the farce "A Lame Excuse" and an oration on the "Necessity of Labor."

Most students came from homes in the area. John Holt Gill, a member of the first graduating class, came in daily by train from his home ten miles west of Rolla. John W. Pack drove a team of horses from his father's farm, six miles from town. Gustavus Duncan rode ten miles on horseback every day. Some students walked several miles to and from school. This inconvenience prompted Duncan to organize a "club" that set up housekeeping arrangements in rented rooms over the Morris hardware store on Pine Street, with a cook and a quiet study area.

The school held its first Commencement on 18 June 1874, with three graduates—Duncan, Gill, and Pack. The proceedings lasted four days, with the first three days being devoted to an examination of the classes. The examinations were public and were "well attended by our citizens and the visitors who honored the city with their presence." The *Rolla Herald* observed that a large number of "distinguished persons from abroad" were present, and Director Williams delivered the charge to the graduates, according to the *Rolla Herald*, "with thoughts that breathe and words that burn." Addresses were given by Albert Todd, who had been active in founding the school, and by John S. Phelps of Springfield, the only surviving member of the commission that had located the university in 1839. Afterward, all repaired to Creusbaur's Hall for a midnight supper and dancing that continued, in the words of the *Rolla Herald*, "into the wee small hours of the morning."

Despite the euphoria generated by such events as the first Commencement, the School of Mines faced serious financial problems. When the Supreme Court of Missouri invalidated the Phelps County bonds, the curators concluded that they could not proceed with con-

Charles E. Wait taught for a couple of years in his hometown of Little Rock, Arkansas, worked as a mining engineer in Arkansas and California, and, at the time of his appointment as director, was serving as chemist with the Alabama Geological Survey.

struction at the Fort Wyman site. Indeed, there was concern for the future of the school itself. The 1870s were years of deep depression in Missouri as in the nation at large, with crop failures, bank closings, and bankruptcies. The Rolla school district faced financial problems even more severe than those plaguing the university; it was becoming increasingly clear that the handsome brick school building was a luxury the district could not afford. After prolonged negotiations the curators bought the school building, now known as the Rolla Building, for $25,000, giving the School of Mines a permanent home.

The acquisition of a building by no means solved the school's financial problems. Faced with niggardly appropriations of $5,000 a year and declining enrollment, Williams resigned the directorship in 1877. He remained in Rolla for a year as director of the geological survey and then returned to Philadelphia. Despite almost insurmountable difficulties, he had established the school, recruited an able faculty, secured a permanent home for the institution, and set the school on the curricular course it would follow through most of its history.

To succeed Williams, the curators chose Charles E. Wait, a twenty-

Wait was single when he arrived, but within two years he married Miss Leila Beasley, described as the "most beautiful woman in Rolla."

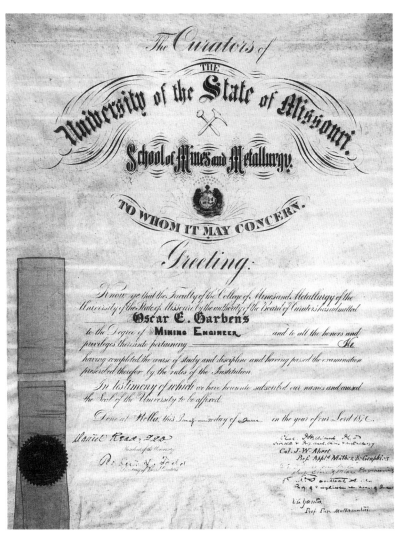

An 1876 diploma.

eight-year-old graduate of the University of Virginia. During his eleven years as director, Wait faced dwindling enrollment and declining support for the institution.

Hoping to attract more students, Professor Douthat, apparently on no authority other than his own, set about to broaden the curriculum. He developed a "Girls Course in Arts" that included classes ranging from music, history, and foreign languages to bookkeeping and calculus. He also founded the Western Musical Conservatory, using the facilities of the Methodist Episcopal Church South. In addition, Douthat felt that the school needed a boarding house for students. Accordingly, he had an old tobacco factory converted into a building that could house sixteen students plus his own family of nine children. The students called it "Poverty Flats." To provide for women, Douthat rented a nearby house.

Douthat's efforts met with strong opposition from the "technical faculty" of the school, and the board of curators adopted a reorganization plan that virtually eliminated Douthat's department. In addition, President Laws thought the technical programs should be moved to Columbia and the normal department in Columbia should be moved to Rolla. This view was shared by some on the board and around the state. In the end, however, the board concluded that no good purpose was served by continued talk of removal. The General Assembly agreed but did pass legislation requiring the School of Mines to adopt a "liberal academic course of study." This essentially was what Douthat had wanted, but by that time he had resigned.

During these trying years the school not unexpectedly experienced considerable faculty turnover—there were four professors of mathe-

A surveying class poses with their instruments, ca. 1890, all decked out in coats, ties, and hats. Daniel Jackling is second from the right.

The chemistry laboratory, completed in 1885, was the second building on the campus. Ultimately known as "Old Chem," the building was used until it was destroyed by fire in 1969.

The chemistry laboratory and the Rolla Building, from an 1885 photograph taken by Director Charles E. Wait.

Before coming to Rolla, William H. Echols, a graduate of the University of Virginia, worked as a railroad engineer and managed a mining company. Only twenty-nine at the time of his appointment, he continued the tradition of youthful directors.

matics in six years. While it is difficult to imagine an engineering curriculum without the study of physics, the school had no professor of physics until 1892 when the board named J. M. Morris, a teacher in the public schools and a member of a prominent Rolla family, to the post. Morris apparently did very well, but a year later the curators abolished the position. Although money for operations remained woefully short, the legislature did appropriate $10,000 for a twelve-room chemistry laboratory.

Director Wait never solved the school's most serious problem, inadequate enrollment. When he became director, enrollment had dropped to 43. It increased to 110 in 1883, but by the time Wait resigned in 1888 to become professor of chemistry at the University of Tennessee it had declined to 50.

To succeed Wait, the board selected William H. Echols, who had joined the faculty a year earlier as a replacement for George Emerson, the last of Williams's faculty to leave. In Echols's three years as director, he exerted substantial influence on the development of the institution. He tried to pattern the school after the Massachusetts Institute of Technology, with courses organized into two divisions, technical and academic.

The class of 1882 in the chemical engineering laboratory.

To head the academic division, Echols chose E. A. Drake, educated at the University of Wisconsin. The technical division operated without a head. Walter Buck Richards from the University of Virginia became head of the mathematics department, and George R. Dean entered the school as a student and an instructor in mathematics. In 1890, Chase Palmer, from Johns Hopkins—and the first Ph.D. to teach at Rolla—became chairman of chemistry. Unfortunately, he left after only a year.

Enrollment began to rise during Echols's tenure, reaching a peak of eighty before he left. To accommodate the increase, Echols secured an appropriation of $5,000 to build a student club. This building, designed by Henry Hohenschild, a local architect who also had drawn the plans for the chemistry laboratory, could house twenty-five to thirty students and seat as many as sixty in the dining hall. Students paid twelve dollars a month for board and room. The grounds, now occupied by three buildings, were beginning to assume some of the characteristics of a conventional college campus. To enhance the environment, Echols constructed sidewalks and built a fence around the campus.

Some years after his graduation, George R. Dean returned to Rolla as a professor of mathematics, serving in that position for forty years, a popular, almost legendary figure. Known as "Old Prof," his eccentric teaching methods were accentuated by his booming voice. Here he enjoys one of the attractions of teaching at Rolla.

The campus in 1890, showing the club house, the chemistry laboratory, and the Rolla Building, with Echols's fence in the foreground.

The football team with Coach Austin McRae, 1893. McRae provided the players with orange and white uniforms, as close as he could come to the school's colors of silver and gold. Interestingly, McRae, who later became director, had also coached the University of Missouri's first football team.

When Echols left to become professor of mathematics and engineering at the University of Virginia, he recommended as his successor a Virginia classmate, Elmo Golightly Harris. Harris was plagued by faculty turnover and even more by controversy over a mining and metallurgy building. Harris had wanted an engineering building, but W. H. Seamon, head of the chemistry department, went forward with his own design for a mining and metallurgy laboratory. When the board accepted Seamon's plan, Harris resigned after only two years. He remained on the faculty, however, as professor of engineering, a post he held for forty years.

One of Harris's most important contributions to the school was the appointment of Austin L. McRae as professor of physics. McRae had a doctorate from Harvard, and he came to the School of Mines from the University in Columbia—where he had been the school's first football coach. He spent most of his active life at the School of Mines, enlarging the work in physics and serving as director from 1915 to 1920. McRae may be best remembered, however, as the father of organized athletics at MSM.

Although students had played baseball in the 1880s and had organized a team called the Ozarks, the Student Athletic Association dates from 1891. A field was graded and enclosed that year, and in 1893 MSM played its first intercollegiate football game, losing to Drury. Professor McRae persuaded the faculty to approve athletic competition and coached the team. During the early years, most "seasons" consisted of one game, and in some years no games were played at all.

To replace Harris as director, the board chose Walter Buck Richards. He was particularly interested in developing the technical aspects of the curriculum, and at the same time he stressed the importance of both English and foreign languages. Richards became so embroiled in controversy that he was able to accomplish little. President Jesse

Elmo Golightly Harris became the third graduate of the University of Virginia to serve as director of the Missouri School of Mines. At the age of thirty, he also continued the tradition of young directors.

Walter Buck Richards, a thirty-year-old graduate of the University of Virginia who had been teaching mathematics at Rolla since 1888, had elaborate plans for the school when he was appointed director in 1893.

Mining and metallurgy laboratory—assaying.

opposed any expansion at Rolla, so relations between Columbia and Rolla grew particularly strained. Richards opposed repeated efforts in the legislature to separate the School of Mines from the university, alienating many people in Rolla. His principal difficulties, however, stemmed from the mining and metallurgy building then being planned. Richards's unsuccessful attempts to reinstate Harris's ideas angered architect Hohenschild, who had become a member of the legislature. Hohenschild had enough influence with the board of curators to bring about the director's dismissal in July 1897.

Testing a steam drill, mining and metallurgy laboratory.

A qualitative analysis class in Old Chem.

Surveying class, 1897. Students by no means "dressed down" for field work.

Norwood Hall was named for J. G. Norwood, dean of the School of Medicine in Columbia. He had no connection whatever with MSM except that he was the father-in-law of J. D. Vincl of Rolla, president of the board of curators.

George E. Ladd, director from 1897 to 1907, a thirty-three-year-old New Englander who had worked for the United States Geological Survey in Texas and Missouri, although he had never taught. He proved to be an extremely popular director, and the school made great progress during his administration, being transformed from what was described as a "country academy" into a genuine college.

In September the board appointed George E. Ladd, a thirty-three-year-old New Englander with a Harvard Ph.D., as director. Ladd was not impressed with the town or the school. Rolla still had no public improvements and no sidewalks outside the small business section. The buildings at the School of Mines were poorly designed and maintained. Hohenschild's club house and mining building were "monstrosities." Indeed, the school seemed to have very little going for it. The president of the Michigan School of Mines had declared that the Missouri school was merely "a country academy." Moreover, Ladd found that neither the board nor the administration in Columbia had much interest in the school; there was strong sentiment for moving the whole thing to Columbia.

Despite these discouraging circumstances, Ladd worked vigorously not only to preserve the School of Mines but also to improve and to expand it, and he achieved remarkable success. The legislature provided money for improved operations, additions to the campus,

This building, originally a dormitory built in 1889, became the director's residence in 1904 and continues to serve as the chancellor's residence.

renovation of existing buildings, and construction of two new buildings: Mechanical Hall, opened in 1902, and Norwood Hall, completed in 1903.

Through the influence of J. D. Vincil, a resident of Rolla and president of the board of curators, the legislature moved the State Geological Survey from Jefferson City to Rolla where it was housed in the Rolla Building. Other campus changes included conversion of the club house, which had been closed, into a residence for the director and moving the library, which had grown to 6,000 volumes, to the

Occasionally, students and faculty broke the routine with trips out of town to visit a mine or to St. Louis to see an industrial plant. Here they enjoy a picnic outing at the Maramec Iron Works, 1891.

first floor of the new Norwood Hall, and the mineralogical museum to the third floor.

Enrollment finally increased, reaching 224 in 1904. The faculty more than doubled in size, growing to twenty-six during Ladd's administration. Ladd brought Austin L. McRae back from the University of Texas and Durwood Copeland from the Michigan College of Mines to chair the Department of Metallurgy. George Dean joined the faculty to teach mathematics. Victor Hugo Gottschalk, another local product, became head of the chemistry department.

Tau Beta Pi, a technical and scientific honorary, was established in 1906, and Theta Tau, an engineering honorary, ten years later. On the social side, Greek letter fraternities made their appearance at MSM by 1903, providing both housing and a variety of activities. Sigma Nu was the first to arrive, and chapters of Kappa Alpha and Kappa Sigma were established later that year. Pi Kappa Alpha followed in 1905, and Lamba Chi Alpha in 1917. The fraternities' annual dances became the social highlights of the year.

In 1880, well over a third of the students in the preparatory department were women. By 1893 women made up forty percent of MSM's enrollment. A year later the legislature abolished the preparatory department, and the enrollment of women drastically declined. In

In 1893, the year this photograph was
taken, women made up forty percent
of students enrolled. When the preparatory department was abolished
by the legislature a year later the
enrollment of women drastically
declined.

Student room, ca. 1897.

1897, only four women attended the School of Mines.

During the 1890s the library in the Rolla building boasted 3,000
volumes, and there were two literary societies that met weekly, the
Philo Society for young men and the Alpha Club for young women.
These years also saw the beginning of the technical societies such as
the Missouri Mining Club, the Electrical Club, the Engineers' Club,
and the Journal Club.

Rolla itself did not offer much in the way of recreational opportunities. There was John Scott's drugstore, where one could meet young
ladies for a soda, and after 1909 there was a motion picture house.
Students frequently gathered at the post office to wait for the mail to

The orchestra, organized in 1907, provided music for campus events, such as dances in Mechanical Hall, and gave concerts in nearby towns.

be sorted, and a trip to the station to watch the train come in provided pleasant diversion.

Somewhat surprisingly, there were quite a few foreign students on campus. As early as 1907 an International Club came into being, with members from India, Russia, Mexico, the Philippines, South America, the Orient, and western Europe. Two years later students established a chapter of the National Association of Cosmopolitan Clubs—the first ever organized at a mining school. The number of students from Latin America continued to increase, and a Latin American Club was formed in 1914.

The Young Men's Christian Association, organized at MSM in 1904, soon became an important element in student life, with a membership that included almost half the students. In addition to recreational activities, representatives of the "Y" met new students at the train in the fall, brought them to the campus, helped them locate board and room, and even assisted with registration.

Director Ladd had a great interest in athletics, particularly football, which he had played in his youth. He encouraged the nascent football program, and in the 1900 season the team played six games, including a game with the university in Columbia. In 1904, the athletic association hired its first football coach, E. F. Boland. The athletic program also included a track team, which competed against the University of Kansas and Washington University in 1907, and a basketball team, which in the same year played Drury College and Washington University. Baseball, begun earlier, was continued.

During his ten years as director, Ladd transformed MSM from a

Football team, ca. 1905.

Lewis E. Young, director from 1907 to 1913, was only twenty-eight years of age at the time of his appointment. His years as director were marked by substantial improvements in faculty and facilities.

"country academy" to a genuine college. Ladd was popular both on campus and in the community, but a small group led by Senator Hohenschild kept up a steady drumfire of opposition. When Joseph Folk was elected governor, with Hohenschild's support, the way was cleared for an investigation of the School of Mines and particularly its director. The trumped-up charges—including the allegation that the director was encouraging the students to learn to play pool—were proved groundless, and the board reaffirmed its support. Ladd, however, weary of controversy, resigned to pursue mining interests in the Joplin area. The board selected Lewis E. Young, a twenty-eight-year-old professor of mining at the Colorado School of Mines, to succeed Ladd. Young guided MSM through six eventful years of progress, generally continuing the course charted by his predecessor.

Student enrollment stayed up, rising as high as 254 and never dipping below 181. With the abandonment of the preparatory department, the student population was made up almost entirely of men. An important exception was Eva Endurance Hirdler, who transferred from Washington University as a junior in 1909. She was something of a curiosity, and on field trips, which had become an organized part of the curriculum, she was required to arrange for a chaperone. She completed the course in mining engineering, but the faculty designated her degree as a B.S. in general science—only a man could be a mining engineer!

Although there was no organized alumni association, in 1910 the students formed the Missouri Mining Association for juniors, seniors, and alumni. Its goal was to expose students to the mining profession and to help alumni keep in touch with their alma mater. Another organization formed in 1910 was the student council, established to provide a vehicle for expressing student opinion. Only a few students could be accommodated by fraternities, and various eating clubs became a useful part of student life. They bore such expressive names as "Grubstakers," "R-Way," and "Training Table."

Students continued to provide most of their own entertainment, and the "Miner's Minstrel," first performed in 1909, became a popular annual event. Even more popular were the "Colonial Minstrels" per-formed by the young ladies of Rolla. The 1909 *Rollamo* reported, "The 'end men' were of course a feature of the evening. . . . Miss Rowe's soubrette songs, 'I'm Strong for You' and 'Love Me Like I Like to be Loved,' were highly successful, causing one young student to eat a whole programme and another youth to shrink to almost inapprecia-ble volume."

The greatest student entertainment of all, though, was the celebra-tion of Saint Patrick's Day, which began in 1908. It all started when engineering students on the Columbia campus invited MSM to send a delegate to their Saint Patrick's Day celebration. The students de-cided to have their own celebration with what remained of the money raised to send their delegate. The organizers spent the night secretly decorating Norwood Hall, posting handbills around town announc-ing a holiday—it was a school day—and requesting all students to meet at the depot at 8:00 a.m. the next day, where they met St. Pat's arrival on a handcar. The *Rollamo* commented, "At 8 A.M. every stu-dent reported at the depot, where they were supplied with green sashes and shelalahs [*sic*]. The students had struck, and a holiday had been established at M.S.M.!"

The parade, led by the MSM band and Saint Patrick, who was clad in a flowing silk robe and holding a mitre, moved to the steps of Nor-wood Hall. George Menefee, the first Saint Patrick, made a "thrilling speech," interpreting the hieroglyphics on the blarney stone found in the Rolla area, proving to all that Saint Patrick was an engineer. The seniors and Director Young were then dubbed Knights of Saint Pat-rick, after which the parade moved on to the town. The historic day ended with a dinner and a band concert on campus.

The celebration soon became more elaborate, and as the years went by new traditions were added. After the first year, St. Pat's Day be-came the responsibility of the junior class, and the next year fresh-men were sent to the woods to gather shillelaghs for all the students. That year a green ribbon was required in order to be admitted to the campus on 16 and 17 March. Snake killing started in 1912 as did the "kowtow." Beginning in 1913 St. Pat rode a manure spreader in the parade. That was also the first year of the masked ball, when the first queen of St. Pat's, Helen Baysinger, was crowned.

In many respects, the major achievement of Young's administration was the construction of Parker Hall. Designed by George Hellmuth (a former student) of Hellmuth and Hellmuth in St. Louis, the building provided for the library (boasting 14,500 volumes), the administrative offices, and the YMCA. Its principal feature was a handsome 550-seat auditorium. In his efforts to improve the campus, Young found an ally in alumnus Daniel Jackling, a highly successful graduate of 1892. Jackling, who had established a student loan fund in 1910, contributed funds to build an athletic field, complete with concrete bleachers, and agreed to help fund a new gymnasium.

Young asked Hellmuth to prepare the design, but here he ran afoul of Henry Hohenschild, who wanted the job for himself and, as be-fore, used political influence to gain his ends. When the board gave

In 1972, as an eighty-eight-year-old grandmother, Eva Endurance Hirdler Greene received a second B.S. degree, this one in mining enineering.

Daniel C. Jackling, a graduate in 1892, worked his way through school, partly as an assistant in chemistry and metal-lurgy, and became one of the country's most successful mining engineers. Students and the school itself were fre-quent recipients of his generosity.

St. Pat arrives in Rolla, 1915.

The "kowtow" to St. Patrick, 17 March 1915, carrying on a tradition begun in 1912.

The "Irish Girl Chorus" in St. Pat's parade, 17 March 1915.

Parker Hall, completed in 1912, honored Luman Frank Parker, a Rolla attorney who had long been a friend of MSM.

the contract to Hohenschild, Young resigned in disgust. The board asked Leon Garrett, a highly successful and popular teacher of mathematics, to serve as acting director, a position he held for a year and a half. Garrett's administration is perhaps best known for its short-lived effort to develop an outstanding football team.

In 1909 MSM (rather than the athletic association) hired the first football coach, F. E. "Spike" Dennie, who also taught physical education and civil engineering. Dennie compiled a respectable record, and E. H. McCleary, who became coach in 1912, improved on that record. His 1913 team lost only to the University of Missouri. In 1914, with Tom Kelly as coach, the Miners did not lose a game, scoring a total of 540 and holding their opponents scoreless. Included in the eight victories was a 9 to 0 defeat of the University of Missouri. The 1914 team was definitely an aberration. Kelly recruited from outside the state, some of his players had difficulty with their studies, and, it was rumored, some of them were paid by townspeople. In any event Kelly left to become director of athletics at the University of Alabama, and MSM settled back to playing with whoever showed up for practice.

Durwood Copeland, professor of metallurgy, took over the directorship in January 1915. He served for less than four months but played a pivotal role in the history of MSM. For several years it had been clear that the school's interests were not being well served in Columbia. President Jesse had opposed expansion, and President Hill had even less enthusiasm for MSM. He thought the whole program should be moved to Columbia. This view was supported by various visiting committees and apparently by a majority of the board of curators. Legislative relief was found in the Buford Act, which provided that MSM could offer the bachelor of science and professional degrees in the basic fields of engineering and in metallurgy, as well as in general science. Although introduced by Senator Buford of Rolla, the legislation actually was written by Copeland and curator S. L. Baysinger of Rolla. Copeland was highly popular in Rolla, but he was persona non grata with Hill and most of the board. On 18 April, two days after the people of Rolla had given a banquet in his honor, he resigned.

Vachel H. McNutt, B.S. in mining engineering, 1910, M.S., 1912, had a brilliant career in oil and potash exploration that brought him great wealth and national recognition. The mineral engineering building, completed in 1987, is named in his honor.

Leon E. Garrett, a popular teacher of mathematics who served as acting director from 1913 to 1915.

The auditorium in Parker Hall.

Austin L. McRae, at fifty-four, was by far the oldest person to have been appointed director. He brought to the position a long record of teaching and research, an interest in athletics, and involvement in the life of the community. His marriage in 1893 to Minnie Wood, daughter of a prominent Rolla family, was an important social event.

To succeed Copeland, the board turned to Austin L. McRae. McRae's early months as director were marred by the curators' refusal to comply with the Buford Act, but he continued trying to increase enrollment and generally building the school. Enrollment reached a peak of 288 in the 1916–1917 year. Virtually all the students were men.

Among the interesting developments in student life was the establishment of *The Missouri Miner* in 1914 as the voice of the students. Published regularly from that time forward, it grew in size and became an important source of news for and about the campus. Another development was the formation of the Metallurgical and Chemical Society from the Missouri Metallurgical Society, organized in 1917 to further the professional interests of the students. Other organizations founded at this time were The Satyrs, an honorary society formed by sophomores in 1916, and the alumni association, tentatively organized in 1915.

While these activities were going on, the attention of both campus and community increasingly turned to the larger issues surrounding the war in Europe. Though McRae could announce in February 1917 that he would give fifty dollars "to the man getting the largest number of new students here next year," by April thoughts of enrollment increases and many other aspects of campus life were being swept away by the tides of war.

# 7 MISSOURI SCHOOL OF MINES

The declaration of war found the Missouri School of Mines in a patriotic fervor. Director McRae, faculty, and students were united on the importance of inculcating patriotism and of contributing to the war effort. The *Miner* discovered that MSM was the only school in the state that did not have a flag pole. "Are we ashamed of our flag?" the editor asked, "or is is that we are indifferent—don't care?"

Urged on by McRae, the Student Council issued an appeal to students and alumni to contribute $350 to erect a flag pole on the campus, "high enough for all to see and revere, and strong enough to last when its builders have answered the 'great call.'" The money rolled in, and on 8 November, the flag was unfurled for the first time from its new standard.

With the declaration of war, many thought that practically every activity at the school should cease in order for the student body to enlist in the army. Finding that the government wanted technical schools to continue operating, MSM stayed open, but many students did march off to war—by the fall of 1917 enrollment had declined to 232.

During this period, school activities changed dramatically. Most obvious among the changes was the reinstitution of military training, abandoned with Colonel Abert's departure in 1877. All first- and second-year men were required to drill from 4:00 to 5:30 p.m. every Monday, Wednesday, and Friday. In the summer of 1918, the War Department established a unit of the Student Army Training Corps at MSM, and for a few months the campus became little more than an army training camp, with soldiers quartered in fraternity houses and in Mechanical Hall. A few months later, the influenza outbreak of 1918 seriously interrupted the detachment's training as well as other aspects of community life. Apparently the malady was not as severe as it was in many other communities—a fortunate condition inasmuch as neither Rolla nor MSM had an infirmary, let alone a hospital.

Armistice brought relief and celebration to Rolla. MSM could take great pride in the contributions of its students, faculty, and alumni. Altogether, 602 men served in the armed forces; 9 gave their lives. Enrollment, which had fallen to 42 in 1918, rebounded rapidly, reaching 562 students by the fall of 1921. More than a third were veterans enrolled in a federally supported vocational education program. The first of its kind in the country, this program enabled many veterans to earn an engineering degree before it was phased out in 1926.

In a sense Director McRae became a casualty of the war. Overextended by the heavy burdens of his office, he became seriously ill in 1917 and never fully recovered. He resigned at the end of the 1919–1920 academic year and died two years later. He had been extremely popular, both on campus and in the community, and had restored a degree

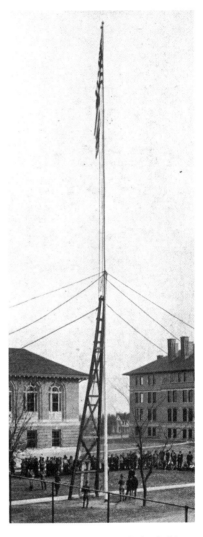

The *Miner* reported, "With the field music playing, and Old Glory waving high above the tallest building in Rolla, the several hundred spectators felt a thrill which only patriotism can cause."

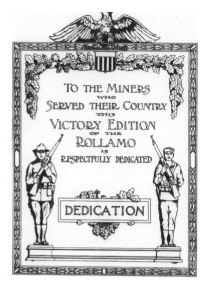

Typical of the spirit of the campus is this dedication page from the 1919 *Rollamo*.

Charles H. Fulton was a German-born metallurgist who had served as president of the South Dakota School of Mines and who at the time of his appointment as director was a professor of metallurgy at the Case School of Applied Science in Cleveland. He served as director from 1920 to 1937, second only to Curtis Laws Wilson in the length of his tenure.

of stability to the school after the tumultuous directorships of Garrett and Copeland.

To succeed McRae, the board appointed Charles H. Fulton. Fulton acted as director for seventeen years, longer than any of his predecessors. He worked assiduously to carry out the mandate of the Buford Act, broadening the curriculum and increasing the number of specialized courses to reflect developments in science and engineering. Under Fulton's leadership, enrollment increased to 680 by the 1931–1932 school year, and the faculty almost doubled in size, though MSM remained primarily an undergraduate college. Mining continued to be an important element in the curriculum, but other specialties, such as civil, chemical, and mechanical engineering, grew rapidly.

The faculty included a number of excellent teachers who were remembered by former students as having had a profound influence on their lives. Among these teachers were Joe Beaty Butler and E. W. Carlton, civil engineering; K. K. Kershner and Walter Schrenk, chemistry and chemical engineering; Samuel H. Lloyd, English and social sciences; C. L. Dake, geology; and George R. Dean, mathematics.

Throughout the period the number of women students continued to be small—about five percent of the total. Many students and to a degree the institution itself tended to be somewhat patronizing of the few women around—the 1925 *Rollamo* wrote fondly of "a bob hair wreck from Rolla Tech, a Co-ed engineer." Gradually, however, the institution began to pay some attention to the needs of women students, appointing first an advisor and then a dean of women.

MSM received even less support than the university in Columbia. This was reflected particularly in the condition of the campus. The only building constructed during Fulton's years was the U.S. Bureau of Mines' Mississippi Valley Experiment Station, completed in 1924.

Although Fulton, in addressing the Chamber of Commerce shortly after his arrival, suggested that the community must assume responsibility for the students' social life as well as housing, there was little a small, isolated town of 2,000 could provide. Student social life continued to be centered on the campus. Faculty members as well as students generally depended on themselves for entertainment and social life. Outings and picnics in the Rolla countryside, on Little Piney Creek, or at Maramec Spring were always popular. With the purchase of grounds for a golf course in 1919, golf became highly popular with the faculty as well as the students.

Among campus rites, none was more sacred than hazing the freshmen. Although abolished during World War I, the practice revived in the 1920s and continued to flourish until World War II. Highlight of the annual fall festivities was the freshman fight, usually a free-for-all in a mud hole between the freshman and sophomore classes.

During these years Commencement took on more color and formality. Beginning in 1922, faculty and graduates assembled in Norwood Hall and, attired in proper academic costume, marched to Parker Hall for the ceremony. Receptions at the director's residence (the Fultons entertained frequently and well), special athletic events, and theatrical productions became a regular part of Commencement.

Support for a broadened curriculum in the 1920s and the 1930s made an impact both on teaching and research and on the faculty as MSM exhibited ingenuity in meeting the needs of their students and their research projects. This 10 1/2 inch reflecting telescope, one of the largest in the state at the time, was built by S. R. B. Cooke, who completed it in 1934 after devoting his spare time for a decade to the effort.

Downtown Rolla at Eighth and Pine, ca. 1923.

The campus, ca. 1926. Jackling Gymnasium stood at the end of what was developing into a mall.

As early as 1919, the *Rollamo* board had sponsored a play, "The College Widow," during Commencement Week. The next year, the Star and Garter was organized to promote "musical and dramatic" events, and in 1921 that society became the MSM Players Club with a competitive membership open to "all students and faculty members, as well as any lady residents of Rolla." The Players Club, advised by Henry H. Armsby of the Department of Civil Engineering, produced two or more plays a year, and performances were always sellouts.

St. Pat's Coronation Ball, 1923.

Students busy at work in the machine shop, ca. 1920s.

In addition to the Commencement Week presentations, the plays became a part of the St. Pat's week festivities and appeared on the General Lecture series inaugurated in 1924. Sam Lloyd, popular professor of English and psychology and for many years head of the Department of Humanities and Social Sciences, ran the General Lecture series, which brought such special guests to the campus as Amelia Earhart, Richard Halliburton, the Don Cossack Choir, J. B. Priestly, Thomas Hart Benton, and Cornelius Vanderbilt.

For students wanting to participate in music groups, several musical organizations were formed. The first MSM Glee Club, organized in 1921, presented a program in Parker Hall under the direction of William D. Turner, head of the Department of Chemical Engineering and Chemistry. However, it was not until 1928 that another glee club was organized. This one, led by Harry Trowbridge, "a leading Rolla vocalist," and later by James S. Cullison of the Department of Geology and Mineralogy, existed until 1933. Finally, in 1942, a glee club of some permanence developed, singing as its most popular song "Fight Missouri Miners" by Fred Waring. In 1926 a band was organized by John W. Scott, owner of Scott's Drug Store, a popular stu-

Tunnel leading into the experimental mine.

Tunnel, hoist, and bin at the experimental mine, an important teaching facility.

dent hangout. Scott, beloved by generations of students, directed the band until his death in 1950.

The St. Pat festivities remained the social highlight of the year. St. Pat continued to arrive on a handcar at the Frisco station, the parades became longer and more elaborate, the "green goo" spread out over more of the town, and the Coronation Ball became more elegant. Even prohibition did not seem to stop the flow of beer during St. Pat's weekend.

In 1924 the student council was replaced by the senior council, which consisted of representatives from every club and fraternity on campus as well as several independents. In 1937 it again became the student council.

Reflecting increased specialization in engineering, a number of

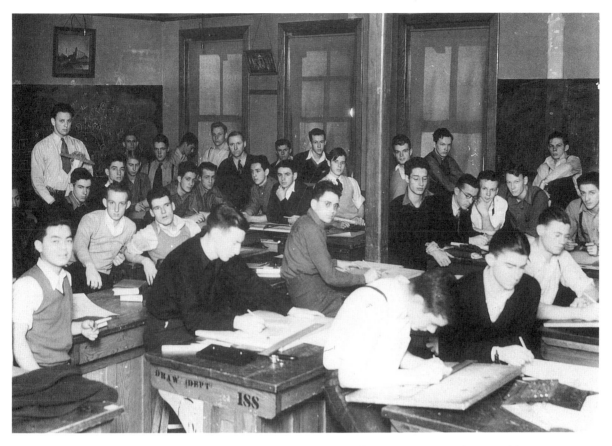

A class in drawing, ca. 1940s. By this date, classroom attire was a bit less formal than it was at the turn of the century.

professional societies assumed the role that had been filled by the student chapter of the American Association of Engineers, organized in 1920 with Professor H. H. Ormsby as its first president. The earliest of these specialized groups was the student chapter for mining and metallurgy, organized in 1921 and affiliated with the American Institute of Mining and Metallurgical Engineers. Chemistry students then formed their own group, "The Diphenyl Dozen," in 1923. Under the leadership of W. D. Turner, head of the chemical engineering department, the group changed its name to the Ira Remsen Society. Later, in 1939 it became a student chapter of the American Institute of Chemical Engineers. Also in 1923, students in civil engineering formed a society that in 1924 became a student affiliate of the American Society of Civil Engineers.

Electrical engineering separated from physics in 1924, and the next year students formed a chapter of the American Institute of Electrical Engineers. Ceramic engineering became a separate department in 1926, and two years later a student chapter of the American Ceramic Society came into being as the Orton Society. The student chapter of mechanical engineers became affiliated with the American Society of Mechanical Engineers in 1930.

The Society of American Military Engineers began as an officers club in 1932. For a time it was known as Scabbard and Blade, and in 1937 it became a part of the national organization. Scabbard and Blade

William R. Chedsey, director from 1937 to 1941. His tenure was troubled by conflicts with President Middlebush and the board of curators over the future of the School of Mines.

Curtis Laws Wilson, dean of the Missouri School of Mines, 1941–1963—with Wilson's appointment, the title of the chief executive was changed from "director" to "dean." His tenure was longer than that of any other chief executive in the history of the institution, and he had as profound an effect on the development of the school as anyone. In their excellent *History of MSM/UMR* Lawrence Christensen and Jack Ridley describe the Wilson years as "A Long Shadow on the Horizon."

sponsored the Military Ball that from its beginning in 1934 became an annual social event of great importance.

During the years between the world wars the athletic program at MSM existed principally to provide recreational opportunities. The Athletic Association was primarily a student organization, and a five-dollar season ticket enabled both students and faculty to attend all athletic events. The "M" Club was formed in 1921 for athletes who lettered in varsity sports, but it floundered and was not reestablished until 1939. The Booster Club, created in 1922, encouraged townspeople, faculty, and students to lend financial support to the athletic program.

Football remained the leading sport, even though there were no great teams. The "big" game of the year was always played with Washington University. The Miners almost always lost, but the game engendered a great deal of enthusiasm, and when it was played in St. Louis numbers of students clambered aboard freight trains—the Frisco's "side-car Pullmans"—for a ride to the city. A notable exception to the dreary succession of losing seasons occurred in 1925, when the Miners, compiling their best record since 1914, lost only to Washington University and to the University of Missouri. So great was the enthusiasm that the 1926 *Rollamo* was dedicated to the team of 1925.

In addition to football, MSM fielded basketball and track teams during the 1920s. There were also golf events, and during the 1930s intercollegiate tennis matches and swimming meets added variety to the athletic fare.

Director Fulton resigned in 1937 at age sixty-three to return to teaching and research. Although he was two years away from mandatory retirement, his long tenure as director had left him with the view that younger men were needed for administrative work. There had been some progress over the years, but MSM had to struggle to keep pace with developing trends in engineering education. MSM's relationship to the university president and to the board of curators was always somewhat tenuous. Although Brooks and Williams were strong supporters of MSM, Middlebush looked on the School of Mines as "Missouri's educational mistake." On campus, the salary cuts necessitated by the Great Depression of the 1930s eroded faculty morale almost to the point of rebellion.

To succeed Fulton, Middlebush selected William R. Chedsey, a fifty-year-old professor of mining at Pennsylvania State College. Chedsey apparently had been given a mandate to narrow the focus of MSM, and he did so by eliminating majors in biology, economics, and English. Even as he cut these programs, he managed to restore the cuts in faculty salaries. Chedsey, however, soon alienated Middlebush and most of the board by pushing too aggressively for improvements. He became embroiled in a public controversy with the president of the board over the need for a dormitory. He also found himself caught up in the separatist movement that erupted once again in the late 1930s. In any event, Middlebush and the board, finding that he was "not the man for the place," forced him to resign.

Chedsey's administration, though brief and tumultuous, brought

To help supply the needs of veterans, many of whom were married, a "Co-op" was opened in an old house. The "parking lot" appears to be full.

considerable progress to MSM. Enrollment almost doubled, reaching 996 during the 1940–1941 year; faculty increased from fifty-nine to seventy-six; the campus appeared to express a greater commitment to research. The most obvious signs of progress, however, were in the appearance of the campus itself. After two decades in which only one new building had been completed, Chedsey in four years managed to build two new structures: Harris Hall, for civil engineering, and a new building for chemical engineering, later named in honor of Walter T. Schrenk.

To bring the school into administrative conformity with the rest of the university and to help quell the separatist movement, the board decided to change the title of the chief administrative officer at Rolla from director to dean. To fill the new post they selected Curtis Laws Wilson, forty-three-year-old chair of the Department of Metallurgy at the Montana School of Mines.

Wilson came to Rolla with a Ph.D. in metallurgy from Goettingen. In their *History of MSM/UMR* Lawrence Christensen and Jack Ridley describe him as "a hard-working, well-organized, efficient, and fiscally conservative administrator who was loyal to his superiors, and . . . [who] expected no less from his subordinates." He remained as dean until his retirement in 1963, the longest tenure of any of the school's chief executives. His years brought great change and explosive growth. It would be hard to name anyone whose influence on the school was more profound.

Wilson had barely settled into his office when the nation was engulfed by World War II. Engineering students were deferred from the draft, and Wilson urged them to stay in school. Enrollment nonetheless declined sharply, falling to 308 in 1944, the lowest since 1918. Social life was curtailed, hazing was abolished, and even St. Pat's was

To meet the needs of the postwar surge in enrollment a number of facilities were converted to new uses. Mechanical Hall, which had been used as a warehouse, was remodeled to house the mining engineering department; the Mining Experiment Station moved off campus, and its building became the home of ceramic engineering; and "Old Chem," now ivy-covered, became a classroom building.

suspended for the duration.

The army had established an engineer unit of the Reserve Officers Training Corps at MSM in 1920, and ROTC had been fairly popular in the 1930s, with about ten percent of the graduates earning commissions in the army. Hundreds of students and recent graduates went off to war, and forty-five lost their lives. The government called on MSM for a number of special training programs, and, in addition, the campus was host to the Army Specialized Training Program.

The war's most significant impact on the campus came after the victory over Germany and Japan as hundreds of veterans utilized their GI Bill of Rights to enroll at MSM for programs in engineering. In the fall of 1946, 2,565 students descended on a campus that could not adequately accommodate half that many. To help meet the crisis the administration moved in fourteen barracks to provide classrooms and housing. Classes and laboratories were scheduled from 7:00 a.m. to 10:00 p.m. six days a week. Several of the older buildings were modified and converted to new uses.

In the midst of all this the separatist issue flared again. Wilson may

The Missouri Geological Survey was moved off campus, and the old Rolla Building, now shorn of its cupola, was given over to the new Department of Humanities and Social Studies.

have touched it off by relieving Clair V. Mann, one of the most ardent proponents of separation, as chair of engineering drawing. Mann resigned from the faculty and took up the cudgel against both Wilson and the university administration. Adding fuel to the flames was a proposal to transfer five senior faculty members, all vocal advocates of separation, to Columbia at a reduction in rank, but with their tenure intact. All five resigned. The alumni got involved, and while a majority appeared to be in favor of separation, a number of leading graduates were either ambivalent or opposed, including Daniel Jackling, Mervin J. Kelly, vice president of Bell Laboratories, and Karl F. Hasselmann, a prominent Texas oilman who was president of the Alumni Association. When a bill designed to free the campus from the control of the university president failed to pass the legislature, the issue died down—and as a serious issue it remained dead.

Moreover, legislative support began to improve. The legislature provided significant evidence of support for a broader curriculum in 1948 when it appropriated funds for a mechanical engineering laboratory. This helped bring accreditation for the curriculum in mechanical engineering by the Engineers' Council for Professional Development and was a further step toward the development of MSM into a comprehensive school of engineering.

By 1951 all engineering departments at MSM had obtained ECPD accreditation, and in the 1950s funds became available for substantial capital improvements. A new power plant was completed, and additions were built to the chemical engineering and mining buildings, as well as to Fulton Hall, the former U.S. Bureau of Mines Mississippi Valley Experiment Station. Electrical engineering, civil engineering, and physics all got new buildings in the mid-1950s.

Improvements in campus facilities and expansion in curriculum and programs were in large part a reflection of President Elmer Ellis's

Oscar Henning, Karl K. Kershner, Floyd H. Frame, Garrett Muilenberg, and Clair V. Mann—five tenured professors who resigned from MSM rather than accept transfer to the University of Missouri in Columbia. The five veteran faculty members were leaders in the effort to secure separation of MSM from the university—or at least from the president of the university—and this effort was widely criticized in Rolla as an attempt to humiliate persons who did not agree with the university authorities. Subsequent to this, an effort was made in the legislature to force separation, but this, like earlier efforts, failed, and the issue eventually subsided.

In marked contrast to an earlier time, the campus by the 1950s had become pleasantly tree-shaded. The new dormitories dominate the south part of the campus.

support of a broadened mission for MSM. Nuclear engineering became an option of metallurgical engineering in 1956, and in 1960, with a grant from the National Science Foundation, MSM established a Computer Center, providing the basis for its development into a leadership role in computer science. Missouri's first nuclear reactor was dedicated on campus in 1961, and construction of a Materials Science

Tau Kappa Epsilon fraternity house, along a stretch that became known as Fraternity Row.

Kappa Alpha fraternity house, another house making up Fraternity Row.

Research Center was begun in the last days of the Wilson administration.

MSM pioneeered in the development of cooperative engineering, a program that permitted students to alternate semesters between classes and jobs, thus providing on-the-job training and financial assistance along with academic education. A number of Missouri's largest corporations as well as the State Highway Department participated. The cooperative program greatly facilitated the career placement of graduates, something that had concerned the school since the 1920s. In 1944, Rex Z. Williams, who had been on the faculty for more than a decade, was assigned responsibility for the placement function. Williams served as an effective liaison between students and employers, initiating the practice of inviting employers to the campus to interview students. Williams left MSM to go into banking,

A parents' day demonstration at the foundry.

Electrical engineering laboratory, 1950s. By this time neckties had completely disappeared, and jeans had begun to make their appearance.

Ceramics laboratory—measuring color with a recording spectrometer.

but in the 1970s he served on the board of curators, the first person from Rolla to serve since before World War II.

Although MSM remained essentially an undergraduate institution, the 1950s and the early 1960s saw some developments in graduate education and research. As early as the 1920s some courses that led to the Ph.D. had been offered at Rolla, but the degrees were awarded by the university in Columbia. In the 1940s, ceramic engineering, geology, mining, and metallurgical engineering obtained authority to offer the Ph.D. By the early 1960s that authority had been extended to chemical engineering, engineering physics, and electrical engineering, and approximately 350 students were enrolled in graduate programs. Among those providing leadership in the development of graduate education and research were a number of departmental chairs, some of them newly arrived: Dudley Thompson in chemical engineering, Harold Q. Fuller in physics, Theodore Planje in ceramic engineering, and Albert W. Schlechten in metallurgical engineering.

The growth in graduate enrollment was a part of the general increase in the student population. The postwar boom peaked during the 1948–1949 school year at 3,025, followed by a sharp decline as veterans completed their educations. During the 1952–1953 year enrollment was at a postwar low of 1,210, but as the baby-boomers started to fill the nation's campuses, MSM's enrollment increased steadily, reaching 3,620 for the 1963–1964 year. To encourage enrollment the campus began holding an "Engineer's Day" for prospective students and their parents.

The increased enrollment dramatized the need for dormitories and a cafeteria. In the absence of these facilities, and to help fill a social gap, the eating club system had expanded, the "Prospectors" organizing in 1914 and "Bonanza" organizing in 1915. Since 1904, students who were not members of fraternities had been forced to find housing in the town. In the early 1940s, however, pressures brought by increasing enrollment and by the construction of Fort Leonard Wood created a housing crisis. Finally, during the 1950s, the university issued bonds to build four dormitories and a cafeteria. A student center, opened in 1960, soon became one of the most popular spots on campus.

The fraternities greatly improved the housing available to their members when a number of them built handsome new houses on Nagagami Road in an area called Fraternity Row. In 1955 the fraternities established a new spring festival, Greek Day—later to become Greek Week—with games, a carnival, and dancing, the proceeds being donated to a Rolla charity.

The Pan Hellenic Council, formed in 1921, worked to improve relations between fraternity men and independents on campus, and to provide a bond between active and alumni Greek-letter men. In 1931 it became the Interfraternity Council. Four years later "Independents," as they had been known for a number of years, formed an organization to enable all students to participate more fully in campus activities.

The student body remained predominantly male, and as late as 1963–1964, the peak enrollment of 3,620 included only 69 women. Nev-

Loading an automatic fraction
collector.

ertheless, as early as 1940 women students had organized a sorority,
Pi Delta Chi. Women were becoming conscious of their role as engi-
neers, and in 1960 they organized a chapter of the Society of Women
Engineers.

As was true at Columbia, black students were discouraged from
applying. When the board denied the applications of two young
blacks from St. Louis in 1950, along with others at Columbia, the
matter went to the courts. Judge Sam C. Blair of the Cole County
Circuit Court ruled that the university must admit qualified blacks to
courses that were not available at Lincoln University. The students at
MSM favored the admission of blacks, and after Blair's ruling there
was no further difficulty, although the number of black students
remained very small until specific recruitment programs were developed in the 1970s. Lelia Thompson, who in 1960 became the first black
woman to graduate from MSM, recalled, "You could walk for days
without seeing another woman or another black."

Football remained the most popular sport, but it also continued to
be strictly an extracurricular activity providing students respite from
a demanding academic schedule. The Miners joined the Missouri
Intercollegiate Athletic Association, and while they occasionally won
a conference championship (as in 1947, 1949, and 1950), they usually

St. Pat leading the parade in his traditional "chariot"—a manure spreader—1939.

The St. Pat's parade—a bevy of beauties bundled up against the brisk March breeze.

placed somewhere in the middle. The 1950 conference championship team also defeated Washington University for the first time in thirty-five years. In addition to football, MSM at this time fielded teams in basketball, tennis, golf, track, swimming, and rifle competition. The 1957–1958 basketball team lost twenty-four games in a row, but they beat Washington University.

The man responsible for Miner athletics for more than a generation was Gale Bullman, first appointed football coach in 1937. His preparation for coaching was as unorthodox as his approach to the game—he had a law degree from Washington University. He taught his boys to enjoy themselves, and he was not particularly concerned when laboratories interfered with practice.

During these years of growth the Alumni Association became

President Ellis and Dean Wilson lead the Commencement procession, 1962. In the background is Jackling Gymnasium, razed in 1965 to make way for the new library.

The end of an era for MSM.

increasingly important in the life of the school. In 1953 the Alumni Association appointed its first full-time executive secretary, Francis C. "Ike" Edwards, who greatly enlarged both the membership and the work of the association. MSM alumni developed into a strong and loyal support group that would become a major force in shaping the destiny of UMR.

As Wilson approached retirement, President Ellis began the search for a new dean. Under Wilson's leadership enrollment had increased by forty percent, the faculty had doubled in size, and the number of students receiving degrees at Commencement had almost tripled. Where there had been fourteen buildings on the campus when Wilson became dean, there were now thirty-two with two more under construction.

To provide leadership for what everyone assumed would be a continued period of growth, Ellis chose Merl Baker, a thirty-nine-year-old professor of mechanical engineering from the University of Kentucky. The growth continued for a time, but the change that took place was more than simple expansion—it was a revolutionary change as MSM became UMR.

# 8 UNIVERSITY OF

## MISSOURI–ROLLA

In less than a year after he became the second dean of the Missouri School of Mines, Merl Baker was named chancellor of the University of Missouri at Rolla. Under Baker's leadership, MSM was transformed from a narrowly focused engineering school existing as a subordinate division of the university in Columbia into a technological university that became a coordinate unit of the four-campus University of Missouri.

As UMR's first chancellor, Baker welcomed the challenge and the opportunity to lead the campus toward what everyone rightly believed would be new heights. He also welcomed the mandate from President Ellis to improve the quality of the faculty, to expand offerings in the social sciences and humanities, to enlarge the graduate program, and to emphasize research.

With approval from Ellis and the board of curators, Baker completely reorganized the campus, creating four schools (mines and metallurgy, engineering, science, and graduate), four departments (humanities, social studies, military science, and physical education), and four research facilities (computer center, materials research center, nuclear reactor, and research center).

At the same time he put together his own administrative team. Dudley Thompson, veteran head of chemistry and chemical engineering, became dean of faculties. Aaron Miles, chair of mechanical engineering, became dean of engineering; Theodore Planje, chair of ceramic engineering, became director of the School of Mines and Metallurgy; Paul Proctor, chair of geology, was appointed director of the

Merl Baker, first chancellor of the University of Missouri–Rolla, presiding at the 1967 Commencement. Seated just behind Baker is President John Weaver. Baker, from the University of Kentucky, was appointed dean in 1963, and in 1964 his title was changed to chancellor. He served until 1973.

Chemical engineering class in Miles Auditorium, 1970s. It is evident that student dress has now become completely informal.

Using the Hydrominer 1, students in rock mechanics cut a bed of coal with water jets.

Dudley Thompson, head of chemistry and chemical engineering, became dean of faculties and director of the School of Engineering in 1964.

School of Science; Wouter Bosch was named director of the Graduate School; and G. Edwin Lorey became director of extension. Miles retired in 1967 and Bosch in 1968. J. Stuart Johnson, dean of engineering at Wayne State University, but formerly of MSM, became dean of the School of Engineering. Robert H. McFarland, a physicist from the Lawrence Livermore Laboratory, was appointed dean of the Graduate School.

In recruiting faculty during this time of growth—enrollment increased from 4,340 in 1964 to 6,416 in 1970—Baker was assiduous in selecting persons from outside the institution with doctoral degrees; former MSM faculty members who stayed on were encouraged to work toward doctorates. As a result, the faculty was both enlarged and transformed, and faculty with doctorates increased from 44 to 80.5 percent during Baker's term.

UMR remained primarily an undergraduate institution, although the number of graduate students increased by more than a third—generally numbering between 500 and 600 in the 1970s. Along with this came an increased emphasis on research. Baker supported research through the establishment of research centers to deal with specific problems—for example, rock mechanics and explosives, materials, and cloud physics—and by encouraging faculty to apply for grants.

One of Baker's major interests was expansion of the curriculum beyond the traditional programs in engineering and science. In this, he was supported by both presidents Ellis and Weaver. The board of curators authorized B.A. degrees in a number of the humanities and social sciences, and in 1970 a College of Arts and Science was organized from the School of Science and Division of Liberal Arts.

Perhaps the most obvious change occurred in the appearance of the campus as new buildings were constructed to meet the needs of expanding enrollment and new programs. Housing had always been at a premium. To help meet the demand for more dormitory space, private operators opened Thomas Jefferson Hall in 1966, a seven-story dormitory just north of the campus, complete with cafeteria, swimming pool, and other amenities. "T.J.," as it was affectionately known, provided relatively high-cost living, but it was always full, and it furnished stiff competition for the eating clubs that traditionally had provided students with low-cost meals. Of the six clubs that existed in the 1960s, only three remained by the early 1970s.

A civil engineering student tests concrete.

The Graduate Center for Materials Research, established in 1964 as the first fruit of Ellis's 1963 decision to locate the university's space center at Rolla, moved into a building of its own in 1967. The building was later named in honor of Martin E. Straumanis, a scientist of international reputation who was one of the first scholars in the center. Under the leadership of William James, its first director, the center developed an important international research program with a nuclear laboratory in France. At home, it conducted cooperative research in the use of biomedical polymers with a group in the medical school at Columbia. Adding further to the research capacity of the campus was a major annex to the physics building, opened in 1967.

In 1970 the humanities and social sciences moved into a new building. Their needs had been made more acute when "Old Chem," the second oldest building on campus, burned 19 October 1969, destroying among other things the social science facilities. A new building for chemistry and chemical engineering rose on the site of "Old Chem." Completed in 1974, it was later named in honor of Walter T. Schrenk, chair of the Department of Chemistry and Chemical Engineering from 1928 to 1956.

Emerging from the experimental mine, gas masks and all.

The academic buildings were funded by a combination of state appropriations and federal grants. The University Center found its source of funds in private gifts and in bonds to be retired by student fees. The $574,000 in private gifts, which was collected in this initial fundraising campaign, was small when compared to results achieved in subsequent years, but it was a good beginning. Moreover, in the process the campus improved its alumni relations and developed the administrative machinery for future fundraising efforts. Key to the success of the enterprise was Frank Mackaman, a young man who arrived from Drake University in 1968 as field secretary for the alumni association and later became director of a combined development and alumni office.

Symbolic of the changes taking place on campus was the decision to raze Jackling Gym and replace it with a separate building for the library. With the construction of the library and the University Center, the South Mall was complete. Landscaping improved its appearance, and an outdoor stage, dubbed the "Hockey Puck," became a popular gathering place for students.

Capping the substantial construction program of Merl Baker's years as chancellor was an impressive new athletic facility just east of

Razing Jackling Gymnasium to make way for the library. The keystone at the top of the building was all that was salvaged from the historic structure.

The Curtis Laws Wilson Library dominates the north end of the mall, center of the campus.

Most students cross the mall at some time during the day.

the golf course at the southwestern edge of campus. Centerpiece of the new complex was the Gale Bullman Multipurpose Building, opened in 1968. Improved facilities were accompanied by a general improvement in the athletic program. Athletic scholarships became available for the first time, and while UMR by no means became an athletic powerhouse, the Miners, competing in the NCAA Division II

Soccer became a popular sport at
UMR.

The Miners could always count on
enthusiastic student support.

Missouri Intercollegiate Athletic Association, began to win more frequently than they had in the past.

The Miners traditionally had done better in sports other than football or basketball, and they continued to field competitive teams in
tennis, golf, track, rugby, and swimming. Baseball, added in the
1960s, and soccer, begun in the 1970s, caught on instantly, with the
Miners winning their share of conference championships in both
sports.

Billy Key, whose influence on Miner athletics was second only to
Bullman's, became basketball coach in 1964, and in 1968 he succeeded
Bullman as athletic director. Key's basketball teams were always competitive, and they enjoyed winning seasons almost from the beginning. In the 1975–1976 year, the Miners won the conference championship for the first time in history.

Football, which had declined in popularity to the point that Baker
and Bullman seriously considered dropping it altogether, revived
under Dewey Allgood and his successor, Charles Finley. The Miners
shared a conference title in 1977 and in 1980, with a 10 to 0 record, won
the conference championship for the first time in history.

All in all, athletics at UMR remained essentially what they had
been at MSM, part of a well-rounded educational program. There
was one aspect of the program, however, that was different—women
were competing in varsity sports. UMR began intercollegiate track for
women in 1969. In 1974, Annette Caruso became the first woman
coach, and by the 1980s women were competing in tennis, soccer,
cross country, swimming, basketball, and softball.

Women's athletics were but one manifestation of the profound
changes that occurred in the student body during Baker's years as
chancellor. As their professional horizons expanded beyond traditional vocations, increasing numbers of women turned to engineering, and for women in Missouri that generally meant a Rolla education. Moreover, with the addition of a liberal arts degree program,
UMR became increasingly attractive to women. As a result, in the
decade between 1964 and 1973 the number of women students jumped
from 57 to 469, more than ten percent of the total. A Women in Engineering scholarship program, started in 1975, also encouraged attendance by women.

Housing, always a problem at Rolla, was particularly acute for
women students. The university took a small step toward a solution
in 1962 when a private dwelling on State Street, with room for fourteen students, was purchased as a women's dormitory. The Thomas
Jefferson Residence Hall had one floor set aside for women—that was
part of its attraction—and in 1969, with the purchase of the old Stuart
Apartments, the space available for women more than doubled. A
few years later, in 1972, McAnerney Hall in the Quad was converted
into a women's dormitory to meet the need for housing women on
campus.

It is interesting that while students at Columbia were engaged in a
much-publicized struggle with board and administration over "intervisitation," students at Rolla quietly achieved the adoption of a policy

Commencement was a proud and happy time.

providing that intervisitation would be permitted pending approval by seventy percent of the residents of a dormitory.

Women gradually found a place in campus activities. In 1962, MSM had formed an organization of women students, and in 1966, UMR reactivated the Society of Women Engineers. In the 1970s, women began to serve on the student council and the student union board. In 1980, Sue Leach became the first woman to serve as president of the student union board, but it was not until 1982 that a woman, Mindy Woodill, was elected to the St. Pat's board.

Perhaps the most telling change of all occurred in 1977 when the students decided that only women enrolled at UMR could be candidates for homecoming queen. As Christensen and Ridley remarked in their history of the school, "Gone were the days when an annual all-school mixer brought busloads of girls from various women's colleges for party weekends."

Like the campus in Columbia, UMR faced difficulty in recruiting black students. Science and engineering were not popular disciplines among young blacks, and the little town of Rolla offered few cultural or social attractions for black students. The administration, nevertheless, made serious efforts to increase black enrollment. A Minority Engineering Program, initiated in 1974, provided scholarships furnished by industry to promising young blacks interested in engineering. By 1982, 63 students had received degrees through the program, and by 1986 the number had reached 129.

Students on the Rolla campus have always been active in the celebration of ROTC Day.

A chapter of Alpha Phi Alpha, the oldest black fraternity in America, came to UMR in 1965. In 1981, a chapter of Alpha Kappa Alpha, a black sorority, was organized. The Association for Black Students, organized in 1969, sponsored an annual black culture week that brought to the campus such well-known figures as Julian Bond, Charles Evers, and Hosiah Williams, together with black entertainers, including the Preservation Hall Jazz Band.

UMR attracted more foreign students than it did American blacks, and the number of foreign students, which had been minimal at MSM, increased to 368 by 1986. The Center for International Programs and Studies (CIPAS), organized in 1968, with Robert Carlile as director, furthered international development projects, cooperative research, and out-of-country degree programs. Through Bobby Wixson and Eunice French, CIPAS took the lead in establishing Missouri's partnership with the state of Pará in Brazil. UMR's most ambitious foreign effort was a five-year program, begun in 1969, to organize an engineering university in Saigon. An innovative program offered graduate courses to ARAMCO employees in Saudi Arabia.

UMR students were described as being relatively conservative in their views. Many wore long hair, a few of the men had beards, and most affected scruffy dress, but they were little touched by the protests that swept the campuses of the country in the late 1960s and the early 1970s. In 1969, the *Miner* editorialized, "Here at the University of Missouri–Rolla we have no student strikes, no riots, no National Guard troops. The town lives and thrives with its college community."

In 1971, a survey by the American Council on Education found that 73 percent of UMR's freshmen thought that colleges were too lax with protesters. Although ROTC was unpopular on many campuses, it flourished at Rolla. Activism related to Vietnam was virtually nonex-

Greek Week carnival.

istent at UMR, but in the wake of the tragedy at Kent State, about 200 students and faculty members gathered on the mall and marched to the library to lower the flag to half-mast. Students who disagreed with the protest formed a wall around the flagpole. There was some verbal confrontation, but the protest dissolved without incident.

Although the campus generally did not provide an atmosphere for protesting, an underground newspaper, *The Good Seed*, was published "to inform the students of the problems of the University and the Rolla community." During its brief existence, however, the newspaper did little more than test the administration's tolerance for obscenity.

Greek letter organizations, in decline during this time on some campuses, prospered at Rolla. In 1972, the year the first national sorority, Kappa Delta, organized a chapter at UMR, there were nineteen fraternities that pledged nearly half the entering freshmen. Within a decade the Kappas were joined by three additional sororities, each with its own house. Panhellenic, the governing body for sororities, took its place alongside IFC, and the annual celebration of Greek Week, inaugurated in the 1950s, continued as a time for fun and community service. The half of the student body not active in fraternities and sororities formed the Independent Organization, which worked well with the Interfraternity Council in the sponsorship of campus events.

The big event of the year remained the annual spring rites in honor of Saint Patrick. It seemed to some old-timers that the celebrants grew less inhibited each year, but the Rolla citizenry seemed to grow more tolerant. The Saturday morning parade brought thousands of visitors to the community and became a major event in the Ozark region. Beginning in 1968, the St. Pat's board inaugurated a new feature, the designation of Honorary Knights of St. Patrick as a means of honoring outstanding faculty, administrators, alumni, and public figures. Appropriately, Chancellor Baker was the first to be dubbed an honorary knight.

St. Pat continued to arrive by rail.

The grandest shillelagh of them all.

Historical accuracy was never allowed to interfere with fun and fantasy in the St. Pat's parade.

The lawn-mower drill team became a regular feature of the St. Pat's parade.

No one ever had too many St. Pat's badges.

"Alice" was the star of every
St. Pat's Day.

While the campus may have seemed like an island of tranquillity in
a sea of unrest, conditions in the country, the state, and the university
at large were having a profound effect on the University of Missouri–
Rolla. During the late 1960s, life at UMR was on a constant upward
spiral. Enrollment increased by more than a third, the size of the
faculty almost doubled, new programs were developed, and new
buildings were dedicated almost every year. In the early 1970s the
spiral reversed. The economy, a decline in the demand for engineers,
and a change in the draft laws conspired to reduce enrollment at
UMR from 6,416 in 1970 to 4,693 in 1974, a decrease of more than twenty-five percent. State appropriations did not compensate for the loss
of fee income—indeed, they were reduced as the number of students
declined—and the chancellor was faced with supporting the enlarged

Streaking comes to Rolla, 1974.

Raymond L. Bisplinghoff, chancellor
of UMR from 1974 to 1976. Bisplinghoff,
former dean of engineering at the
Massachusetts Institute of Technology,
came to UMR from the National Science Foundation, where he was deputy director. He left Rolla to become
vice president for research at Tyco
Laboratories, Inc.

faculty, sustaining the new programs, and paying for the new buildings (some of which had been financed with the expectation that the
bonds would be amortized by increased student fee income) with
drastically reduced resources.

The burdens seemed insurmountable. Faculty morale, already at a
low ebb, plummeted further as a result of the uncertainties over "Role
and Scope." Baker's struggle with the complex problems of the campus seriously undermined his health, and announcing that he could
no longer bear the burdens of office, he resigned to accept a position
on the staff of the university president. For the next year following
Baker's resignation, Dudley Thompson, dean of faculties and a veteran MSM administrator, served as acting chancellor.

In October 1974 Raymond L. Bisplinghoff, deputy director of the
National Science Foundation, became chancellor. Bisplinghoff arrived
at Rolla during the height of the energy crisis, with enrollment down
and the state's economy in decline. He perceived UMR as uniquely
positioned to help Missouri solve its complex problems, and he
pushed vigorously for increased support—from the federal government and private sources as well as from the state. He brought the
Governor's Missouri Energy Council to the campus and organized the
Institute of River Studies, funded by the U.S. Army Corps of Engineers. Enrollment began to increase as engineering became popular
once again, and the campus was making good progress when in
November 1976 Bisplinghoff suddenly announced that he was resigning, effective 1 January, to become vice president for research at Tyco
Laboratories, Inc.

Students in hard hats gather in front
of the experimental mine.

Underground operations in the
experimental mine.

Even well-organized engineers find it difficult to avoid clutter in their dormitory rooms.

Jim C. Pogue, professor of English, served as Bisplinghoff's provost and dean of faculties, and during the 1977–1978 year he served as interim chancellor.

Jim C. Pogue, whom Bisplinghoff had appointed provost, was named interim chancellor. Pogue served for nineteen months before he returned to teaching, and despite the fact that he was a professor of English literature—it had never occurred to anyone that a non-engineer could ever be chancellor at Rolla—he was popular with both faculty and alumni. During this time, the development office in 1977 organized the Order of the Golden Shillelagh as a major gifts club to expand private fundraising efforts. Charter members included loyal alumni who were engaged in significant engineering activities all over the world.

The long search for a new chancellor came to an end in the summer of 1978 with the appointment of Joseph Marchello. He remained for eight years and, aided by his wife, Louise, provided UMR with vigorous, effective leadership. Marchello moved quickly to put his stamp on the campus, reorganizing it completely and replacing most of the senior administrators. When he had finished, UMR had a College of Arts and Science, a School of Mines and Metallurgy, and a School of Engineering. Providing campuswide oversight were the offices of chancellor, provost, and administrative services. The Graduate College and Extension Division were abolished as separate units, and their functions were transferred to the three academic units while their deans were placed under the provost.

The personnel changes accompanying the reorganization were complicated and for a time upsetting. Marvin W. Barker of Mississippi State University became dean of arts and science, succeeding Adrian Daane, who became graduate dean. In mines and metallurgy, Theodore J. Planje, longtime respected teacher and administrator, died suddenly in 1980 and was replaced by Don L. Warner, professor of geological engineering. James E. Halligan, whom Bisplinghoff had appointed as dean of engineering, resigned to go to the University of Arkansas and was replaced by Robert L. Davis, professor of engineering mechanics. Tomlinson Fort, Jr., of Carnegie-Mellon University became provost, but after a couple of years he resigned and was replaced by John Park, chair of physics. At that time the position was changed to vice chancellor for academic affairs. Joseph D. Wollard, business officer, became executive director of administrative services.

By 1982 enrollment reached 7,795, an increase of about forty-five percent in five years. Part of the growth came from new programs and new emphases, particularly in computer science. New equipment enabled the campus to innovate in the teaching of computer-aided design/computer-aided manufacturing (CAD/CAM) and robotics. When the National Science Foundation gave Thomas R. Faucett, professor of mechanical engineering, $250,000 to develop the capabilities of the CAD/CAM system, UMR became a national leader in the use of CAD/CAM and robotics in undergraduate instruction.

Reflecting further specialization, the department of metallurgical and nuclear engineering was divided into two separate departments. In the basic sciences, the Department of Physics developed a national reputation for research and innovative teaching, stemming from an NSF departmental development grant in the 1960s, and an observatory opened in the 1970s. In 1981, Laird Schearer became the first UMR faculty member to receive the university's presidential research award.

New degree programs in arts and science substantially broadened the options available to UMR students. By the 1980s it was possible to earn undergraduate majors in economics, English, history, psychology, and philosophy, as well as to do considerable work in art, music, and theater. Professors in the humanities began to receive recognition as well as those in the sciences. The University of Missouri Press published James Wise's *Sir Thomas Browne's "Religio Medici" and Two*

Joseph M. Marchello, former provost for the Division of Mathematics, Physical Sciences, and Engineering at the University of Maryland, served as chancellor from 1978 to 1985, when he resigned to become president of Old Dominion in Virginia.

John T. Park, chair of physics, became vice chancellor for academic affairs in 1983. After Marchello left Rolla in 1985, Park served as interim chancellor for one year.

A new method of cleaning shell cases, using waterjets, developed at UMR.

Band practice.

The band occasionally left campus to accompany the football team or to give concerts in the surrounding towns.

Computers early became an integral part of the instructional process at UMR.

*Seventeenth-Century Critics*; Douglas Knight received international recognition for his research into Shakespeare's signatures; in 1982 Douglas Wixson became the first UMR faculty member to receive the university's Thomas Jefferson Award.

Students also enjoyed increasing extracurricular opportunities in the arts. KUMR-FM, the 100,000 watt stereo radio station, opened in 1973, offering both experience in broadcasting to students and public radio to the Ozarks. Performance opportunities were in abundance. Bands under the direction of David Oakley were particularly popular. A university orchestra provided symphonic opportunities. The glee club, long a popular singing group, was complemented by the university choir, composed of both men and women. Christmas performances by the Madrigal Players delighted university and townspeople alike. The UMR theater, directed by Margie Boston, presented a play each semester. While the campus performing arts series offered students high-quality entertainment, the Remmers Special Lecture/Artist series, inaugurated in 1979 through the generosity of alumnus and industrialist Walter Remmers and his wife Miriam, carried forward the idea of the old General Lecture Series.

A further enlargement of student horizons came about through the establishment of the Smurfit-Alton Packaging Fellowship, which supports an exchange between faculty and students at UMR and University College, Dublin, Ireland. This furnished another example of campus enrichment through private support; it also provided a kinship much enjoyed by the campus that celebrates the day of St. Patrick with such vigor and enthusiasm.

Marchello recognized the importance of developing a research faculty, and he used the curators' professorship program to that end. Stig Friberg, professor of chemistry, in 1979 became the first person appointed curators' professor. Others who have received the honor are Delbert Day, ceramic engineering; Walter Eversman, mechanical and aerospace engineering; Thomas O'Keefe, metallurgical engineer-

Performances by the Madrigal Players became an important part of the holiday season.

ing; Ronald Olson and Laird Schearer, physics; David Summers, mining engineering; and Wei-Wen Yu, civil engineering.

Aided by funds from the 1980 state bond issue and increased private gifts, Marchello continued an ambitious program of building renovation and construction. The Rolla Building, oldest on campus, was renovated and restored to its original appearance, including its old bell tower. The chancellor's residence was restored to its 1889 appearance, a charming—if somewhat quaint—Victorian house.

The Department of Engineering Management, founded in 1968, had developed a Ph.D. program, and under the leadership of Bernard Sarchet had become a major source of assistance for businesses all over Missouri. In order to house the department in adequate quarters, E. A. Smith of Tulsa, Oklahoma, and other alumni provided $500,000 toward the total cost of $2.5 million.

Marchello's most ambitious building project, involving the most extensive fundraising effort in the institution's history, was an $18 million mineral engineering building to be constructed at the northwest corner of the campus. Harry H. Kessler and his wife kicked off the $3.5 million fundraising drive with the gift of an interest in a producing mine valued at $250,000. Success of the effort was assured when Mrs. V. H. McNutt of San Antonio, Texas, gave $2 million. This was the last of "Momma Mac's" philanthropies on behalf of MSM/UMR.

President Gerald Ford inaugurates the Remmers Special Lecture/Artist series, 1979. Applauding are Walter and Miriam Remmers, who established the series.

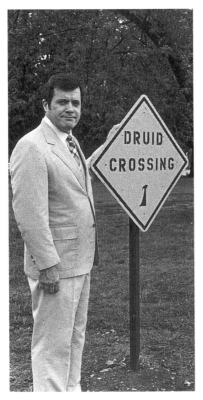

Joseph Marchello at the site of the future Stonehenge, a particular interest of his.

The widow of Vachel H. McNutt, a 1912 graduate and founder of the nation's most important potash company, "Momma Mac" not only carried on the business after her husband's death in 1936 but also became increasingly involved in activities at Rolla. The V. H. McNutt Foundation provided scholarships and other assistance for the Department of Geology. Mrs. McNutt traveled to Rolla at least once a year to meet with "her boys" and to visit with faculty, administrators, and students. She received the first Doctor of Humane Letters ever conferred at UMR in 1967, the first woman to receive an honorary degree from the school. Her last trip to the campus, shortly before her death in 1984, was to participate in the inaugural ceremonies for what was to become Vachel H. McNutt Hall.

As construction started on McNutt Hall, a unique monument was being built adjacent to the site. Characterized as one of the world's outstanding engineering projects, and a sophisticated early computer, Stonehenge had caught the imagination of faculty, students, and alumni. UMR Stonehenge was completed in 1986 as a one-half-scale partial reconstruction of the ancient megalith on Salisbury Plain in England.

Marchello resigned in 1985 to become president of Old Dominion University in Virginia. After an extended national search, during which John Park served as interim chancellor, President Magrath and the board of curators appointed Martin Jischke, dean of engineering at the University of Oklahoma, to the post. Martin and Patricia Jischke, with their two young children, arrived on campus 28 April

The half-size "working model" of Stonehenge at the northwest entrance to the campus. The granite used in the monument was cut with water jet techniques developed by the Rock Mechanics and Explosives Research Center.

The restored Rolla Building.

The cupola goes back on the old Rolla Building. Louise Marchello was particularly interested in preserving the historic buildings on campus, directing her attention to both the Rolla Building and the chancellor's residence.

1986. They found an institution secure in its mission and confident in its ability to carry it out.

The original Rolla Building, restored to its former glory, dominated a campus of seventy acres arrayed with buildings constructed over a century to provide for the needs of a school that had changed from an institution with a narrow, vocational curriculum to a modern scientific and technological university. The faculty was becoming increasingly well-known for the quality of its research and teaching, and alumni in prominent positions all over the world attested to the quality of the education they had received at MSM and UMR. Nostalgia for MSM was being replaced with pride in UMR.

Martin L. Jischke, dean of engineering at the University of Oklahoma, became chancellor in 1986.

# Kansas City

# 9 UNIVERSITY OF
## KANSAS CITY

The University of Kansas City traces its origins to the years before World War I when community groups and civic leaders began to express an interest in the establishment of a university. The need was self-evident. Kansas City had a high-quality junior college as well as Rockhurst College, founded by Jesuits in 1910, Park College in Parkville, and William Jewell College in Liberty. In addition, Kansas City had a number of private professional schools—dentistry, law, music, and pharmacy. The nearest universities, however, were the University of Kansas, 40 miles to the west, and the University of Missouri, 120 miles to the east.

Despite the obvious need, the idea of establishing a university in Kansas City was a long time in coming to fruition. The Chamber of Commerce appointed a succession of committees to study the matter, and in 1925 a committee headed by A. Ross Hill, former president of the University of Missouri who had retired in Kansas City, urged the community to move forward to establish a university. While the committees deliberated, Kate W. Hewitt, widow of a former president of the Kansas City Dental College, offered the Methodist Church 147 acres of land at State Line Avenue and 175th Street on which to found a college, an effort resulting in the establishment of Lincoln and Lee University. For a time this plan competed with the Chamber of Commerce effort, which in 1929 had chartered the University of Kansas City. Finally, the two groups came together in support of a nonsectarian University of Kansas City.

The person most responsible for giving the idea direction and moving it toward realization was William Volker. He provided money to buy forty acres of land north of Brush Creek from the trustees of the Nelson Gallery, and in December 1931 he purchased the William S. Dickey mansion and eight acres of land south of Brush Creek. Volker was dedicated to the cause of the university, contributing over two million dollars until his death in 1947. With the purchase of the Brush Creek site and the Dickey mansion, the university not only had an accessible campus—the Hewitt land was considered too far south—it also had a handsome building and a magnificent tract of land in the heart of what was developing into Kansas City's cultural district. The trustees, under the leadership of Ernest E. Howard, worked to open the university as soon as possible. Providing daily leadership was Ernest H. Newcomb, former president of Central College for Women in Lexington, Missouri, who at considerable personal sacrifice had been the driving force of both the Lincoln and Lee and UKC efforts and who, as secretary of the board of trustees, administered the university for the first three years of its existence.

Although the trustees had only $2 million of the $5 million they had hoped to raise, with encouragement from Volker, they decided to

Late in life, William Volker commented, "Among the things I have tried to do in this city, I am sure the University will pay the biggest dividends to the most people. . . . Certainly it is the best investment I have ever made."

Ernest E. Howard served as chairman of the board of trustees from the establishment of the university to his death in 1953.

Ernest Newcomb, secretary of the board of trustees, administered the university from 1933 to 1936. In 1984 the Old Library was named Newcomb Hall in his honor.

Rustic wooden signs contributed to the parklike atmosphere of the campus.

begin operations in the fall of 1933. Newcomb labored heroically to hire a faculty, to draw up a curriculum, and to prepare the Dickey mansion for use as a university building. On 1 October—a beautiful autumn Sunday in Kansas City—two thousand people gathered on the lawn south of the Dickey mansion to dedicate the new university. Dr. Harold Brown, the first professor of chemistry, recalled that the faculty "were all enthused with the challenge of starting a new university. We were looking far ahead to a future." It was indeed a time of hope and realization for Kansas City. Despite the Great Depression, the inauguration of the university was followed within two months by the opening of the William Rockhill Nelson Gallery of Art and Atkins Museum and by the first performance by the Kansas City Philharmonic Orchestra.

The university began classes as scheduled on 2 October, with a faculty of 18 and a student body of 260. The Dickey mansion, located on the highest spot in Kansas City, provided elegant if not altogether efficient facilities. The mansion housed all university activities, except science classes, which were held in the greenhouse. The carriage house served as power plant and gymnasium.

Although Newcomb served as chief administrative officer, academic matters were placed in the hands of a dean, Orin G. Sanford, who had been assistant state superintendent of public instruction for Missouri. Sanford helped to recruit an able young faculty and to develop the initial curriculum, but he had very little administrative authority; the trustees tended to run the university directly or through Newcomb. This precipitated a crisis before the first year was out. When the trustees declined to renew the contracts of three popular professors, the students went on strike, and there was a general call for the appointment of a president to provide leadership for the institution.

The trustees responded by naming J. Duncan Spaeth. Spaeth was a likable man, but he did not generate much interest in the presidency. He did not assume office for a year after his appointment. Then his wife died and his own health deteriorated. Moreover, the internal conflicts characterizing the institution's first year continued in exacer-

The dedication ceremony was described by the *Kansas City Times* as "conscious of destiny."

J. Duncan Spaeth, first president of the university, served only from 1936 until 1938, when he resigned because of ill health. Here he is shown with students.

The lovely lawns surrounding the Dickey mansion, with their stately trees and grassy hillsides, provided an idyllic campus setting. Here students pose in front of the building before resuming their academic activities.

Among the features of the Dickey mansion were marble floors and marble fireplaces. Here an English class meets in an elegant upstairs room that later became the chancellor's office.

The south patio of the Dickey Mansion provided a pleasant place for students to gather, as attested by these members of the first student body.

Orin G. Sanford, formerly assistant state superintendent of public instruction for Missouri, served as dean from 1933 until 1938, when he became dean of men, a position he held until 1941. He continued as professor of education until his death in 1948. Here he is shown with a group of students in his office.

bated form. In particular, Spaeth had problems with Newcomb, who continued to act as executive secretary even after a president was appointed. Late in 1937, after little more than a year in office, Spaeth asked to be relieved of his administrative duties preparatory to resigning.

Despite internal feuding and administrative difficulties, the institution had developed rapidly. The junior and senior years were added,

Beginning with the first graduation in 1936, Commencement on the Quadrangle was an important and much cherished event. This procession occurred in 1939 or 1940.

and in June 1936, at the first Commencement, 80 graduates received their diplomas. By 1937 enrollment had increased to 700, and the faculty numbered 46. Largely because of the generosity of William Volker, several new buildings were added. A science building opened in 1935, and a library, completed in the spring of 1936, hinted at the development of an open quadrangle south of the Administration Building, as the Dickey mansion came to be known. A Liberal Arts Building, begun in the spring of 1937 with funds given by Lena Haag, gave further form to the campus. In 1936 Volker purchased a commodious house on the east side of Fifty-first and Rockhill to be used as a home for the president.

Ilus W. Davis, a member of the first class, later recalled: "It was fun! It was exciting! . . . We were there to receive an education and incidentally to do all of the things that had to be done to bring a university into being."

At Spaeth's suggestion, the trustees named Clarence R. Decker as vice president and gave him responsibility for daily management of the university. Before the year was out they had named him president. Decker served as president of the university from 1938 to 1953, a longer tenure than any chief executive in the history of the institution, and he had a profound influence on its development. Young, articulate, athletic, musical, the new president was highly popular with students, faculty, and community leaders.

Decker quickly put his stamp on the university. Newcomb, forced into a subordinate position, soon resigned. Earlier, Dean Sanford, caught between Decker and Newcomb, had resigned to become a professor of education, a position he retained for many years. Decker's views on education had been greatly influenced by Robert Hutchins, president of the University of Chicago. Decker thought of the university as a classical academy with a curriculum centered on the humanities. He had little use for science and less for professional education. He vigorously opposed intercollegiate athletics and national Greek-letter organizations, and the students apparently accepted these restrictions on campus life with good grace.

The young university nevertheless developed traditions. Freshmen were required to wear blue and gold beanies, and walk counterclockwise around the quadrangle, at pain of being tossed in the pond for failure to follow the rules. Denied intercollegiate athletics, the students developed a lively, healthy program of intramural sports with

A pleasant little pond east of the Carriage House added to the bucolic setting. The pond, a favorite gathering place for students, gave way to progress in the early 1970s.

These students appear to be appropriately dressed for Hobo Day, later called Bum Friday, which traced its origins to a student strike conducted in the spring of 1934 as a protest against the failure of the trustees to renew the contracts of three popular professors.

both men's and women's athletic associations. There was particularly strong support for women's gym classes. Denied the opportunity to join national fraternities and sororities, they developed local clubs in great numbers. More than forty clubs were organized in the first ten years of the school's existence, and almost every student belonged to at least one.

Even though they had just one national Greek-letter organization—Alpha Phi Omega, a national scouting fraternity—the students

The Tophatters, ca. 1939, a forerunner of the performing arts at the university.

Initially, the University Players performed in a tent.

formed both the Interfraternity Council and the Panhellenic Council to coordinate and to govern the social clubs. An elected student council tried to exercise control over all student activities. Students could keep up with the various campus organizations through the *University News*, which covered student activities on a weekly basis, and the *Kangaroo*, which recorded campus life on first a monthly and then an annual basis.

Two students do not seem to notice
Alexander Cappon, long-time faculty
member and founding editor of *The
University Review*, descending the
steps of the Administration Building,
the name given the Dickey mansion.

Clarence Decker served as president of
the university from 1938 to 1953, the
longest tenure of any chief executive
in the history of the institution. Here
he is shown with President Truman on
the south porch of the Administration
Building, just before the President's
speech, 28 June 1945.

In the beginning, music and theater were primarily extracurricular
activities, although the University Singers, led by Everett Hendricks,
began to exhibit qualities of musicianship that would come to charac-
terize performances given by many university musical groups. A
university orchestra was started under the direction of Sir Carl Busch.
The Music Club and the Tophatters club provided social as well as
musical opportunities. The University Players started as the Varsity
Players, with William Troutman as director, and although there was a
lively interest in drama, theatrical groups had no satisfactory place to
perform; some plays were given in tents.

Despite low salaries and inadequate facilities the university was
able to attract an exceptionally good faculty. Some members of the
faculty, such as Harold Buschman, John Ciardi, Henry B. Hill, Lawrence Kimpton, and Hans Morgenthau, left after a few years to build
their reputations elsewhere. Others, however, stayed to devote their
lives to building the new university, among them Hugh W. Speer,
education; John R. Hodges, economics; Alexander Cappon, English;
William L. Crain, foreign languages; Sidney E. Ekblaw, geology; Norman Royall, mathematics; Marathon High, physics; Ernest Manheim,
sociology; and Helen Jo Crissman, director of publications. Decker
frequently augmented the faculty by bringing to the campus leading
figures from literature and the arts to give lectures or to serve as
short-term visiting professors. The Deckers used these visits as occasions to entertain trustees and other leading citizens in their home.

Commencement and special convocations also brought noted public figures to the quadrangle. President Truman received the university's first honorary degree there in 1945, and Averell Harriman gave the
Commencement address in 1951.

As the nation moved toward World War II, the university continued to grow. In the fall of 1941, enrollment stood at 1,280, the highest in history. Liberal arts still dominated the curriculum, but the
university was no longer just a liberal arts college. The incorporation
of a number of Kansas City's well-established professional schools
into the university initiated a change in the fundamental nature of the
institution.

The School of Law was established with the incorporation of the
Kansas City School of Law in 1938. Founded in 1895, the Kansas City
School of Law had operated in a number of downtown office buildings until 1926 when it secured a building of its own on Baltimore
Avenue. At that time it had a student body of more than seven hundred (mostly part-time) and a faculty of fifty-two (also part-time). By
the Depression, however, with enrollment under two hundred, affiliation with the university seemed the only route to survival. Benjamin F. Boyer became dean shortly after affiliation and served in that
capacity until 1947. Two members of the original faculty, John Speca
and John Scurlock, continued with the university until their retirement.

The School of Dentistry, added in 1941, originated in the 1919 merger of the dental department of the Kansas City Medical College,
founded in 1881, and the Western Dental College, established in 1890.

A Saturday painting class, taught by Joseph Fleck, meets on the grounds later occupied by the Linda Hall Library, mid-1940s. Fleck, one of a number of artists-in-residence during the Decker years, stands in the middle of the picture, his hand to his chin.

Andre Maurois was one of a number of notable persons who served as visiting professors during the Decker years. He endeared himself to Kansas Citians by writing, "Who in Europe, or in America for that matter, knows that Kansas City is one of the loveliest cities on earth? . . . Few cities have been built with so much regard for beauty."

During his time as artist-in-residence, Alexander Archipenko created the two large columns that grace the Rockhill Road exit.

Luis Quintanilla served as artist-in-residence, 1940–1941. During his time at the university he painted the Don Quixote frescoes in Haag Hall.

Chemistry lab was serious business. The science building, completed in 1935, provided badly needed facilities. Later, after the completion of the Kenneth A. Spencer Chemistry Building, the old science building became the home of the Department of Art and Art History.

Students and faculty pose in front of the Western Dental College's new building at Eleventh and Locust, ca. 1900. After the merger with the dental department of the old Kansas City Medical College, the school moved to a building at Tenth and Troost where it was located at the time it became part of the university.

The School of Dentistry was well-established in its own building at Tenth and Troost, and Dean Roy Rinehart soon became a dominant force in university affairs.

The School of Pharmacy, absorbed in 1943, dated from 1886 when it was established as a department of the old medical school. Although druggists in the area supported the college fairly well, a loss of students during the war inspired it to seek university affiliation, and it did so with Theodore T. Dittrich as dean. Fortunately, well-equipped

Dr. Rinehart's class, 1902, takes the form of a dental clinic. Roy J. Rinehart had been dean of the Dental School since the 1920s, and following the merger with the university in 1941 became a dominant figure in university affairs. Following Clarence Decker's resignation in 1953 he served for a few months as chief executive of the university. He continued as dean until his death in 1957.

Dr. Rinehart's first office, ca. 1900.

space was available in the new Chemistry-Biology Building, constructed in 1942 as a gift from William Volker.

In addition to absorbing the three professional schools, the university continued to add to its physical plant in the early 1940s. Swinney Gymnasium opened in 1941 to provide the campus for the first time with adequate indoor facilities for physical education and recreation. Over the entrance, words by John Ciardi remind students that "Exercise renews the body, supports the spirit and keeps the mind in vigor," and admonish all to "run hard, leap high, throw strongly and endure."

World War II brought growth to a halt and completely transformed the university. During this time, when Swinney Gymnasium became

Swinney Gymnasium, the gift of E. F. Swinney, chairman of the board of the First National Bank.

Swinney Gymnasium provided a facility for instruction in all kinds of athletic endeavor, including self-defense.

a barracks for Army Air Force cadets, enrollment of regular students dropped precipitously—twenty-two percent in the second semester of the 1941–1942 school year—and most of the students were women. The School of Law abandoned daytime classes and concentrated its instruction in the evening courses. Most of the dental students, domiciled in Epperson House, continued their education as part of the Army's Specialized Training Unit or the Navy's V-12 program. Aside from the fact that the campus at times looked like a military post, the impact of war soon began to be felt in the casualty lists. Of the nine hundred students and former students who served in the armed

Epperson House, given to the university by J. J. Lynn in 1942, one of a number of large homes that became a part of the campus.

Most of the regularly enrolled students during World War II were women. This group poses on the south steps of the Administration Building.

Harold L. Holliday, the first black to be admitted to the university, entered the law school in 1947. He graduated and became one of Kansas City's leading political figures.

forces, twenty-nine lost their lives.

At the end of the war male students returned to the campus, UKC, in common with virtually every college and university in the country, faced the need to accommodate large numbers of returning veterans. The university had no dormitories, classroom and laboratory space was limited, administrative services were inadequate, and the small faculty was unable to meet the demands of rapidly rising enrollment. By the fall of 1946 the student body numbered 3,350, a gain of sixty percent in one year.

The postwar years saw the admission of the first black students to the university. At the urging of both Decker and the faculty, the trustees in 1947 opened the university to all students, regardless of race or color, who met the entrance requirements. By January 1948, seven blacks were enrolled. Although the number of black students remained small, KCU had changed its whites-only policy.

New faculty members were hired and class schedules were adjusted. The admissions staff was enlarged to handle the heavy flow of applicants; among those added was returning veteran Richard Bolling, who worked as an admissions counselor before making his initial run for Congress. Epperson House became a makeshift dormitory, but for the most part the university depended on residents in the neighborhood to provide rooms or apartments for students who did not live at home.

Five war surplus buildings helped to relieve crowded conditions. Three of them housed the School of Pharmacy and first-year dental students as well as general classes. The other two were the student union and the University Playhouse, which had been the post theater for Camp Crowder. Decker had a particular interest in the theater,

"Bum Friday" lunch in front of the old Student Union at Fifty-first and Rockhill.

and the university spent some $300,000 converting the old Army movie building into a first-class professional house. The stage was larger than most New York stages; wing and backstage facilities were of professional quality. New seats comfortably provided for an audience of 510 persons. Led by John Neufield, the theater flourished from the beginning. Patricia McIlrath, who arrived in 1954, built an outstanding Department of Theater and developed the Missouri Repertory Theatre, which she founded in 1964, into one of the nation's leading regional theaters.

In 1949 the university bought eight houses along Pierce Street from the Nelson Trust. Built originally by William Rockhill Nelson as model workingmen's homes, the houses were rented to faculty for a few years and then were converted into offices. The only new building constructed during these years was the School of Law. Dedicated in 1950, the new building made it possible for the law school under the leadership of Dean Marlin M. Volz to expand both its curriculum and its enrollment. A legal aid clinic provided practical experience, and the *Law Review* gave opportunities for research and writing.

The fireplace patio in front of the University Playhouse provided a pleasant place for meetings, such as this alumni gathering in 1959, and to spend intermission during theatrical performances.

As the years wore on, it was clear that Decker was coming to the end of his time as an effective leader. He remained popular in the community and with the trustees, but faculty and students were becoming increasingly restive under his refusal to push for growth and his determination to maintain the university as a small, elitist institution. Faculty were distressed over low salaries, inadequate facilities, and governance practices that were so arbitrary as to have drawn censure from the American Association of University Professors.

Decker's problems coalesced in the spring of 1952 while he was on leave in the Far East. Robert Mortvedt, vice president since 1947, serving as acting president in Decker's absence, dug into the university's operations and found finances in disarray and enrollment declining, a gloomy picture in contrast to the rosy hue with which Decker had portrayed the university's condition.

Mortvedt laid the condition of the university before the board, and despite the votes of no confidence in Decker passed by the faculty and students, most of the trustees, and particularly Ernest E. Howard, continued to support the president. When Decker returned in the fall of 1952 he found the university in turmoil. Several members of the administration submitted their resignations: Mortvedt; Norman Royall, who had succeeded Mortvedt as dean of liberal arts; Dittrich, dean of pharmacy; and John Barnett, registrar and assistant dean of liberal arts. At first the board refused to accept the resignations, but then they relieved Mortvedt and Royall from all administrative responsibilities. Finally, 23 February 1953, the board accepted the resignation Decker had submitted in November.

Decker remained as president until the end of the year, presiding over the May Commencement as his last official act. More than 3,500 people filled the quadrangle to watch 444 graduates receive their diplomas and to pay tribute to the retiring president—even after his difficulties on campus, Decker continued to be popular with the

trustees and many in the community. Everyone sensed that it was the
end of an era. Decker's view of the university as a small classical
academy devoted to the arts and the humanities fell before the growing demand for a more practical education.

Roy J. Rinehart served as executive administrator until Earl J.
McGrath arrived in the fall to become the university's third president.
With McGrath's leadership the university moved quickly to broaden
its mission. The School of Business Administration was founded in
1953, with Charles E. Gilliland as dean, and the School of Education
was established the following year, led by Hugh W. Speer, who acted
as dean for almost a decade. In addition to appointing deans for the
new schools of business administration and education, McGrath
selected Leslie Eisenbrandt to replace Theodore Dittrich, who had
resigned as the dean of pharmacy at the end of the Decker administration. In the College of Liberal Arts, which John Barnett continued to
oversee as dean, bachelor of science programs in science, home economics, and medical technology broadened the university's appeal,
and at the master's level new programs were offered in theater, city
planning, and public administration. To accommodate the needs of
adults who wished to take short, non-credit courses at night, an Evening Division was established with William Weifenbach as dean. In
1958 the name was changed to Division for Continuing Education,
and Berndt Kolker became dean, a post he held until 1963, also serving as vice president for development.

In 1953, Wheadon Bloch became dean of students, serving with
great effectiveness during two difficult decades as student life was
expanded in many ways. Two years after his appointment, KCU
acquired a dormitory, a four-story brick structure. At the ground-
breaking ceremonies in June, McGrath predicted that the dormitory,
making it possible for students to live at the university, would "fun-
damentally change the atmosphere of the campus." Furthermore,
during Bloch's term, national Greek-letter organizations were approved, a debate team was organized, and for the first time in its
history the university ventured into intercollegiate athletics, fielding
a men's basketball team. The Kangaroos opened against Rockhurst
College on 24 January 1954, losing 53 to 92, and went on to play a ten-
game schedule, mostly with junior college and club teams.

Omicron Delta Kappa, a national leadership society for men, came
to campus in 1956, joining Delta Alpha, a senior women's leadership
society, and Torch and Scroll, a scholastic honor society. The Alumni
Association, organized in 1936, joined with the students in sponsor-
ing homecoming events and in promoting school spirit. The steady
parade of celebrities characterizing Decker's years was reduced to an
occasional visiting lecturer. In 1955 Eleanor Roosevelt spoke in the
Playhouse; the capacity crowd included President and Mrs. Truman.

A number of additions to the faculty during McGrath's years would
leave indelible marks on the institution: Joanne Baker, music; George
Ehrlich, art and art history; Morton Goldman, psychology; Elmer
Horseman, law; Patricia McIlrath, theater; William Rost, pharmacy;
Genevieve Roth, dentistry.

Dr. and Mrs. Earl McGrath in front of
the president's home at the southeast
corner of Fifty-first and Rockhill.
McGrath, former United States Commissioner of Education, served as
president from 1953 to 1956.

An exciting moment in a game with William Jewell College.

McGrath was proving to be a popular president when suddenly in May 1956 he announced that he was resigning to become director of an educational institute at Columbia University in New York. Mc-Grath had been ambitious for the university and had brought about rapid expansion of course offerings, activities, and services. The community, however, was not prepared to pay the necessary costs to keep him. McGrath had urged the trustees to change the title of the chief executive, and Richard Drake, who had succeeded Mortvedt as vice president for academic affairs, was appointed acting chancellor. When a year-long search failed to produce a more satisfactory candidate, the trustees removed "acting" from Drake's title.

Drake was inaugurated with great fanfare, the ceremony being carried live by six television stations. More than four million people viewed the ceremonies as the university inaugurated new leadership for its second quarter-century. Lawrence Kimpton returned from the University of Chicago to give the inaugural address, and it appeared that despite financial problems the university would continue to progress. Throughout the inaugural year, the university continued to celebrate its second quarter-century with lectures, symposia, concerts, and plays. For a while it seemed that UKC did have a future as a private institution.

In 1958 Margaret Hashinger gave her home at 5106 Cherry to the university. This lovely Tudor house with its splendid garden became the chancellor's residence, and the older residence on Rockhill Road was converted to offices.

Drake made a number of significant appointments, including Hamilton B. G. Robinson as dean of the School of Dentistry and Carleton F. Scofield as director of graduate studies. Fred Lewis, named as dean of the law school, rescued the school from the threat of losing accreditation and started it on the road to a position of eminence. The reputation of the law school was greatly enhanced when alumnus Charles E. Whittaker was appointed to the Supreme Court of the United States.

The university acquired a major addition in 1959 when the trustees of the Kansas City Conservatory of Music voted to merge with KCU. The Conservatory, founded in 1906, had merged with the Horner Institute in the 1920s and had developed an enviable reputation for performance and instruction in performance. This addition brought a valuable property just west of the Kansas City Art Institute, including newly constructed Grant Hall, a gift of William T. Grant, and an experienced faculty including pianists Joanne Baker, Walter Cook, Wiktor Labunski, Marjorie Ounsworth, and Herbert Six; violinists Dorothy Brown, Dorothy Rendina, and Eugene Stoia; and percussionist Charmaine Asher. Stanley Deacon and Martha Longmire taught voice; Everett Hendricks, choral music; Francis Buebendorf and LeRoy Pogemiller, theory and composition. Russell Patterson was responsible for orchestra, opera, and horn. Archie Jones of the University of Texas became dean and Lyle Kennedy, who had been serving as acting director of the Conservatory, assistant dean.

Archie Jones, dean of the Conservatory of Music at the time it became a part of the university.

Community involvement in the university was greatly enhanced by the establishment of the University Associates in 1958. Designed to bring social, cultural, and educational leaders of the community into the university family, the University Associates from the beginning worked effectively to interpret the university and the community to each other. James M. Kemper served as the first president of the organization that developed a membership of several hundred. The trustees got new leadership, as John A. Morgan, a young, aggressive, and thoughtful business executive, who had been instrumental in

Shown at the founding dinner of the University Associates, 9 October 1958, are David Beals, John Taylor, John A. Morgan, Patricia Morgan, and Richard Drake. In 1959, Beals, chairman of the board of trustees from 1953 to 1959, was the first recipient of the Chancellor's Medal, given each year at the associates' annual dinner. Taylor, a prominent Kansas City business executive, was one of the founders of the University Associates. Morgan, also a founder of the associates, served as chairman of the board of trustees from 1959 to 1963 and was instrumental in effecting the merger between the University of Kansas City and the University of Missouri. Drake served as chancellor from 1956 to 1961.

Obviously, this student intended to be well prepared.

organizing the University Associates, became chairman, replacing David Beals.

Another major force in the cultural life of the community was the Cockefair Chair, inaugurated in 1960 as a means of honoring Carolyn Benton Cockefair, long-time teacher of English literature who was a great favorite of both students and townspeople. Norman Cousins served as the inaugural lecturer, and under the leadership of Selma Feld the Cockefair Chair developed an endowment that enabled it to present distinguished lecturers and opportunities for short courses in the humanities.

In 1959 ground was broken for what would become the popular University Center. Financed by private contributions and by a government loan, the million-dollar structure provided the university for the first time with an adequate facility for conferences and meetings as well as with dining and lounge areas.

For the many students enrolled part-time in the university, the relationship to campus was limited to classroom contacts, and they found the classroom experience rewarding. In addition to faculty who had arrived earlier, students had opportunities to study under such persons as Norman L. Schwartz in dentistry; Margaret Dudley, Martin Levit, Mary Lee Marksbury, and Hazel Browne Williams in education; Frederick R. Mcleod in English, Eldon Parizek in geology, Reverdy Gliddon in management, and Solomon Levy in philosophy. Edwin J. Westermann of the Department of History had become dean of the College of Liberal Arts, Kenneth J. LaBudde was director of the library, and Leo J. Sweeney was registrar and director of admissions.

For full-time students living either on or off campus, the university provided a fairly complete array of student activities, with clubs, social organizations—Chi Omega, the first national sorority on cam-

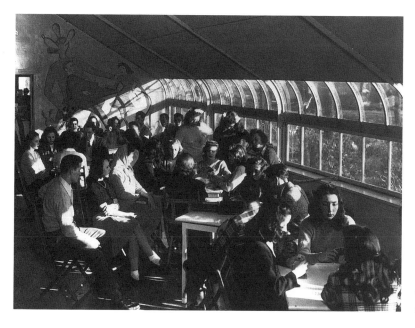

The old greenhouse served for a time as a student union.

pus, was established in 1961—and honor societies. The All Student Association provided opportunities for budding politicians and gave some direction to student activities.

Superficially, KCU seemed to be in good shape, but there were ominous signs of serious difficulty. Faculty salaries were a disgrace, the campus bore the scars of inadequate maintenance, and the half-empty new dormitory stood as a monument to enrollment problems that were almost at crisis stage. Symbolic of the school's condition was the decision in the spring of 1961 to discontinue the operation of KCUR-FM, founded in 1957 and developed into a National Public Radio affiliate under the leadership of Sam Scott, and to abolish inter-collegiate athletics for budgetary reasons. The students responded to the decision on athletics with what were described in the *Kangaroo* as the "March Riots," which featured a huge bonfire "as the starting spark of the students' drive to bring sports back to the campus."

Student efforts proved unsuccessful because the problem was monetary in nature. The Kansas City community simply had not been able to provide the resources needed to maintain the university, let alone to build it into the kind of institution its founders had dreamed about. The utter hopelessness of the situation caused Richard Drake, who had never been much interested in fund-raising, to call it quits in May 1961.

The trustees turned to Carleton Scofield, vice president for academic affairs and widely popular on the campus and in the community. Scofield agreed to accept appointment as acting chancellor if the trustees would activate a chancellor selection committee at once with the understanding that he would not be a candidate for the post, and if they would restore $12,375 for KCUR-FM to the budget. Both conditions were accepted, and Scofield took on the task of trying to save the university.

Carleton F. Scofield served as the last president of the University of Kansas City and the first chancellor of the University of Missouri–Kansas City. Scofield joined the faculty in 1953 as director of graduate studies and later became vice president for academic affairs. He was appointed acting chancellor in 1961 and president in 1963. His efforts in the months leading up to the merger with the University of Missouri were critical to the success of the enterprise. In 1983 the Administration Building was named in his honor.

The University of Kansas City becomes the University of Missouri at Kansas City, but the tradition of the rustic signs continues.

It was a hopeless task. Study after study had shown that unless the trustees were able to raise a substantial endowment it would be impossible for the university to continue as a private institution. Increasingly, community leaders—particularly Homer Wadsworth, president of the Kansas City Association of Trusts and Foundations, which had taken the lead in funding efforts to seek a solution—were coming to the conclusion that the only course left for the University of Kansas City was affiliation with the University of Missouri, even though some trustees bitterly opposed such an affiliation.

Scofield made a trip to Columbia to sound out President Elmer Ellis on the possibility of a merger and found him receptive to the idea. Absorbing the University of Kansas City would be an important step toward taking the university to the state's two largest cities. After a protracted and difficult negotiation, the way was cleared for the merger of the two institutions, if funds could be secured from the legislature. At the urging of Governor John M. Dalton, the legislature authorized the university to acquire the University of Kansas City and establish a campus in St. Louis; after intense lobbying, particularly from Morgan and other Kansas City leaders, the legislature also provided the necessary funding. At high noon on 23 July 1963, the University of Kansas City became the University of Missouri at Kansas City.

# 10 UNIVERSITY OF
## MISSOURI–KANSAS CITY

Although there was some nostalgia for the old University of Kansas City, most people associated with the institution were soon swept up in the excitement and the promise—and at times the frustration—of the new University of Missouri at Kansas City. Most seemed to agree with the *Kansas City Times*, which stated, "There are no limits for U.M.K.C. . . . It would be difficult to exaggerate the importance of this development."

Carleton Scofield, whose title had been changed from acting chancellor to president shortly before the merger, was named chancellor of the new campus. Whereas he had spent the previous two years trying to keep the ailing university's doors open, he now found himself struggling with the problems of explosive growth. Although tuition was maintained at earlier levels for one year to help pay off accumulated debts, enrollment in the fall of 1963 was 4,394, an increase of 46 percent. When fees were dropped to the University of Missouri level in 1965, enrollment jumped to 6,114.

To accommodate the flood of students the university added forty-seven new faculty members in 1964 alone. Many of them moved on, but included in the number were some who would continue for years as members of the faculty: William B. Eddy, administration; Eric Bransby, art; William Milstead, Norlan Henderson, and Henry Mitchell, biology; Layton McCoy and John Connally, chemistry; Robert Farnsworth, English; Paul Liebnitz, mathematics; Hans Uffelman, philosophy; James Phillips and Richard Waring, physics; Max Beatty, theater; and Bernard Grabowski, pharmacy.

Students fill out registration forms on the steps of Pierson Hall.

Miller Nichols, prominent Kansas City business and civic leader and a long-time member of the University of Kansas City Board of Trustees, whose leadership in acquiring land surrounding the Volker campus made possible university expansion.

The Kangaroo receives greetings from another famous Kansas Citian.

Facilities proved more difficult to expand. Long-neglected maintenance absorbed much of the money available for capital improvements, and the only new construction was the completion of the Katz Pharmacy Building on which KCU had been forced to suspend work. Tureman House, a handsome building west of Epperson House donated by Mrs. Marie P. McCune, alleviated some of the problems caused by expansion, and, in the fall of 1965, Oxford Hall, formerly occupied by St. Paul School of Theology, and an adjoining carriage house (Epworth House) became home for the School of Business and Public Administration. Shortly thereafter, the UKC trustees, who under the merger agreement stayed in existence as a support group for UMKC, acquired the Vandegrift mansion at Fifty-fifth and Ward Parkway. They sold it and used the funds to buy property near the campus, thus beginning a program of land acquisition that under the leadership of Miller Nichols provided the campus with badly needed room for expansion.

The library faced particularly critical conditions. For a while books were stored in the City Library. Then the Federal Aviation Agency's building at 4825 Troost Avenue was leased for use by the library. This building, which ultimately was purchased by the university and converted into a consolidated student and administrative services building, was leased on and off for two decades to house various departments.

Scofield made a number of important administrative appointments. John Dowgray became dean of faculties and was heavily involved in the recruitment of new faculty. Patrick Kelly, a member of the law school faculty, became dean of the law school. Jack D. Heysinger of the University of Wichita was appointed dean of the School of Business and Public Administration. Shirley Hill, a brilliant young professor of mathematics education, took over as acting dean of education when Hugh Speer resigned. Although she resisted further administrative assignments, she won wide recognition as a faculty leader both on campus and in the university as a whole, and she became one of the nation's leading figures in mathematics education. Responsible for law and order on the campus were two men who would play key roles in the unrest of the late 1960s and the early 1970s, both in Kansas City and in Columbia—Harvey Cottle and Ronald Mason.

Scofield reached the mandatory retirement age in 1965. He had provided leadership for the transition of the university from private to public status. In recognition of his unique role in the history of the institution, the old Dickey Mansion, office for both presidents and chancellors, was named in his honor.

To succeed Scofield, President Ellis appointed Randall Whaley. Dynamic and aggressive, Whaley, and particularly his wife, Mim, became instantly popular in Kansas City and favorites of the trustees. The Whaleys brought a steady parade of notables to the campus for speaking engagements, among them Marvin Kalb, Pierre Salinger, Dick Gregory, and F. Lee Bailey.

The university continued to grow. Enrollment reached 7,891 in 1966 and 8,418 in 1967. The School of Graduate Studies was established in

1966, and Wesley J. Dale, chair of the Department of Chemistry at
UMC, became its first dean. Other new deans were William Strickland, who replaced Leslie Eisenbrandt in Pharmacy, and Calvin
Gross, former superintendent of schools in New York City, who
became dean of the School of Education.

It was a heady time, but Whaley did not get along well with members of the central administration and particularly with John Weaver,
the new president. The principal problem was Whaley's opposition to
the concept of a single university adopted by the board of curators.
Whaley's efforts pleased the trustees and others in Kansas City who
wanted as much autonomy as possible for UMKC, but the response
was not positive in Jefferson City or in Columbia. There were also
administrative difficulties, involving delays in moving campus plans
along and difficulties in keeping within the budget. By the summer of
1967, Whaley had no choice but to resign.

He announced his resignation, effective 31 December, over the
Labor Day weekend. The curators accepted but relieved him of his
duties immediately. Whaley's resignation, which took many people
by surprise, created a minor uproar on the campus and in the community, and exacerbated the ill will that had developed between
Weaver and the curators on one side and the trustees on the other
side over the relationship between the central administration and the
campus—ill will that would take a long time and much patient effort
to ameliorate.

After a year in which Hamilton B. G. Robinson, dean of the Dental
School, served as acting chancellor, the curators named James C.
Olson, vice chancellor for graduate education and research at the
University of Nebraska, chancellor. Commenting on Olson's appointment, Homer Wadsworth, president of the Kansas City Association
of Trusts and Foundations and a prime mover in the community,
stated, "The main piece of unfinished business in Kansas City is the
creation of a true university. It will not be easy. The university and
this community have never pulled together on the oars. The new
chancellor will need help, and he will need sympathy, too, for this is a
difficult job."

Fortunately, the community seemed ready to begin to pull together
with the university. Robinson had done much during his year as

Chancellor Randall Whaley presents
an alumnus of the year award to Supreme Court Justice Charles E. Whittaker, a graduate of the law school.

Dr. Hamilton B. G. Robinson, dean of
the School of Dentistry from 1958 until
his retirement in 1975. He developed
the Dental School into one of the largest in the United States and was instrumental in securing funds for the
school's new building. He served as
acting chancellor from 1967 until 1968.

James and Vera Olson enjoy Christmas music by the Heritage Singers in
the chancellor's residence. Lower right
is Vinson Cole, a student who went on
to become an internationally ac-
claimed opera singer.

Norman Royall, professor of mathematics from 1947 until his retirement in 1975, at the dedication of Royall Hall, 1983. Royall, a legendary figure on the campus, was a leader in the university's effort to develop a foundations program in general education. He served as dean of the College of Arts and Science from 1947 until 1953.

acting chancellor to help heal the wounds; Brice Ratchford as president was considerably more conciliatory than Weaver had been. Almost from the beginning James and Vera Olson found Kansas City and particularly UMKC's principal support groups—the University of Kansas City Trustees, the University Associates, the Women's Council, and the Alumni Association—ready and willing to support their efforts.

*The Kansas City Star* commented that the new chancellor "has taken over his duties at a time of maximum opportunity." One aspect of that opportunity was a $23 million building program that Weaver had implemented, and the early years of the Olson administration were characterized by frequent ground-breaking and dedication ceremonies. The first building completed was the new library, a handsome $3 million structure, built with state funds and a contribution from the Sunderland Foundation. Next to be completed on the Volker Campus was the $5 million biology-chemistry complex, with the chemistry half being named in honor of Kenneth A. Spencer in recognition of the contribution of the Kenneth and Helen Spencer Foundation.

With the completion of the biology-chemistry building, the Department of Art and Art History moved into the old science building, establishing a little gallery, which under the leadership of Hollister Sturges and Craig Subler came to be, in the words of Donald Hoffman, art critic for *The Kansas City Star*, "the most imaginative place in the city for contemporary art."

In 1973 the School of Education moved into a new $2.8 million building. This new kind of "little red schoolhouse" provided UMKC with the most advanced instructional facilities available, with computer terminals, a television distribution system, and a multimedia auditorium. Conservatory classes took up the vacated space in Epperson House.

The General Library, winner of an urban design award.

The Kenneth A. Spencer Chemistry
Building, named in recognition of the
contribution of the Kenneth and
Helen Spencer Foundation.

Filling in the south quadrangle on the Volker campus, a $1.3 million
addition to Haag Hall—later named Royall Hall, in honor of Norman
Royall, long-time professor of mathematics and beloved campus cur-
mudgeon—connected Haag Hall and the Geology Building. A museum established with the assistance of Dr. Richard Sutton enriched the
Geology Building, and a parking structure, a bookstore, an animal
laboratory, and an air-conditioning system completed this period of
construction on the Volker Campus.

UMKC's development was guided by a ten-year plan for the statewide university that the curators adopted in 1968, and, indeed, this
plan probably had more impact on UMKC than it did on any other
campus. It provided that, in addition to furnishing opportunities for
a broadly based undergraduate education, UMKC would concentrate
in three main fields—the health sciences, the performing arts, and
programs particularly related to the needs of an urban area.

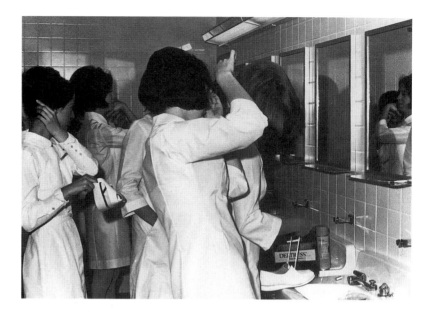

Dental hygiene students making
important preparations.

Ruth Ann Russell and Lois Trani welcome Walter Cronkite, son of a Dental
School alumnus, who spoke at the
Dental School's centennial luncheon,
1981.

In the health sciences, the School of Dentistry moved into a new
$7.5 million structure on Hospital Hill in the spring of 1970. Dean
Robinson was instrumental in securing building funds, with a state
appropriation of $1.5 million being supplemented by $4 million in
federal funds and by $2 million in private contributions. Dedicated 1
March, the imposing brick structure, the largest clinic in the country,
provided space for six hundred dental students, one hundred dental
hygiene students, and one hundred graduate students.

The dental alumni, a large and loyal group scattered all over the
country, included some of the nation's leading practitioners. In the
1969–1970 year, for example, three United States dental services were
headed by UMKC graduates: Dayton D. Krajicek at the Veterans
Administration; Lee M. Lightner of the Air Force; Robert B. Shira of
the Army. The alumni gathered in Kansas City each year in March for

E. Grey Dimond speaking at the ground-breaking ceremonies for the Truman Medical Center, 8 September 1973. Dimond, provost for the health sciences from 1969 to 1979, was instrumental in developing UMKC's innovative six-year medical school. Listening here, left to right, are Charles Curry, Robert Sweeney, Dr. Edward Twin, and Senator Edward Kennedy.

three days of fun, fellowship, and fund-raising, accompanied by substantial courses in continuing education.

Robinson retired in 1975 after seventeen years of service. After a period in which Russell Sumnicht served as acting dean, Marvin Revzin of the University of Southern California was appointed dean. Revzin came to the deanship at a time when the demand for dentists was beginning to decline, bringing with it the need for hard choices in the Dental School. He managed those choices with great skill, retaining the loyalty of both the faculty and the alumni, until ill health forced his retirement in 1982.

The decision to build the Dental School on Hospital Hill was part of a long-range plan for a major health science complex there, including a medical school. The complicated and controversial story of the creation of the medical school is beyond the scope of this book. Outside the university the two prime movers were Homer Wadsworth and Nathan Stark, senior vice president of Hallmark Cards and president of the board of Kansas City General Hospital. Stark, in particular, orchestrated the political process through which the medical school came into being. Within the university, Vernon Wilson, vice president for academic affairs and former dean of the School of Medicine at UMC, played a key role, as did Richardson K. Noback, associate dean for Kansas City in the Columbia Medical School and executive director of General Hospital, who became the first dean of the UMKC School of Medicine.

The prime architect of the medical school and its innovative six-year medicine program was E. Grey Dimond, a brilliant cardiologist, formerly of the University of Kansas but more recently of Washington, D.C., and Rancho Santa Fe, California. Dimond, who served first as a consultant to the chancellor and later as provost for the health sci-

Truman Medical Center.

ences, led the planning for the six-year medical school, an "open medical school" using resources from the community and faculty from the university's other schools to teach a curriculum that enabled a high-school graduate to receive a bachelor's degree and the M.D. in six years. The program was closely observed around the country and on the campus. To help monitor progress, a distinguished group of consultants to the chancellor, including health care professionals from some of the country's most prestigious institutions, spent several days on campus each year to assess developments and give suggestions.

The school opened in the fall of 1970 with forty students enrolled, the plan being to gradually increase enrollment until there were six classes of one hundred each. Although enrollment did not develop as rapidly as expected, the school grew steadily, serving as a national model in medical education. In 1974 a $13.25 million building was completed, providing state-of-the-art facilities for instruction. Truman Medical Center, a $35 million structure connected to the Medical School, together with Children's Mercy Hospital, adjacent to the Dental School, served as the school's principal teaching hospital, although hospitals throughout the community were used for clinical instruction.

A School of Nursing, established in 1979, added to the opportunities. The School of Pharmacy, led by Donald Sorby, who replaced William Strickland as dean in 1975, participated fully in Hospital Hill programs, although it remained on the Volker Campus. The Eye Foundation, under the leadership of Felix Sabates, opened a major

Eph Ehly watches as an aspiring conductor puts her singers through their paces.

The Swinging Choraliers, led by William Fisher, were a popular USO attraction.

teaching, treatment, and research facility in 1987 as part of the overall Hospital Hill complex. The health sciences became a dominant feature of UMKC, and UMKC in turn developed into the largest provider of health science professionals in Missouri.

The performing arts, second of UMKC's major thrusts, also enjoyed substantial expansion. Emphasizing performance, the Conservatory of Music, having affiliated with UKC in 1959 and functioning as the university's School of Music, provided a number of performance groups of substantial reputations: the University Singers, directed first by Everett Hendricks and then by Eph Ehly; the Choraliers, directed by William Fisher; The Accordionaires, directed by Joan Sommers; the Jazz Ensemble, directed by John Leisenring; a percussion group, directed by Charmaine Asher-Wiley; and the Civic Orchestra, directed first by Bruce McIntyre and later by Glenn Block. Among individual performers on the faculty, Witkor Labunski con-

The Volker String Quartet in residence at the university occupies a unique niche in the cultural life of the Kansas City community. Shown here are Tiberius Klausner, Hugh Brown, Charles Stegeman, and Robert Battey, each of whom has earned individual artistic recognition.

tinued to enthrall audiences in piano recitals almost until his death in 1974. Carrying on the tradition of piano teaching and performance were Joanne Baker, Richard Cass, John McIntyre, and Ruth Anne Rich. James Evans and John Obetz developed wide reputations as organists; Richard Knoll, tenor, developed an international reputation for his operatic roles.

Composer Gerald Kemner, later joined by James Mobberley, experimented with electro-acoustic music, and Wanda Lathom developed an innovative program in music therapy on the campus. In addition, the Institute of American Music under Jack Ralston acquired major collections of musical Americana, and a tradition in dance providing support for the Kansas City Ballet evolved under Tatiana Dokoudovska. Archie Jones, the original dean, retired in 1969 and was replaced by Joseph Blankenship, chair of the Department of Music at the University of New Mexico. He resigned in 1976 and was succeeded by Lindsey Merrill, dean of the School of Music at Kent State University and director of the Blossom Festival.

In the Department of Theater, Patricia McIlrath, surrounding herself with a small but extremely competent staff—including Max Beatty, Francis Cullinan, Susan Dinges, Robin Humphrey, Felicia Londre, and Vincent Scasselati—created one of the region's major programs in drama. Its centerpiece was the Missouri Repertory Theatre, founded in 1964 to carry on the tradition of professional theater dating from the dedication of the Playhouse in 1948. Assisting McIlrath was James D. Costin, a playwright with experience as business manager of the American Ballet Theater. Under McIlrath's guidance

The Performing Arts Center provides excellent teaching and rehearsal facilities for ballet.

and that of some of the world's outstanding directors who came as visiting directors for a play or a season, a competent corps of professional actors developed the Missouri Rep into one of Kansas City's brightest cultural jewels. Meanwhile, the student theater was developing a substantial reputation, and "Fashion" was chosen in 1975 for presentation in the American College Theatre Festival in the Kennedy Center in Washington.

The major problem for both the Conservatory and the Theater was lack of space for performance, practice, and instruction. The Conservatory's facilities included Grant Hall, a well-designed structure, although too small for burgeoning enrollment and an expanded program, a large old house, and a barn. The Theater had only the deteriorating old wooden playhouse, beloved by many on campus and in the community but wholly inadequate.

A way to alleviate the common problems of the Conservatory and the Theater was to build a Performing Arts Center to serve the needs of both. Realizing that the General Assembly of Missouri probably could not be persuaded to provide the full cost of such a building— the project frequently was referred to in Jefferson City as "that sing-

The theater department's 1984 production of "Harbledown," with music and lyrics by Mark Houston. Left to right: Martin Coles, Kevin Doyle, Val Fagan, Nikki Dixon, and Ty Richardson.

The stone mask stood guard at the old University Playhouse.

in' and dancin' building"—it was determined that part of the cost
would have to come from private sources, and a campaign for private
funds got underway, led by Eugene M. Strauss, assisted by Paul
Henson, Dutton Brookfield, Cliff C. Jones, Robert Patterson, and
Charles Price. The University of Kansas City Trustees, with Coleman
Branton providing particular leadership, raised $3 million; Helen
Spencer came forward with a gift of $2 million earmarked for the
theater; and the legislature appropriated $6.5 million. Ground was
broken in 1974, and in 1979 the building was dedicated.

Urban affairs, including the urban-related aspects of the schools of
business, education, and law, together with a number of other activities, became the third leading thrust of UMKC during this time of
expansion. The School of Business, actually called the School of Administration, offered programs, including graduate work, in both
business and public administration. The program in business administration remained largely theoretical, and the school earned accreditation by the National Association of Collegiate Schools of Business.
In public administration, the school, under the leadership of William
B. Eddy, worked closely with city and county governments. The Center for Management Development provided resources of value to
management in both the profit and non-profit sectors.

The faculty of the School of Education, like that of the School of
Business, tended to be highly theoretical. Dean Gross, however, with
his New York City experience, understood the problems of urban
education, and various members of the faculty worked well with the
schools in the city. This effort was expanded when J. Joseph Doerr
became dean. The Center for the Study of Metropolitan Problems in
Education, founded by Daniel U. Levine and Robert Havighurst,

W. Coleman Branton, who, in addition
to providing significant leadership in
the final stages of the Performing Arts
Center's fund-raising campaign, was
the first chair of the board of the Missouri Repertory Theatre.

The Performing Arts Center, including the Spencer Theater and the White
Recital Hall.

Patricia McIlrath and Helen Spencer
with the Performing Arts Center in the
background.

Selma Feld, a founder and leading
supporter of the Cockefair Chair, helps
Chancellor George Russell dedicate
Cockefair Hall.

proved to be of major assistance to the Kansas City School District.

The School of Law, under the leadership of Pat Kelly, became increasingly professional and full-time. The night school was abandoned when it was found that classes would not be large enough to justify a separate J.D. program if the same standards required for regular, full-time students were applied to applicants for night school. To provide opportunities for working lawyers to obtain additional education, an LL.M. program, taught principally at night, was instituted. With the appointment of Robert Freilich of New York University, an authority on urban law, the Law School developed a major specialty in the field, and *The Urban Lawyer*, a publication of the American Bar Association, was domiciled at UMKC.

As the demand grew for legal education and as the reputation of the Law School increased, facilities became crowded beyond capacity, and the building on Rockhill Road became a source of embarrassment, threatening the school's continued accreditation. A new building was opened in 1979. The building, financed by public and private funds, included the Leon E. Bloch Library, named in recognition of a $250,000 gift from Henry and Richard Bloch. With the completion of the new Law School, the old building was remodeled for use by various departments in the humanities and named Cockefair Hall in honor of Carolyn Benton Cockefair.

UMKC continued to emphasize its involvement in various aspects of the life of the community. *The University Review* was continued under the name *New Letters*, with David Ray, a nationally recognized poet, as editor. KCUR increased its power to 100,000 watts and began broadcasting around the clock. Further interaction with the community was through a number of special-purpose organizations. The Family Study Center was founded and carried forward under the patronage of Martha Jane Starr. The Community Studies Institute, an independent research organization, became affiliated with the university. The Ethnic Awareness Center was developed; the Women's Center, a research and action-oriented group, was led by Ruth Mar-

The School of Law, including the Leon
E. Bloch Law Library.

golin; the Women's Council, organized by Martha Jane Starr and Georgia Spencer in 1967, sought to involve community women in the life of the campus; and a program in Judaic Studies, financed largely by members of the Jewish community, added to the offerings of the College of Arts and Science. Many of the community activities were coordinated by the Division for Continuing Education, headed by Walter Wright, with Jane Berry and Michael Mardikes as assistant deans.

The campus extended itself still further into the community when it was asked to take over the Independence Residence Center, operated by Central Missouri State University. The center, located adjacent to the Truman Library, was renamed the Truman Campus and ultimately became the site of most of the instruction in the coordinated engineering program developed under the direction of Donald Smith in cooperation with the University of Missouri–Columbia.

A number of important administrative changes—aside from appointments in the health sciences and education, already mentioned—took place during the Olson administration. John Dowgray resigned as dean of faculties to become vice president of the University of Tulsa. He was replaced for a few months by Richard Armitage of Ohio State University, and then by Wesley Dale—with Armitage's appointment the title had been changed to provost. Dale was succeeded as graduate dean by Herwig Zauchenberger of the Claremont Graduate School. Edwin Westermann retired as dean of the College of Arts and Science, and was replaced by Robert J. Corrigan, a political scientist from the University of Iowa. Corrigan resigned after two years to become vice chancellor at the University of Maryland-College Park, and he was replaced by George Dahlgren, a chemist from the University of Cincinnati. In 1970 Wheadon Bloch, who had been dean of students since 1953, returned to teaching. Gary Widmar, associate dean, took over as dean of students.

Students gather in protest against the Vietnam War, May 1970, with Swinney Gymnasium in the background.

Registration is serious business.

During the Olson administration enrollment increased each year—where there had been nine thousand in 1968, there were more than eleven thousand in 1976. An unusually high percentage of UMKC students were graduate and professional students, and the student body was essentially a commuter group. Students were older than the average college student—and considerably more serious and socially conscious than students of an earlier generation. They reacted with concern to the killings at Kent State University in May 1970, but while there were some short-lived sit-ins and some rallies, there were no widespread protests. Students were, for the most part, preoccupied with their own concerns—getting through school and getting a job.

A much-publicized and highly controversial expression of social concern was the first Robert F. Kennedy Memorial Symposium organized by the All Student Association in February 1969. The subject was "Dissent," and ASA managed to gather almost every prominent "dissenter" in the country for the event. The symposium was widely publicized, generating a fire-storm of criticism, but the board of curators refused to interfere. The symposium proceeded as planned, and without incident. The success of the first venture prompted ASA to repeat the effort in succeeding years, devoting most of their program money to a one-week spectacular in which prominent speakers would gather to discuss specific topics—"Mass Media," "Diminishing Man," "Technology," "Morality." Although less controversial than the first one, they were always stimulating and attracted large audiences from the community as well as from the campus.

The first RFK Symposium was followed by Afro-American Week, also supported by ASA, at which Mohammed Ali was the principal speaker. Black students, never a large percentage of the student body, continued to seek identity and a role on the campus. The university

Ken Kesey and others at the first Robert F. Kennedy Memorial Symposium.

Many black students participated in Afro-American Week.

The tug-of-war was always a highlight of Bum Friday.

A "big" dance in Pierson Hall.

Elmer F. Pierson gave the funds to make possible construction of a large multipurpose auditorium-ballroom (Pierson Hall) as part of the University Center.

sought to increase minority enrollment through active recruitment and through such programs as "Upward Bound" and "The Transitional Year." By 1978, 634 black students were enrolled, but that constituted only six percent of the total. Hispanic students, an even smaller minority, also sought to make their presence on campus felt through a series of annual festivals. Among their leaders was Tony Salazar,

Coach Darrell Corwin and David Smith during an exciting moment in a Kangaroo basketball game. The Kangaroos moved out of NAIA athletics in 1987 when UMKC became a corresponding member of NCAA–Division I.

UMKC women battle traditional foe Rockhurst College.

later to become prominent in the revitalization of Quality Hill in Kansas City.

Although UKC had offered an active social scene, students at UMKC generally exhibited little interest in traditional student activities. A few students belonged to fraternities and sororities, and occasionally there were "big" dances in Pierson Hall, but for the most part social life was individual and not university related. Honor societies, however, flourished—Omicron Delta Kappa, Phi Kappa Phi, and a newly organized chapter of Mortar Board, among other societies in the professional schools. "Bum Friday" was one event from the old days that retained its popularity as an annual spring event.

Intercollegiate basketball was revived in 1969, with former Missouri Tiger star Bill Ross as coach, but most students had little interest in the NAIA games, even on the one occasion when the Kangaroos went to the national tournament. The alumni exhibited more interest in basketball than did the students.

The alumni became an increasingly active group, interested in much more than athletics. The Alumni Association, encompassing the alumni organizations of the various schools, engaged in a wide variety of activities in support of the campus. Highlight of the year was the annual Alumni Awards Banquet. The names of those receiving "Alumnus of the Year" awards bore testimony to the widening influence of the university. Among these individuals were Jay Dillingham, prominent Kansas City businessman; Clarence M. Kelley, director of the Federal Bureau of Investigation; Frank Kelly, associate director of the Center for the Study of Democratic Institutions; Kansas City mayor Charles B. Wheeler; and William G. Hyland, editor of *Foreign Affairs.*

UMKC seldom awarded honorary degrees, but the tradition was revived in 1974 when two distinguished Kansas Citians were honored at Commencement: Arthur Mag and Laurence Sickman, director of the Nelson Gallery. Mag, a member of the board of trustees since the founding of KCU, had been a key figure in bringing about the merger.

When Brice Ratchford resigned as president in May 1976, the curators asked Olson to assume the role of interim president. In March 1977 he was appointed president. Provost Wesley J. Dale, who had been a key figure in the Olson administration and had handled a number of important and delicate assignments, served as acting chancellor until a new chancellor could be found. In August 1977, the curators appointed George A. Russell, vice chancellor for research and dean of the Graduate College at the University of Illinois, chancellor of UMKC.

Russell continued to move UMKC toward becoming a university of the first rank and maintained close ties between the campus and the community, particularly in the field of economic development. Despite flattening enrollment and financial stringency, he was remarkably successful in achieving his goals. Early on he shaped the administration to fit his own style of operations, ultimately creating a structure headed by four vice chancellors. Eugene P. Trani of the University of Nebraska became vice chancellor for academic affairs; Joseph J.

Doerr, dean of the School of Education, became vice chancellor for administrative affairs; Gary Widmar, dean of students, became vice chancellor for student affairs; and William J. French, formerly assistant to the chancellor, became vice chancellor for development.

To replace Doerr as dean of the School of Education, Russell promoted Eugene E. Eubanks, assistant dean, to the post. Eubanks, the first black in the history of the campus to serve as a dean, moved the school to new levels of cooperation with the public schools of the area, particularly with the Kansas City School District. Eubanks himself became widely recognized for his leadership in public education.

Through the process of attrition Russell had an opportunity to appoint new deans in all the schools. George Dahlgren resigned as dean of the College of Arts and Science, and was replaced by Eldon Parizek, long-time chair of the Department of Geology; when he reached retirement age, Max Skidmore of New Mexico State University took his place. In the School of Administration—soon to be called the School of Business and Public Administration—Jack Heysinger decided to return to teaching, and was replaced by Eleanor Schwartz of Cleveland State University. Schwartz, the first woman to head a school other than the Nursing School, became vice chancellor for academic affairs in 1987 when Trani left to become vice president for academic affairs at the University of Wisconsin. When Pat Kelly retired as dean of the School of Law, he was replaced by Pasco Bowman, dean of the Law School at Wake Forest University. With Bowman's appointment as judge of the Eighth Circuit Court of Appeals, Robert Popper, assistant dean, took over the post. In medicine, Harry Jonas, long-time Independence gynecologist who had been active in public life, replaced Richardson Noback, who decided that he wished to return to teaching. Michael J. Reed of of the University of Mississippi succeeded Marvin Revzin as dean of the School of Dentistry, and Robert W. Piepho of the University of Colorado replaced Donald Sorby in Pharmacy. In the Conservatory of Music, David Kuehn of California State College at Long Beach succeeded Lindsey Merrill.

Russell also sought wherever possible to improve the scholarly competence of the faculty, both in new appointments and in making use of such incentives as curators and professorships especially funded by the University of Kansas City trustees. Within five years approximately fifty members of the faculty had been the beneficiaries of the short-term trustee professorships established in 1982.

Russell undertook a number of new initiatives, including a program in computer science and the establishment of a School of Basic Life Sciences, headed by Marino Martinez-Carrion of the Medical College of Virginia, which further strengthened the biological and health sciences. The computer science program, a cooperative effort with United Telecommunications, Inc., which provided $2.5 million toward its support, was directed by Richard W. Hetherington. The Richard A. Bloch Cancer Management Center, established with funds furnished by Richard and Annette Bloch, provided an innovative approach to the treatment of cancer. The Center for Academic

Acting Chancellor Wesley J. Dale with Chancellor's Medal recipients Joyce C. Hall and Donald J. Hall, at the University Associates' annual dinner, 1977. In 1987 Adele Hall became the third member of the Hall family to receive the prestigious award.

George A. Russell, appointed chancellor in 1977. A native of Bertrand, Missouri, Russell came to UMKC from the position of vice chancellor for graduate education and research at the University of Illinois. During more than a decade of service, he has improved the quality of the institution and integrated it more fully into the life of the community, particularly in the area of economic development.

Since 1979 the Marvin and Rose Ann Carr Millsap Memorial Trust has brought
outstanding musical artists to the Conservatory of Music in Kansas City.
Pictured (from left front) are Margaret Donnell, Conservatory alumna with the
Lyric Opera of Kansas City; Margaret Hillis, in residency in 1985 as the Lorena
Searcy Cravens Distinguished Visiting Professor; Diana Walker, Conservatory
alumna with the New York City Opera; Eph Ehly (standing), director of the
Heritage Chorale and Civic Chorus; David Kuehn, dean of the Conservatory;
UMKC Chancellor George A. Russell; Ralph Klapis, Consevatory alumnus,
formerly with the Lyric Opera; arts benefactor Marvin Millsap; and Richard
Berry, Conservatory alumnus on the voice faculty of the Lamont School
of Music.

Mary Clark Dimond shows visitors from the Peoples Republic of China
material from the Edgar Snow Memorial Collection.

Henry W. Bloch, C. Peter Magrath, Governor John Ashcroft, and George Russell break ground for the Henry W. Bloch School of Business and Public Administration.

Development, directed by Deanna C. Martin, developed a wide reputation for its work in helping students improve their learning ability. The Department of English, encouraged by substantial gifts from Rheta Ṣosland Hurwitt, a long-time campus patron, pioneered in the improvement of undergraduate writing.

The Conservatory of Music benefited from an artist-in-residence program established with funds provided by Marvin Millsap of Forsythe, Missouri, in memory of his wife, a former student. The Department of Theater similarly benefited from a million dollar grant from the Hall Family Foundations. To facilitate community support of the professional theater, the Missouri Repertory Theatre was placed under the control of a separate not-for-profit corporation, with James D. Costin as executive director and Patricia McIlrath as artistic director. To relieve McIlrath of part of her burdens, Jacques Burdick of Adelphi College was appointed chair. When McIlrath retired, George Keathley, well known for his work in the theater and television in Chicago and New York, became artistic director.

Students enjoy a break from classes in
the Newcomb Hall lounge.

The university steadily expanded its international horizons. From
the early 1970s, E. Grey Dimond had taken a lively interest in the
improvement of relations between the United States and the Peoples
Republic of China. Through his efforts and those of his wife, Mary
Clark Dimond, the papers of Edgar Snow were deposited in the
university library. Under the leadership of Henry Mitchell, exchange
arrangements were also established with ten universities in China,
and a number of universities in Korea, Africa, and Europe, including
Moscow State University.

In the School of Business and Public Administration, new programs in labor studies, banking, and direct marketing were established—the latter, led by Martin Baier, with support from a grant by
the Direct Marketing Foundation of New York. The Cookingham
Institute of Public Administration, named in honor of L. P. Cookingham, Kansas City's legendary city manager, further developed the
school's substantial program in public administration, and much
needed expansion to Oxford Hall more than doubled the space available. In recognition of a million dollar gift from the H&R Block
Foundation, the school was renamed the Henry W. Bloch School of
Business and Public Administration.

Russell was particularly concerned that the university play a major
role in Kansas City's economic development. In 1984 a Center for
Business Innovation was established to assist in the development of
technologically based businesses. Shortly thereafter the most ambitious project in the history of the university was unveiled—a $270
million new campus to be developed with private funds on university-owned land between Brush Creek and Forty-seventh Street. The
"North Campus," as it was called, would house university functions
and technologically based business and industry.

Heralding a new era of prosperity for UMKC, the University of
Kansas City Trustees launched a fund-raising campaign to provide
$18.5 million for the enrichment of university activities and offerings.
They called it the "New Horizons" campaign. When they finished—

The quadrangle, scene of the founding convocation, remains the heart of the campus.

ahead of schedule—they had raised not $18.5 million but $21.7 million.

When UMKC celebrated its fiftieth anniversary in 1983, 750 faculty members were offering 1,500 courses to 11,500 students. There were 47 undergraduate degree programs, 47 master's programs, and 15 Ph.D. programs. Three campuses occupied 132 acres. As the University of Missouri approached its sesquicentennial, the horizon beckoned to a bright future indeed for its Kansas City campus.

# St. Louis

# 11 UNIVERSITY OF

## MISSOURI–ST. LOUIS

The University of Missouri–St. Louis, youngest of the four campuses, traces its origins to the University of Missouri–Normandy Residence Center, which enrolled its first 205 students at the old Bellerive Country Club, 15 September 1960. For Ward Barnes, superintendent of the Normandy School District, President Ed Monaco and other members of the Normandy school board, and the people of Normandy generally, it was not only the realization of a long-held dream but also the beginning of an effort to establish a full-fledged campus of the University of Missouri in St. Louis.

There was no question about the need. Although St. Louis had two well-established private universities and a number of small, church-related colleges, it was the largest city in the United States without a public institution of higher learning. When the Bellerive Country Club moved further west in the county and put its property up for sale, Barnes persuaded the voters of Normandy to bond themselves in the amount of $600,000 to purchase the property, and the way was cleared for the establishment of a junior college.

The old Bellerive Country Club in Normandy was an ideal site for a campus. Located about two miles east of Lambert International Airport, it encompassed a beautiful, rolling tract of 128 acres, with a handsome clubhouse, tennis courts, and a large swimming pool. The pond came to be known as Bugg Lake.

Arnold Grobman presents University of Missouri–St. Louis's first Chancellor's Medal to Ward Barnes. Barnes, superintendent of the Normandy School District, was instrumental in the establishment of a campus of the University of Missouri in St. Louis.

Meanwhile, Barnes had negotitated an agreement with President Elmer Ellis providing that the university would furnish the educational program for the junior college if the school district would be responsible for the property and guarantee a beginning enrollment of at least one hundred students. Ellis was easy to deal with; he clearly saw the need for the university to establish a presence in St. Louis.

The new school was an immediate success. The clubhouse had been remodeled over the summer to provide four lecture rooms, thirteen classrooms, a cafeteria, a lounge, a library, and an office. The school opened in 1960 with eleven faculty members approved by Dean Francis English of the College of Arts and Science in Columbia. C. E. Potter, principal of Normandy Senior High School, became the center's administrator. The center was clearly much more than a Normandy enterprise, with students from all over the area seeking admission. It was also much more than the Normandy School District could maintain.

Barnes pressed the university to take over the operation entirely, and the board of curators agreed to acquire the property for a nominal sum without restrictions. Legislation introduced by Senator Robert Young and Representative Wayne Goode resolved legal complications and the way was cleared for the university to take over the Normandy center. On 13 July 1963—the same day the University of Missouri–Kansas City campus was established—the board of curators authorized payment of $100,000 to the Normandy School District for the property and the equipment used in the center and directed negotiations with architects Hellmuth, Obata, and Kassabaum of St. Louis for the design of the initial buildings. A month later the board formally established the St. Louis campus and accepted the plans of the architects for a classroom building and a science building, ordering "all future buildings to be uniform in general design and use of materials." On 15 September, in the presence of fifteen hundred people, Ellis, board president James Finch, Governor Dalton, and Ed Monaco formally dedicated the St. Louis campus of the University of

Parking structures helped to alleviate one of the university's most serious problems. They were heavily used during both day and evening classes.

Missouri, and "UMSL," as it was known for a time, was ushered into existence.

To head the new campus, Ellis chose a close friend, James L. Bugg, Jr., chair of the history department at UMC and a highly respected member of the faculty. Although active on faculty committees, Bugg had never been tempted by an administrative career. Ellis was persuasive, however, and the opportunity to lead in the creation of a new institution provided a challenge Bugg could not resist. The new dean selected two Columbia campus friends for his first appointments: H. E. Mueller, assistant director of admissions, as director of admissions; and John Perry, comptroller of the hospital, as business manager. As his academic second-in-command, Bugg hired Glen Driscoll, professor of history at the University of South Dakota, whose initial appointment was as chair of the Division of Social Sciences.

There were challenges aplenty. School opened in September with 673 students—Potter had told Bugg that the old clubhouse could not accommodate more than five hundred. Somehow the school managed to squeeze the students in, but their cars were another problem. Latecomers parked wherever they could find a space. Even after the parking lot had been expanded, parking problems remained for many years. Within the clubhouse, faculty members shared small cubicles for offices, and students studied wherever they could find a place to sit. The library, with three thousand volumes, was crowded into the rear of the building, and a cafeteria in the basement served food from vending machines.

If the clubhouse had seemed crowded with 673 students, it was filled to overflowing in the fall of 1964 when 1,038 day students enrolled. To accommodate the demand for more space, Bugg created an Evening Division, and its initial enrollment was 1,601. This was more than the clubhouse could possibly accommodate, and some of the evening classes were taught in the Normandy Junior High School. Arthur Mallory, assistant superintendent of the Parkway schools, became the first head of the division. When he left after a few months to become president of Southwest Missouri State College, the post

Traffic posed a problem from the beginning.

went to Joy Whitener, assistant superintendent of the Webster Groves School District. UMSL became even busier at night than it was during the day, as people with full-time jobs took advantage of the opportunity to continue their education.

Working closely with the Evening College was the Extension Division, which had been responsible for many of the university's efforts in the St. Louis area. Virgil Sapp, head of extension in St. Louis, became director of extension for the campus and took the lead in developing innovative programs of education and service. Of particular importance was the work of Margaret Fagin, director of women's programming, whose efforts encouraged many adult women to attend college.

As classes began in 1965, the campus was moving rapidly toward the achievement of full university status. During the summer Bugg's title had been changed from dean to chancellor, and the College of Arts and Science had been organized with Driscoll as dean. By 1967 the initial departments, including history, mathematics, modern foreign languages, sociology/anthropology, and social work, had been expanded to include administration of justice, biology, chemistry, economics, English, fine arts, philosophy, physics, political science, and psychology. The divisions of education and business administration were expanding and in 1966 became schools, led by Adolph Unruh and Emery Turner. Both schools easily received professional accreditation—the School of Business was the youngest in the country to receive full accreditation.

The new departments and the many new students required a substantial number of additional teachers. Moreover, in 1965 a junior year was added to the curriculum, and a year later a senior year was added. Bugg was determined to recruit a high-quality faculty, and he succeeded to a remarkable degree, hiring for the most part promising young Ph.D.s from good institutions. Interestingly, as Blanche Touhill points out in *The Emerging University*, they formed the university along traditional lines rather than the innovative ones Bugg originally had envisioned.

With the addition of a junior year, enrollment skyrocketed—in the

Students studied wherever they could find a place to sit in the old clubhouse.

fall of 1965, 2,504 students were enrolled in the day program and 2,254 in the Evening Division, including 300 students in a cooperative master's program in education with UMC. Graduate work had not been part of the original plans for UMSL, but the demand was so great that the campus moved with seeming inevitablity toward offering master's level work in a number of fields. Finally, in 1968 a graduate school was established with Driscoll as dean.

The crowd on the first day of classes, 1965, created a traffic jam worse even than that of opening day in 1963. Despite the efforts of policemen and university personnel, traffic at the entrance to the campus was blocked for almost an hour; once on the campus, there was no place to park.

Benton Hall, the first new classroom-laboratory building, was supposed to have been ready for occupancy by the beginning of the school year, but it was not until the second semester that all of it was ready for use. Meanwhile, the old clubhouse continued to be used, with some classes held in nearby churches and some in storefronts along Natural Bridge Road. Students and faculty accepted the inconveniences with good grace, and a sense of camaraderie was devel-

The St. Louis Symphony performs on the lawn.

A student Carmen strikes a seductive pose in a performance by the University Players.

oped that would not have existed on a larger, better-equipped campus. Moreover, a second classroom building was under construction, and plans were being developed for a new library and a second science building.

The students at UMSL were quite unlike those found on a residential campus. They commuted from all over the area; many of them were older than the traditional student, substantial numbers were married with families, and most of them worked. Generally, they were very bright and energetic. Only a minority was interested in traditional student activities and campus life. Harold Eickhoff, appointed dean of student affairs in 1964, worked hard to develop a sense of community on the campus. Bugg shared Eickhoff's views and was especially interested in involving students in campus governance. He appointed an advisory committee and worked closely with the student association.

From the beginning students evinced a lively interest in music and drama, with limited curricular offerings being expanded through an active extracurricular program in the arts. There were concerts on the lawn, and student groups performed regularly. The University Players performed a variety of plays with verve and talent. The University Chorus, organized in 1965, developed into the University Singers, a group which sang at Carnegie Hall in 1977 and at the Kennedy Center in 1986.

There was considerable interest in athletics. Chuck Smith was hired in 1966 as director of athletics and basketball coach. He re-

The University Singers perform at the National Cathedral in Washington.

mained on the campus to develop a sound, healthy—and usually winning—Division II program. To create interest in athletics among the students, Eickhoff and Smith persuaded the Student Affairs Committee to sponsor a contest to select a mascot, resulting in the UMSL Riverman. A few athletic scholarships were made available from the proceeds of the student activity fee, and, in the 1966–1967 year, UMSL began intercollegiate athletic competition in men's basketball.

With no facilities, the Rivermen practiced in the gym at Normandy Junior High School and played their "home" games wherever they could—at Concordia Seminary, or in Kiel Auditorium or the Arena. They had a good first season, winning twelve and losing seven games. In 1969 the Rivermen advanced to the NAIA national championships in Kansas City, but lost to High Point, North Carolina, in the first round. Their best season ever, during the 1971–1972 year, was their first in the new Mark Twain Building. They won the NCAA Division

Chuck Smith proudly points to the site of the new field house.

Women's Basketball at UM–St. Louis. Shown here is Myra Bailey with a career total of one thousand points.

Papageno performs for TV, apparently to advertise an opera workshop. Limited curricular offerings in the arts were expanded through an active extra-curricular program.

The Rivermen drew large crowds in the Mark Twain Building.

II Midwest Regional but were defeated by Roanoke College in the first round of the quarterfinals.

In baseball, begun in 1969, the Rivermen were more successful, advancing to the regional tournament six times, and to the College World Series in 1972, 1973, and 1977. The most successful teams of all, however, were those in soccer, inaugurated as an intercollegiate sport in 1968. Under Coach Don Dallas, the Rivermen made fourteen consecutive appearances in the NCAA tournament between 1972 and 1985. They won the national championship in 1973 and were MIAA conference champions in 1981, 1982, 1983, and 1985. In 1981 the legislature, with an unsolicited appropriation, provided $50,000 to light the soccer field.

Beginning with basketball and volleyball in 1974, UMSL began to field women's teams in intercollegiate competition. The Riverwomen got off to a good start in basketball, with a 15 to 1 record, but following that they seldom had a winning season. In 1976 the volleyball team posted a 24 to 1 record, but over the years lost about as many games as they won. The same was true with field hockey. As was the case with men's sports, the most successful women's sport was soccer, begun in 1981, with a series of winning seasons, post-season tournaments, and national rankings.

Both men and women enjoyed active intramural programs. Intercollegiate athletics were generally supported by an allocation of student fees, but athletics were not the only activities funded by student fees. A number of campus organizations received regular allocations, as did the student newspaper, *The Current*, first issued 18 November 1966. During their first year, staff members of *The Current* won three of ten awards in the Missouri College Newspaper Association's spring contest in the Class A category of four-year schools with more than one thousand students.

Because of the character of the student body, extracurricular activities involved a relatively small attendance. Likewise, there was little

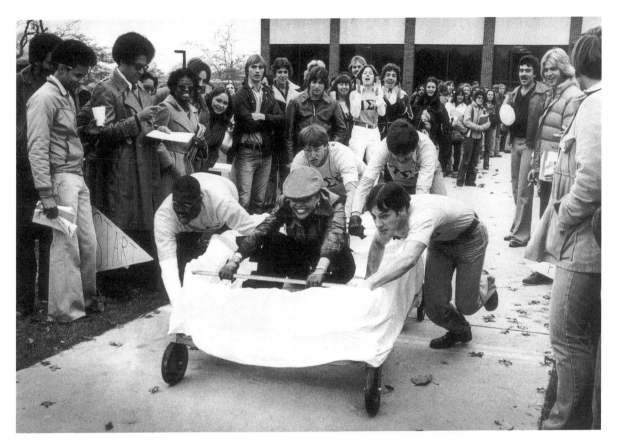

Greek Week festivities provided a showcase for student ingenuity.

of the student protest that rocked the country's campuses in the late 1960s and early 1970s. There were heated debates and occasional demonstrations about ROTC, free speech, the war in Vietnam, and the place of black Americans on the campus, but the only "sit-in" was a demonstration on the hill above Bugg Lake to express discontent over the lack of adequate cafeteria facilities.

Bugg was much concerned with finding ways to encourage academic achievement. An honors convocation was held each semester. This ceremony, attended by students, faculty, friends and family, was followed by a reception, which was sponsored by the Faculty Women's Club. Later, honor societies were established to encourage scholarship. By far the most impressive ceremony of the early years was the first Commencement, held in June 1967, and celebrated with three days of festivities. Commencement remained a well-attended event, in all respects a community ceremony. Leading citizens of St. Louis or members of the faculty served as Commencement speakers, and important figures in the community received honorary degrees.

Glen Driscoll enjoys chatting with a group of Wilson Fellows.

The first graduates organized an Alumni Association, and in the fall of 1967, the university established an alumni office, with a member of the first class, Lois Brockmeier Schoemehl, as its first director— a position she held until she became first lady of St. Louis. Although young and few in number, the Alumni Association immediately went to work on behalf of the campus. It organized "Serendipity Day" to

Chancellor Bugg talks with students during a demonstration against the lack of adequate cafeteria facilities. The demonstration began at 11:15 in the morning and lasted until 4:15 in the afternoon with an hour and a half break for lunch. Bugg later recalled that he was worried at first, but when the demonstrators decided to break for lunch he knew that he did not have a really serious problem on his hands.

Students were put to work assembling furniture for the new Benton Hall.

acquaint high school students and their parents with the campus. In 1968, the Alumni Association inaugurated an alumni citation for good teaching, with the first award going to Emery Turner. The association also began a program of scholarships.

In addition to adding substantially to the educated work force of St. Louis, UMSL alumni increasingly came to occupy positions of leadership, particularly in the public sector. Vincent Schoemehl became mayor of St. Louis; Thomas Villa, president of the St. Louis Board of Aldermen; and John Mahoney, president of the St. Louis Board of Education.

In the fall of 1968, Bugg announced that he was leaving UMSL to become president of Old Dominion University in Norfolk, Virginia. Although the announcement came as a shock to the campus, close associates were not surprised. Bugg had been restive for some time over what he perceived to be the growing bureaucracy of the central administration after Ellis's retirement. Moreover, he was becoming concerned that the campus would not be able to expand sufficiently to meet the needs of the community. He was particularly concerned over his failure to obtain an engineering program.

Whatever the future might hold, the preceding six years had been a time of great achievement. Enrollment had increased from 673 to 8,891, the faculty from 22 to 257; the old clubhouse had been augmented by Benton Hall, completed in 1967, Clark Hall, 1968, and Thomas Jefferson Library, 1969, with five more buildings under construction; the general operating budget had increased from $350,750 to $7,833,311.

President Weaver appointed Driscoll as interim chancellor and established a committee to search for Bugg's replacement. Driscoll

A chapter of Alpha Phi Omega, national service fraternity, came to the campus in 1966. Soon a number of social fraternities and sororities achieved national recognition. Highlight of the year was Greek Week, held each spring to promote friendly competition and work in community service projects, and generally to have a good time.

The ducks on Bugg Lake, campus favorites in all seasons, with Benton and Stadler halls in the background. Bugg Lake, the eighteenth-hole water hazard at the old Bellerive Country Club, was named by the students in honor of James Bugg, the first chancellor, who served from 1965 until 1969 when he resigned to become president of Old Dominion University in Virginia.

had been part of the campus's administrative team almost from the beginning. He knew virtually everybody on campus and generally was highly popular. As the search wore on, it became increasingly clear that he was the logical choice for the permanent appointment, and in November "interim" was removed from his title.

Driscoll's vision for the campus included developing graduate programs and expanding its urban mission. Although Driscoll was not able to add as many new programs as he had hoped, the campus did begin to offer the Ph.D. in psychology and chemistry in 1971. Master's programs in biology, mathematics, and English were approved, but implementation was delayed for lack of funds.

The new chancellor had more success with further developing the role of the campus within its urban setting. Using the newly estab-

Everett Walters and Glen Driscoll sample the punch at a campus reception.

Bugg Lake provided a good source of materials for biology laboratories.

KWMU soon became an important part of the cultural life of St. Louis.

lished curators professorship program, Driscoll persuaded Norton Long of the University of Illinois, one of the country's leading authorities in public administration and urban politics, to take the directorship of the Center for Metropolitan Studies, developing it into an important and respected force in St. Louis life. The School of Education moved toward greater involvement in the life of the city when William Franzen of the University of Toledo, an authority on urban institutions, was appointed dean. Encouraged by Franzen, the School of Education developed close relationships with the elementary and secondary schools of the area, and individual faculty members became active in the urban outreach program.

The campus extended itself further into the community when KWMU went on the air in the summer of 1972. It became the originating station for the broadcasts of the St. Louis Symphony on National Public Radio. A classroom in Lucas Hall became Gallery 210, providing small but remarkably effective exhibit space, which under the leadership of Jean Tucker of the Center for Metropolitan Studies became a significant addition to the St. Louis art scene.

Driscoll was concerned that UMSL provide educational opportunity for all segments of the St. Louis population. The campus established what was known as Project UNITED (University Needs in the Education of the Disadvantaged) to provide counseling and tutorial assistance for disadvantaged students, most of whom were black. The number of students who took advantage of the services offered

Construction dominated the campus during the sixties and the seventies.
When this photograph was taken in 1969, construction was just beginning
on the Penney Building and the Social Sciences–Business Administration
complex. The old clubhouse remained, and the large fir tree that stands near
the northeast entrance of the Penney Building was being protected during
construction.

One young customer has found what
he wanted at the annual book fair
sponsored by the Faculty Women's
Club.

The University Center became a popular and much used facility.

Mary Brewster in the office of Project
UNITED.

by Project UNITED grew steadily, as did the black enrollment. By the
late 1970s UMSL had more black students than any other institution in
the state, including Lincoln University.

More new buildings were opened during Driscoll's term than during the term of any other chancellor in the school's history. In 1970, a

Commencement at UM–St. Louis was always a family affair.

Librarian Susan Freegard utilized beer cases and student help to move into Thomas Jefferson Library.

Thomas Jefferson Library.

The SSB Tower, completed in 1971, dominates the campus skyline.

"The Underground," in the University Center, completed in 1971, alleviated crowded cafeteria conditions that had plagued the campus from the beginning.

new science building, named for Lewis J. Stadler, famed geneticist on the Columbia campus, was completed. In 1971, faculty and students occupied five additional new buildings: the J. C. Penney Continuing Education Building; Lucas Hall, named for Jean Baptiste Charles Lucas, a prominent St. Louis pioneer; the Mark Twain Building, which gave the campus first-class athletic facilities as well as a place to hold Commencements and large convocations; the Social Sciences and Business Building and Tower; and the University Center. All were new buildings funded by state appropriations, except the J. C. Penney Building, which was funded primarily by the sale of a warehouse donated to the university by J. C. Penney for use in Continuing Education.

The new buildings provided space that allowed UMSL to grow. In the fall of 1972, enrollment reached 11,477, a number which suddenly made UMSL the largest university in St. Louis and the second largest in the state. In terms of program offerings, however, UMSL's potential for further growth remained constricted, particularly at the graduate level. Driscoll had hoped that "Role and Scope," President Ratchford's planning effort, would open the door to program expansion, but the final version was disappointingly tentative in its provisions.

Driscoll announced in August 1972 that he was leaving the university to become president of the University of Toledo in Ohio. Ratchford immediately appointed dean of faculties Everett Walters interim chancellor and organized a committee—including for the first time two students—to search for a new chancellor. Walters's interim year came to an end 1 September 1973, with the arrival of Joseph R. Hartley, vice president of Indiana University, as the new chancellor.

Hartley presided over the tenth anniversary celebration of the campus for two days in October. With an enrollment of over twelve

Homecoming was never as big an event at UM–St. Louis as on many traditional campuses, but some organizations took note of the occasion.

Awaiting the signal to begin the Commencement processional are Curator William H. Thompson, C. Brice Ratchford, Emery Turner, and Governor Christopher Bond.

thousand, UMSL had graduated seventy-five hundred students. Driscoll, who returned for the occasion, talked about the "ten-year miracle" being celebrated; President Ratchford said the campus could become "the finest higher level university the state has known." At the same time the campus was still seeking its way in the community and in the university at large, and there were no assurances that resources would become available to make possible the dreams of 1963, let alone the dreams of 1973.

Hartley remained less than a year, resigning in March to return to Indiana to enter a family business. With Hartley's resignation, it was clear that the revolving door in the chancellor's office was becoming one of UMSL's major problems. This time Ratchford turned to Emery Turner, dean of the School of Business Administration. Turner had been on campus since 1962 when he was the only professor of business at the Normandy Residence Center. He had been the principal architect of the School of Business Administration, and he knew the campus as well as anyone. Despite his veteran status, he was only forty years of age.

Joseph Hartley looks on as the birthday cake for the tenth anniversary of the University of Missouri–St. Louis is cut.

Turner plunged into his new task with characteristic vigor, trying to salvage as much as possible for the campus in the final version of Role and Scope being readied for the curators' stamp of approval. He was not particularly successful. Although the plan authorized the development of graduate programs in the arts and sciences, business, and education, it provided virtually nothing in the way of authority to develop the career-oriented programs in which the St. Louis community was expressing increased interest. Moreover, officials of both Washington University and St. Louis University were beginning to voice concern over the growth of graduate programs at UMSL, and that view was being reflected in the attitudes of the newly created Missouri Coordinating Board for Higher Education, which had the authority to approve or to disapprove new programs at public col-

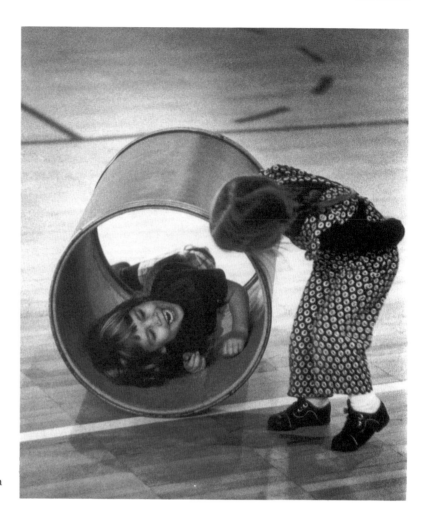

The Child Development Center provided community service as well as an educational laboratory.

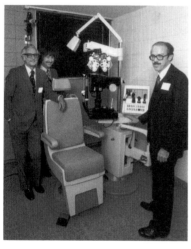

One of Arnold Grobman's major achievements was the establishment of the School of Optometry. He is shown here with Jerry Christensen, the first dean. Grobman, an internationally known biologist, served as chancellor from 1975 until his retirement in 1985.

leges and universities.

As dean of the School of Business Administration, Turner had been actively involved with the St. Louis business community; as interim chancellor he expanded that involvement. A satellite center established at Lindbergh High School brought the campus closer to students in South County. On campus a Child Development Center began operations, and women's athletics received official recognition with the establishment of athletic scholarships available to women. Looking to the future, Turner urged the acquisition of nearby Marillac College, which was for sale, and the establishment of a School of Optometry.

Turner's interim year came to an end 1 April 1975, with the arrival of Arnold B. Grobman as UMSL's fourth chancellor. Grobman, an internationally known biologist, came to UMSL from the University of Illinois-Chicago Circle, where he was serving as special assistant to the president of the University of Illinois. He served as chancellor for a decade, bringing stability to the chancellor's office and the campus, and through a combination of ingenuity and persistence moved the campus toward his vision of a comprehensive urban university. The most obvious achievements of the Grobman years were the purchase

Among the eight buildings on the Marillac campus was this handsome library.

of Marillac College and the establishment of the schools of optometry and nursing.

The acquisition of Marillac College added 43.5 acres and eight buildings to the campus—for the first time UMSL had surplus space. The School of Education and the Department of Music moved to the South Campus (as Marillac came to be called), and in due course the schools of optometry and nursing were located there. The School of Optometry, with Jerry Christensen as dean, opened in the fall of 1980 with thirty-six students. Enrollment grew steadily, and the first degrees were granted in 1984. The School of Nursing, led by Shirley Martin, opened in the fall of 1981 with 112 students. Other degree programs added during Grobman's years reflected his interest in expanding the curriculum available to career-oriented students: baccalaureate degrees in speech communications, applied mathematics, administration of justice, social work, public administration, and physical education; master's degrees in public policy administration, accounting, psychology, and management information systems; a doctoral degree in education.

Although UMSL's need for space had changed, two new buildings were completed on the North Campus the same year Marillac was acquired: the general services building and the administration building, Woods Hall, named in honor of Howard Woods, a former member of the board of curators. With the completion of Woods Hall, the old Administraton Building, long deemed unsafe, was razed and the swimming pool was filled in. UMSL was beginning to take on many

Workmen put the finishing touches on "Profile Canto A," one of two pieces of sculpture on campus by the internationally known sculptor Ernest Trova, a native St. Louisan. The other Trova sculpture is located in the Alumni Circle near the Natural Bridge entrance to the campus. The sculptures are on loan to the University of Missouri–St. Louis from Adam Aronson of Clayton and Gene Spector of St. Louis.

Almost from the beginning, campus life was enriched by the presence of foreign students. Chancellor Grobman had a great interest in international education, and under his leadership and that of K. Peter Etskorn, associate dean of the Graduate College, and Ed Fedder, director of International Studies, student exchange opportunities were developed with a number of institutions in Europe and in Asia.

of the physical attributes of a mature campus. More important, the young and promising faculty members hired in the early days had matured into scholars of substantial reputation.

From the beginning Grobman sought to integrate the campus more effectively into the community. Emphasizing the importance of community relationships in the reorganization of the administrative structure, he created a vice chancellorship for community affairs and appointed Everett Walters to the post. The Chancellor's Council, organized to provide a means of securing advice and assistance from community leaders, was a vital link between the campus and the community. Studio Set became a community support group for cam-

Everett Walters, interim chancellor, 1972–1973, served as vice chancellor for academic affairs, 1971–1976, and vice chancellor for community affairs, 1976–1979.

When the old clubhouse was razed, the circular drive was preserved and some of the bricks from the old building were used to construct a low wall and several small benches on the grassy commons in front of the library. Alumni Circle, at the head of the commons, was enhanced by Ernest Trova's sculpture.

pus radio station KWMU. Virginia Edwards, a community leader in the arts who served as assistant to the chancellor for cultural events, developed a concert series that established a solid position in the community.

At the end of his first year Grobman presented what he called a Report to the Community. This became an annual event. Attended by hundreds of alumni and civic leaders, it provided Grobman with a splendid platform from which he could urge greater support for the university. In his tenth and last report, given 9 May 1985, Grobman said, "I think our past decade of modest progress constitutes a solid and firm foundation upon which to build an improved community resource, in public higher education, to serve the St. Louis metropolitan region. We are not there yet, but we do appear to be on the verge of a resurgence of university service to St. Louis."

Grobman was too modest in his assessment of achievements. Despite severe financial constraints the campus had made substantial progress in the expansion of programs, the addition of facilities, and the improvement of relations with the St. Louis community. It was a record of which he could be justifiably proud.

The swimming pool in the Mark Twain Building provided facilities for community service.

The Jordan Foundation, under the leadership of Robert Neill, former curator from St. Louis, helped the university exchange an inadequate chancellor's residence for this handsome house at 9 Bellerive Acres where Arnold and Hulda Grobman each year entertained thousands of people from the campus and the community.

President C. Peter Magrath and St. Louis Mayor Vincent Schoemehl (a UM–St. Louis graduate) welcome Chancellor Marguerite Barnett. Barnett, who came to the university from the City University of New York, where she was vice chancellor for academic affairs, was the first black woman ever to head a college or university campus in Missouri.

Grobman's successor, Marguerite Ross Barnett—formerly vice chancellor for academic affairs at the City University of New York, and the first black woman ever to head a college or a university campus in Missouri—moved quickly to build on the progress of the past. She was immediately and stunningly successful. Enlisting the sup-

The North Campus, UM–St. Louis, from Natural Bridge Road.

port of key St. Louis leaders, she formed "Partnerships for Progress" to develop relationships between the university and the community to further sustain economic growth and vitality. Monsanto, launching the program with a $500,000 unrestricted gift, was followed by others, and during the year UM-St. Louis (Barnett dropped the use of "UMSL") received corporate pledges of more than $2.4 million.

As the university approached its sesquicentennial, the newest campus celebrated its twenty-fifth anniversary. In noting that fact, Chancellor Barnett observed, "Twenty-five years ago, men and women of vision dreamed of a public university of stature for the St. Louis region. Today, we dream of a world-class university working to keep St. Louis dynamic, vital, and prosperous. . . . Our ambition is great but so is our potential." Both assessments seemed to be correct.

# University of Missouri

# 12 THE STATEWIDE
## UNIVERSITY

In the beginning the University of Missouri was thought of primarily as a Columbia institution. Most of the students were from Boone County or other nearby counties in central Missouri, and representation on the board of curators was weighted toward the area. It was not until 1867 that the General Assembly appropriated state funding from its revenues to support the university. Through the next century, however, there were various indications that the state legislature increasingly realized the need to support a public university that would serve interests statewide.

With the passage of the Morrill Act, the College of Agriculture had been located in Columbia; mining interests in the southeastern part of the state motivated the establishment of the Missouri School of Mines in Rolla. In response to the needs of the two state institutions, in 1875 the state constitution assured that the university governing body would have representation from throughout the state by requiring that no more than one curator could reside in a single congressional district.

The move toward reaching a wider Missouri public began early in the history of the university. In the early years of the twentieth century, professors began to give lectures in St. Louis, Kansas City, and smaller cities around the state. In 1910 the curators established an Extension Division to conduct off-campus education in a more organized fashion. Four years later the Smith-Lever Act established a federally supported system of agricultural extension, and the University of Missouri became a leader in providing educational opportunities for farmers in all parts of the state.

Relatively speaking, the two large cities were less adequately served than the rural areas. Almost two-thirds of the students came from Kansas City and St. Louis, and the university offered programs in continuing education in both cities, but it was apparent to both cities—Kansas City and St. Louis were the two largest cities in the United States without public institutions of higher education—by the 1950s that local public institutions were essential. At the same time President Ellis was concluding that the university needed a presence in the two cities if the university were to play an effective role in a state steadily becoming more urban.

Although the vehicles for expansion were quite different, both campuses were established in 1963. In Kansas City the financially troubled University of Kansas City, a private institution, was incorporated; in St. Louis the public junior college established by the Normandy School District was taken over. The result was the most significant development in Missouri's higher education since the founding of the University of Missouri in 1839.

Newly painted and lighted for the celebration of the sesquicentennial, Jesse Hall continues to be the center of the campus at UM–Columbia.

The addition to Ellis Library, UM–Columbia, completed in 1987, provided badly needed space for the growing collections of the university libraries and the State Historical Society of Missouri.

The School of Law, UM–Columbia, which began life in the old "Law Barn" and then moved to Tate Hall, looked forward to occupying spacious new quarters in 1988.

The multicampus university being a fairly new development in American higher education, there were few models to provide guidance for Ellis and the board as they sought to develop an administrative structure for the expanded university. They innovated to meet local conditions but generally followed patterns developed in California and in North Carolina. At first Ellis simply added responsibilities to his own staff in Columbia, with Vernon Wilson, dean of the medical school, playing a key role in the adminstration of the four campuses. Ellis soon found, however, that duties related to the smooth operation of the four campus system needed to be carried out separately from the Columbia campus. At this time he appointed John Schwada, dean of faculties, as chancellor, and separated himself from the campus to act as chief adminstrator for the system.

In 1966, Ellis reached the statutory retirement age of sixty-five. His twelve years as president had brought changes more profound than those in any comparable period in the entire history of the university.

Elmer Ellis, president from 1954 until
his retirement in 1966, transformed the
university from a single-campus institution with a detached school of mines
into a four-campus university serving
the entire state.

The search and selection committee that recommended the appointment of
John C. Weaver to succeed Elmer Ellis as president. Seated: board member
Robert Neill of St. Louis, and former board president James Finch of Jefferson
City, representing the alumni; standing: board members William H. Billings
of Kennett and Oliver Ferguson of Fredericktown. A. G. Unklesbay, professor
of geology at the University of Missouri–Columbia, represented the faculties.
Unklesbay became vice president for administration in 1967, serving in that
position until his retirement in 1979.

Vernon Wilson, dean of the medical
school at UM–Columbia, played an
increasingly important role of assisting the president in the administration
of the four-campus system. In 1967 he
became vice president for academic
affairs, a position he held until 1970,
when he resigned to become an assistant to the Secretary of Health, Education and Welfare. Wilson worked
closely with E. Grey Dimond in the
establishment of the medical school at
UM–Kansas City.

He was a beloved father figure who would be hard to replace. After
an exhaustive national search, the board chose as the new president
John C. Weaver, vice president for academic affairs at Ohio State
University. A native of Wisconsin, with his degrees from the University of Wisconsin, Weaver brought to Missouri a broad background of
experience in midwestern public universities, including Kansas State
University, the University of Nebraska, and the University of Iowa.

Weaver's inauguration, in which representatives of all four campuses participated, was one of the most elaborate ceremonies the
university had ever staged. Actually, it was the first formal inauguration the university had held since 1923, when Stratton Brooks became
president. There were other notable differences with the appointment
of Weaver. The president, while continuing to live and work in Columbia, became increasingly removed from the Columbia campus.
Weaver moved his office to University Hall as soon as it was completed in the spring of 1970; Schwada took over what had been the
president's office. The Schwadas moved into the president's house,
and the Weavers lived in a rented house on Burnam Road while a new
presidential residence was being constructed. That residence, on a
bluff overlooking Hinkson Creek, was not finished before the
Weavers left Missouri to return to Wisconsin.

V. H. McNutt Hall, completed in 1987, provides more than 150,000 square feet of classroom, office, and laboratory space for mineral engineering at UM–Rolla. The building was funded through a combination of private and state money, with the largest private grant being given by Mrs. V. H. McNutt, long-time supporter of the university.

Weaver spent his years at Missouri trying to implement board policy establishing one university with four campuses. His efforts created tensions on the campuses, and three chancellors—Bugg, Schwada, and Whaley—resigned in part at least because of differences with the president. The curators, however, solidly supported Weaver in his efforts to implement their policies, and Weaver was able to establish an administrative structure that, though considerably modified by his successors, continued to provide the pattern of operation for the university system.

In an effort to maximize the advantages of the multicampus system, a number of functions were administered on a systemwide basis for the benefit of all campuses, notably extension, the Western Historical Manuscripts Collection, the research reactor, the Sinclair Farm, and the University Press. Under the leadership of Vernon Wilson, whom Weaver appointed vice president for academic affairs, the president's office became heavily involved in the encouragement of research. As vice president for extension, Ratchford took the lead in organizing outreach programs on the urban campuses, and in particular he developed a series of urban problem-solving seminars that proved to be both popular and useful. Construction, business, the budget, and finance were generally controlled by Ray Bezoni and Dale Bowling of the central administration, and A. G. Unklesbay, professor of geology at UMC, whom Weaver appointed vice president for administration, played a key role in the day-to-day affairs of the university. Phil Connell, who had served as executive assistant to a number of presidents of the University of Iowa, was brought in to fill a similar role at Missouri.

John C. Weaver delivering his inaugural address, 18 April 1967. Weaver served as president from 1966 to 1970, when he resigned to become president of the University of Wisconsin. To Weaver fell the responsibility of implementing the board of curators' policy establishing one university with four campuses. He also presided over a period of great growth and severe campus unrest.

Students at UM–Rolla learn the art and science of metals casting.

UM–Rolla pioneered in the teaching of robotics. Here students are learning how to use a robot.

Weaver's years as president were filled with controversy, but they were also years of substantial growth. Enrollment increased by almost thirty percent, and state appropriations increased by almost seventy percent. In addition, the state provided about $50 million for capital improvements, much of which was spent on the urban campuses.

In October 1970 Weaver suddenly announced that he was leaving Missouri to become president of his alma mater, the University of Wisconsin. The board appointed C. Brice Ratchford interim president, and in June 1971 he was appointed president. A native of North Carolina with a Ph.D. in agricultural economics from Duke University, Ratchford had come to Missouri in 1959. He had reshaped extension in Missouri and increasingly had come to be relied on by both Ellis and Weaver as an adviser and lobbyist in Jefferson City.

Ratchford generally continued with the administrative team he had been a part of during the Ellis and Weaver administrations. Paul Nagel, former dean of Arts and Science at the University of Kentucky, replaced Wilson as vice president for academic affairs; Ardath Emmons, who had supervised the building of the reactor, succeeded Raymond Peck as vice president for research; and Carl Scheneman became vice president for extension.

Although Ratchford relaxed somewhat the rigid internal controls established by Weaver, he maintained strict control of the university's relationships with the governor and the General Assembly. Stirling Kyd assumed responsibility for lobbying efforts in Jefferson City, but Ratchford continued to be active in the state capitol. Another group with which Ratchford worked directly was the alumni of the university. As a major step toward bringing the alumni together on behalf of the university, Ratchford encouraged the organization of the Alumni Alliance made up of representatives of the four campus alumni associations.

Ratchford's administration is perhaps best remembered for its controversial planning effort, known popularly as "Role and Scope." Ratchford was convinced—and rightly so—that the university could not continue to grow indefinitely and that the General Assembly

C. Brice Ratchford, president from 1971 to 1976, carried forward a comprehensive planning and reassessment effort to establish a role and scope for each campus and systemwide unit.

At UM–Kansas City, Swinney Gymnasium was greatly expanded by the addition of a multi-use recreational center designed to serve students, faculty, and townspeople.

At UM–Kansas City, the old Shields mansion was expanded to provide handsome and functional space for the Henry Bloch School of Business and Public Administration, named in honor of Henry Bloch, chairman of H&R Block and a major benefactor of the school.

could not be depended on to fund program expansion through continued increases in appropriations. He saw a need to modify the growth-oriented Ten-Year Plan adopted during the Weaver administration, and as interim president he convened a group of faculty and administrative leaders for a series of meetings to consider the university's future in the light of changing demographic and economic conditions. Appointed president, Ratchford continued his efforts to reorganize the university under a plan that would avoid duplication by assigning each campus and systemwide unit a specific role and scope within the overall mission of the institution.

A preliminary draft of the plan created an uproar on the Columbia campus as faculty and administrators perceived a diminution in programs, particularly at the graduate level, in favor of developments on the other campuses. The plan went through several revisions, and when the curators finally approved it in the summer of 1974 little was changed at UMC, although opportunities for program expansion were severely curtailed.

The academic plan served the university well for a decade, providing a framework for orderly change during a period of restricted resources. Ratchford, however, never recovered from the effects of the controversy surrounding its development. Earlier efforts to expand the role of extension beyond agriculture had left a legacy of ill will among farm leaders throughout the state, and when the *Maneater* revealed a controversial state relations plan, which would use exten-

The walkways that connect the biology building and the Kenneth A. Spencer Chemistry Building at UM–Kansas City provide a place to linger as well as a place to cross.

sion personnel to pressure legislators, his opponents, both in Columbia and around the state, mounted a crescendo of criticism that made his position almost untenable. Health problems brought on by stress and weariness weakened his ability to combat his enemies, and he had no choice but to resign.

To succeed Ratchford, the board appointed James C. Olson, chancellor of the University of Missouri–Kansas City, first as interim president and then, in March 1977, as president. While still serving as interim president Olson faced an explosive issue relating to an 8,000 acre wooded tract of land in St. Charles County known as Weldon Spring. The university had acquired the land as a gift from the federal government after World War II and was using part of it for agricultural research. The board of curators had concluded that the land would be of greatest value to the university if it were developed into a

James and Vera Olson caught by a photographer on the Rolla campus. Olson served as chancellor of the University of Missouri–Kansas City from 1968 to 1976. He was appointed interim president in 1976 and president in 1977, a position he held until his retirement in 1984.

"The Monday morning gang," President Olson's staff just before its regular weekly meeting. From left to right, James R. Buchholz, vice president for administrative affairs; Melvin D. George, vice president for academic affairs; Duana Linville, assistant to the president for legislative affairs; Guy M. Horton, assistant to the president for public relations; and Phil Connell, assistant to the president.

multi-use residential, business, and industrial area. This ran afoul of St. Louis interests determined to maintain the land for recreational purposes.

Things seemed to be at a standoff, when the *Missourian* reported that the university had permitted some of the trees in the area to be cut, primarily to thin the forest. Some of the trees happened to be fine old walnuts and it was revealed that the tree-cutters had made a handsome profit on the lumber, which provided tantalizing oppor-

Protests against South African investments were more persistent at Columbia than anywhere else, but they did spread to the urban campuses as well. This photograph was taken at UM–St. Louis.

tunities for both the press and St. Louis politicians. Finally, after a protracted and complicated set of negotiations, the curators sold all but 700 acres to the Conservation Commission for $12 million, and the money was set aside as an endowment to support faculty research. Each year, in addition to providing grants for specific faculty research projects, the Weldon Spring fund supports a ten thousand dollar Presidential Research Award.

During his term Olson reduced the number of vice presidents from six to two. Melvin D. George, formerly professor of mathematics at UMC, brought back by Ratchford to serve as vice president for academic affairs from the University of Nebraska, where he was dean of Arts and Science, continued in that role with responsibilities expanded to include research and extension. James R. Buchholz of the Rochester Institute of Technology was appointed vice president for administrative affairs. They performed brilliantly as they helped to steer the university through the fiscal troubles that beset virtually all institutions of higher learning in the late 1970s and early 1980s.

The state of Missouri had never provided adequate support for its university, and though there were substantial increases in appropriations during this period, the gains frequently were absorbed by inflation. Faculty salaries remained a critical problem, with increases too frequently having to be wrung out of existing resources through a painful, wrenching process of reallocation. The principal burden of reallocation fell on the chancellors—now except for Arnold Grobman at UMSL an altogether new group (Barbara Uehling at UMC, George Russell at UMKC, Joseph Marchello at UMR)—and for each it was a continuing struggle. A ray of light in the fiscal gloom developed in 1980 as the voters approved a $600 million bond issue for capital improvements at state institutions. The university, and particularly Duana Linville, assistant to the president for governmental affairs, furnished much of the leadership for the campaign.

Governor John Ashcroft adds a brick to the new science building at UM–St. Louis as President C. Peter Magrath looks on.

As the years wore on it was becoming increasingly clear that Ratchford's academic plan, which had served the university well for almost a decade, was in need of revision. In 1982 the curators launched a comprehensive planning exercise to prepare the university for the twenty-first century. The process, while not as elaborate as the "Role and Scope" efforts of a decade earlier, involved an outside consultant and committees on each of the campuses. Even more than in earlier plans, institutional aspirations were attuned to fiscal realities.

In May 1983 Olson announced that he would retire 1 July 1984. At his retirement, he was sixty-seven and had stayed on longer than he had intended when first appointed. The search process failed to produce a successor by 1 July, and Vice President George was appointed interim president. On 18 June 1984 the curators announced that C. Peter Magrath, president of the University of Minnesota, would become the seventeenth president of the University of Missouri. He distinguished himself as an individual with a deep commitment to and broad experience in public higher education, serving as president of both the American Association of Universities and the National

The SSB Tower dominates the skyline at UM–St. Louis and serves to dramatize the changes that have taken place at the old Bellerive Country Club in less than a quarter century.

Association of Land Grant Colleges and State Universities during his first year in office in Missouri.

Magrath, who assumed office 1 January 1985, immediately made his presence felt on the campuses and around the state. He took up the task of implementing the newly adopted Long-Range Plan, placing special emphasis on the university's role in the state's economic development. He asked St. Louis industrialist Charles E. Knight to head a study of the structure, a study that resulted in an acceleration of the process of decentralization begun under Ratchford and Olson.

Within a short time there was an almost complete change in the top administrative team. Vice President George, appointed president of St. Olaf College, was replaced by Jay Barton, formerly president of the University of Alaska. James Buchholz, who resigned to become vice chancellor for administrative affairs at Washington University, was succeeded by James McGill of the University of Oregon. There

C. Peter Magrath faced student activism on the question of the university's South African investments from the first day of his arrival in 1985, as evidenced in this photograph, taken at his inauguration. Under his leadership a program of divestment was begun.

were new chancellors on three of the campuses: Haskell Monroe, UM–Columbia; Martin Jischke, UM–Rolla, and Marguerite Barnett, UM–St. Louis.

Increasingly, Missouri's business and political leaders came to appreciate the critical importance of the university to the state's economic and cultural well-being, and the university was poised to play an ever more important role in the life of the state. The oldest public institution of higher learning west of the Mississippi River was also eternally new. What had begun as a small local academy with an uncertain future had become a vast statewide institution with an annual budget of more than $600 million, enrolling 53,000 students on four campuses where they were taught by 7,500 faculty members, many of whom were part time. There were extension centers in every county and in the city of St. Louis. Alumni occupied positions of leadership in every community in the state. The university had become the state's most important resource.

# INDEX

## A

Abert, Colonel James W., 133, 134, 153
Academic Hall, **C,** 5, 14, 16, 26, 27, 29–32, 33–34, 51, 58, 112, 115. *See also* Jesse Hall
Accordionaires, The, **KC,** 223
Administration Building, **KC,** 197, 200, 206, 213, **StL,** 259
Administration, School of, **KC,** 227, 233
Aery, Shaila, 114
Afro-American Week, **KC,** 230–31. *See also* Association for Black Students; Black Culture Week; Black Students
Ag Club, **C,** 45
Agricultural College Building, **C,** 31
Agricultural Engineering Building, **C,** 120
Agricultural Experiment Station, **C,** 81
Agriculture, College of, **C,** 14–16, 19, 27, 34, 37, 44–45, 70, 80, 81, 98, 267; complex, **C,** 51
Albrecht, William A., 81
Aldrich, Ina, 22
Ali, Mohammed, 230
All Student Association (ASA), **KC,** 213, 230
Allard, Winston, 81
Allen, Edward A., 35
Allen, Nelson, 133
Allen, Thomas S., 4, 5
Allgood, Dewey, 176
Alpha Club, **R,** 146
Alpha Kappa Alpha, 178. *See also* Sororities
Alpha Phi Alpha, 178. *See also* Fraternities
Alpha Phi Omega, 198, 251. *See also* Fraternities
Alpha Pi Alpha, 107. *See also* Fraternities
Alumni, mentioned, **C,** 9, 62, 98–99, 101, 103, 118, 120, 121, 125, **R,** 148, 153, 163, 166, 169–70, 179, 184, 187, 188, 189, **KC,** 208, 220, 232, **StL,** 261, **UM,** 270, 273, 281; alumni-student lunch, **C,** 125; alumnus of the year award, **KC,** 217; awards banquet, **KC,** 232; relations office, **R,** 173
Alumni Alliance, **UM,** 273
Alumni Associations, **C,** 29, 47, 56, 118, 125, **R,** 135, 148, 152, 163, 169–70, 173, **KC,** 209, 218, 232, **StL,** 249–50
Alumni Center, **C,** 104, 113
Alumni Circle, **StL,** 261
American Association of Engineers, 159
American Association of Univer-

sities, 74, 278
American Association of University Professors, 66, 109, 208
American Association of University Women, 45
American Bar Association, 228
American Ceramic Society, 159
American College Theater Festival, 117
American Institute of Chemical Engineers, 159
American Institute of Electrical Engineers, 159
American Institute of Mining and Metallurgical Engineers, 159
American Society of Civil Engineers, 159
American Society of Mechanical Engineers, 159
Andy's Corners, **C,** 87
Anniversaries, University of Missouri: **StL,** 10th, 256; **C,** 75th, 50; 100th, 74; **UM,** 125th, 103
*Argus, The,* **C,** 38
Archipenko, Alexander, 201
Armitage, Richard, 229
Armsby, Henry H., 156
Army Air Force, 204
Army Specialized Training Program, 162
Army's Specialized Training Unit, 204
Arnold, Thomas A., 18
Aronson, Adam, 259
Art and Art History, Department of, **KC,** 202, 218
Art, Department of, **C,** 9, 10
Art History and Archaeology, Department of, **C,** 113
Artley, A. Sterl, 99
Arts and Science, College of, **C,** 55, 64, 82, 95, 96, 105–6, 111, **R,** 172, 184, **KC,** 229, **StL,** 244
ASA. *See* All Student Association
Ashcroft, John, 235, 278
Asher-Wiley, Charmaine, 211, 223
Association for Black Students, **R,** 178. *See also* Afro-American Week; Black Culture Week; Black Students
Association of American Universities, 34
Association of Collegiate Alumni, **C,** 45
Asterisk Club, **C,** 38
*Asterisk, The,* **C,** 38
Astronomy, Department of, **C,** 36
Atchison, David Rice, 3
Athenaean Society, **C,** 8–9, 29, 64
Atherton, Lewis W., 97
Athletic Associations, **C,** 41, **R,** 147, 151, 160, **KC,** 198

Athletics: mentioned, **C,** 38, 39–41, 51, 53, 62, 75, 83, 88, 113, 118, 120–21, 123, 125, **R,** 141, 147, 154, 160, 168–69, 173, 175–76, **KC,** 197, 204, 209, 213, 232, **StL,** 246–48, 256; athletic fields, **C,** 41, 68, **R,** 149; directors, **C,** 41, 88, 121, 123, 149, 176, 246; scholarships, 103, **StL,** 247, 258; women's, **C,** 41, 43, 56, 68, 122, 124, **R,** 176, **StL,** 248, 258. *See also* Baseball; Basketball; Field Hockey; Football; Golf; Rugby; Soccer; Swimming; Tennis; Track
Atkins Museum. *See* Nelson Gallery and Atkins Museum
Atwater, James, 116

## B

Baier, Martin, 236
Bailey, F. Lee, 216
Bailey, Myra, 248
Baird, Charles, 57
Baker, Joanne, 209, 211, 224
Baker, Merl, 170–73, 176, 179, 182
Baker-Park Dormitory, **C,** 80. *See also* Housing
Ballet, **KC,** 224, 225. *See also* Performing Arts
Band, **C,** 20, 39, 88, 122, **R,** 186. *See also* Performing Arts
Banning, James H., 112
Barkelow, Bruce, 118
Barker, Marvin W., 184
Barnes, Mary, 125
Barnes, Ward, 241–42
Barnett, John, 208, 209
Barnett, Marguerite Ross, 262–63, 281
Barnwarming, **C,** 45, 87
Barton, Jay, 279
Baseball, **C,** 39, 62, 90, 122, **R,** 141, 147, 176, **StL,** 248. *See also* Athletics
Basic Life Sciences, School of, **KC,** 233
Basketball, **C,** 62, 88, 122–24, **R,** 147, 160, 169, 176, **KC,** 209, 232, **StL,** 246–48. *See also* Athletics
Bass, Eli E., 4, 5
Bass, Everett, 22
Battey, Robert, 224
Bauman, John, 118
Baysinger, Helen, 149
Baysinger, S. L., 151
Beals, David, 212
Beasley, Leila, 136
Beatty, Max, 215, 224
Behrens, Gloria, 94
Belden, Henry M., 35
Bellerive Country Club, **StL,** 241, 251, 279
Benjamin, A. Cornelius, 107

Bent, Henry E., 70
Benton, Thomas Hart, 39, 92–93, 157
Benton Hall, **StL**, 245, 250
Berenger, Tom, 118
Berry, Jane, 229
Berry, Lloyd, 112
Berry, Richard, 234
Beta Theta Phi, 22. *See also*
    Fraternities
Bezoni, Ray, 271
Bible College of Missouri, **C**, 51
Billings, William H., 270
Bingham, George Caleb, 10, 29
Biology Building, **StL**, 275
Biology-Chemistry Building, **KC**, 218
Biology, Geology, and Museum
    Building, **C**, 31, 33
Bisplinghoff, Raymond L., 182, 184,
    185
Black Culture Week, **R**, 178. *See also*
    Afro-American Week; Association
    for Black Students; Black Students
Black Students: enrollment, **C**, 82–84,
    88, 111, **R**, 168, 177–78, **KC**, 206,
    230–31, **StL**, 252–53; faculty, **C**, 111;
    fraternities, **C**, 107, **R**, 178; home-
    coming king and queen, **C**, 125;
    sorority, **R**, 178. *See also* Afro-
    American Week; Association for
    Black Students; Black Culture
    Week
Black Studies, **C**, 111
Blair, Francis Preston, 19
Blair, Judge Sam C., 84, 168
Blankenship, Joseph, 224
Bledsoe, Alfred, 10–11
Bliss, Philemon, 17, 24
Bloch, Annette, 233
Bloch, Henry W., 62, 228, 235, 274
Bloch, Richard, 228, 233
Bloch, Wheadon, 209, 229
Bloch, Henry W., School of Business
    and Public Administration, **KC**,
    235, 236, 274
Bloch, Leon E., Law Library, **KC**,
    228. *See also* Library
Bloch, Richard A., Cancer Manage-
    ment Center, **KC**, 233
Block, Glenn, 223
Bloodworth-Thompson, Linda, 118
Blount, Don, 116
Bluford, Lucile, 83. *See also* Black
    Students
Board of Curators. *See* University of
    Missouri Board of Curators
Board of Trustees. *See* University of
    Kansas City Board of Trustees
Boarding Clubs, **C**, 21–22, 24, **R**, 137.
    *See also* Housing
Boland, E. F., 147
Bolling, Richard, 206
Bond, Christopher, 257
Bond, Julian, 178
Bondeson, William B., 111, 116, 118
Boone County, 3, 5, 14, 26, 40, 81, 267

Booster Club, **R**, 160
Bosch, Wouter, 172
Boston, Margie, 186
Botts, Tom, 62, 90, 122
Bowling, Dale, 271
Bowman, Pasco, 233
Boyer, Benjamin F., 200
Boyle, Hal, 70
Bradley, General Omar N., 76
Brady, Thomas A., 80
Brady Commons, **C**, 80, 102
Bransby, Eric, 215
Branton, Coleman, 227
Brewer, Chester L., 41
Brewer Field House, **C**, 62, 68, 78, 88
Brewster, Mary, 253
Briggs, Fred N., 93
Brookfield, Dutton, 227
Brookings, Robert, 46
Brooks, George C., 111
Brooks, Stratton D., 50, 55, 56, 65–66,
    160, 270
Brown, Charlie, 107
Brown, Dorothy, 211
Brown, Harold, 194
Brown, Hugh, 224
*Brown* v. *Topeka*, 84. *See also* Black
    Students
Brownlee, Richard, 97
Broyles, Frank, 88
Buchholz, James R., 276, 277, 279
Buebendorf, Francis, 211
Buford Act, 151–52, 154
Bugg, James L. Jr., 243, 244, 246, 249,
    250, 271
Bugg Lake, **StL**, 241, 249, 251, 252
Bullman, Gale, 176
Bullman, Gale, Multipurpose Build-
    ing, **R**, 175
Bum Friday, **KC**, 198, 207, 231, 232
Bunker, Herbert, 106
Bunn, Ronald, 115
Burdick, Jacques, 235
Burnett, Robert A., 82
Busch, Carl, 200
Buschman, Harold, 200
Business Administration, Division
    of, **StL**, 244
Business Administration, School of,
    **KC**, 209
Business and Public Administration,
    School of, **C**, 50, 67, 99, 103, **KC**,
    216, 236
Business, School of, **KC**, 227, **StL**, 244
Butler, Joe Beaty, 154
Byler, William H., 118
Byler, William H., Awards, 118

**C**

CAD/CAM System, **R**, 185
Cadet Band, **C**, 39. *See also* Band
Cafeteria, **R**, 166, 173, **StL**, 243, 250,
    256
Callaway County, 3, 5

Campus Plan, prior to 1900, **C**, 15
Cappon, Alexander, 200
Capshaw, Kate, 118
Carideo, Frank, 62
Carlile, Robert, 178
Carlton, E. W., 154
Carriage House, **KC**, 198
Caruso, Annette, 176
Case, A. A., 118
Casey, Greg, 118
Cass, Richard, 224
Center for Academic Development,
    **KC**, 233–35
Center for Business Innovation, **KC**,
    236
Center for International Programs
    and Studies (CIPAS), **R**, 178
Center for Management Develop-
    ment, **KC**, 227
Center for Metropolitan Studies,
    **StL**, 252
Center for the Study of Metropolitan
    Problems in Education, **KC**, 227
Ceramic Engineering, **R**, 159, 162;
    laboratory, **R**, 166
Chalybeate Spring, **C**, 51
Chancellor's Council, **StL**, 260
Chancellor's Festival of Music, **C**,
    116. *See also* Music
Chancellor's Medal, **KC**, 212, 233, **StL**,
    242
Chancellor's Residence, **C**, 17, 111,
    112, **R**, 144, 189, **KC**, 211, 217, **StL**,
    262
Chapel, **C**, 7, 13, 26, 29, 34, 45, 92. *See
    also* Academic Hall; Green, A. P.,
    Chapel; Jesse Hall
Chapman, Carl, 61, 63
Charters, W. W., 49
Chedsey, William R., 160–61
Chemical Engineering, **R**, 163; labo-
    ratory, **R**, 139
Chemistry-Biology Building, **KC**, 203
Chemistry Building, **C**, 56
Chemistry, Department of, **C**, 20, 36,
    70, **R**, 141, 145, **StL**, 244; laboratory,
    **C**, 31, 32, 33, **R**, 138, 139, 140, **KC**, 202
Chi Omega, 212. *See also* Sororities
Child Development Center, **StL**, 258
Childers, L. F., 81
Children's Mercy Hospital, 222
Christensen, Jerry, 258, 259
Christensen, Lawrence, 160, 161, 177
Christman, Paul, 62
Ciardi, John, 200, 203
CIPAS. *See* Center for International
    Programs and Studies
Civic Orchestra, **KC**, 223. *See also*
    Music
Civil Engineering, Department of, **R**,
    163
Civil Rights Commission, 83
Civil War. *See* War
Claiborne, Craig, 70
Clark, Larry, 117

Clark Hall, **StL,** 250
Club House, **C,** 21, **R,** 140, 144, **StL,**
    242, 243, 245, 250, 253, 261. *See also*
    Housing
Cobb, Irvin S., 64
Cobbs, Marvin, 125
Cockefair, Carolyn Benton, 228
Cockefair Chair, **KC,** 212, 228
Cockefair Hall, **KC,** 228
Coffey, Dan, 118
Cole, Vinson, 217
Cole County, 3, 84
Coles, Martin, 226
*Collegian,* **C,** 19, 38
Collegium Musicum, **C,** 117. *See also*
    Music
Columbia, 5, 7, 12, 14, 18, 21, 29, 31, 45,
    81, 82, 100, 103, 106, 113, 137, 142,
    143, 151, 171, 176, 177, 267, 270
Columbia College, 4
*Columbia Herald,* 46, 47
*Columbia Missourian,* **C,** 38, 82, 276
Commencement, **C,** 7, 12, 13, 29, 33,
    42, 50, 55, 58, 76, 84, 86, 92, 93, 94,
    102, 106–7, 112, 113, 125, 127, **R,** 135,
    154, 156, 170, 171, 177, **KC,** 197, 200,
    208, **StL,** 249, 254, 256, 257
Commerce, School of, **C,** 49
Committee on Forensic Activity, **C,**
    64–65
Community Studies Institute, **KC,**
    228
Computer Center, **R,** 164, 171
Computer Science, **R,** 185, **KC,** 233
Computers, **C,** 99, 105–6, **R,** 185, 186,
    **KC,** 218
Conley House, **C,** 119
Connally, John, 215
Connaway, John R., 34
Connaway Hall, **C,** 104
Connell, Phil, 271, 276
Conservatory of Music, **KC,** 211, 223,
    225, 234, 235. *See also* Music
Continuing Education, Division of,
    **KC,** 209. *See also* Evening College;
    Evening Division
Cooch, William, 133
Cook, Walter, 211
Cooke, S. R. B., 155
Cookingham, L. P., 236
Cookingham Institute of Public
    Administration, **KC,** 236
Coolidge, President Calvin, 63
Cooper County, 3, 5
Cooperative Education, 165
Copeland, Durwood, 145, 151–52, 154
Corrigan, Robert J., 229
Corwin, Darrell, 232
Costin, James D., 224, 235
Cottle, Harvey, 216
Courtney, Gladys, 112
Cousins, Norman, 212
Covington, Joe E., 98
Cowan, Leslie, 80
Craig, Cleo, 94

Crain, William L., 200
Cramer, Bruce, 80
Crews, Monte, 39
Crim, Betty, 118
Crissman, Helen Jo, 200
Croft, Huber O., 81
Cronkite, Walter, 220
Crow, Herbert Carl, 38
Crowder, Enoch H., 20, 22
Crowder Hall, **C,** 75
Croy, Homer, 39, 93
Cullinan, Francis, 224
Cullison, James S., 157
Curators, Board of. *See* University of
    Missouri Board of Curators
Curators Professorship Program, **R,**
    186, **StL,** 252
Curators Scholarships, **C,** 22, 118
*Current, The,* **StL,** 248
Curry, Charles, 221
Curtis, Harry A., 81
Curtis, Winterton C., 69
Curtis Hall, **C,** 69
Curtis Laws Wilson Library, **R,** 175.
    *See also* Library

**D**

Daane, Adrian, 184
Dahlgren, George, 229, 233
Dairy Department, **C,** 81
Dake, C. L., 154
Dale, Wesley J., 217, 229, 232, 233
Dallas, Don, 248
Dalton, John Hall, 72
Dalton, John M., 93, 103, 214, 242
Daniel, Walter, 112
Davenport, Herbert J., 50
Davis, Fred, 118
Davis, Ilus W., 197
Davis, James, 127
Davis, Joni, 124
Davis, Robert L., 185
Davis, Secretary of War Dwight F., 63
Day, Delbert, 186
Dayan, Moshe, 118
De Voto, Bernard, 64
Deacon, Stanley, 211
Deal, Jean, 104
Dean, George R., 139, 145, 154
Debate Team, **KC,** 209
Debating Club, **C,** 45
Debating Society, **C,** 64
Decker, Clarence R., 197, 200, 201,
    206, 208–9
Defleur, Lois, 115
Defoe, Luther M., 69
Delich-Bentley, Helen, 82
Delta Alpha, 209. *See also* Sororities
Dennie, F. E. "Spike," 151
Dentistry, School of, **KC,** 200, 202,
    217, 220, 221, 222
Depression of the 1930s, **C,** 67, 74, 77,
    95, **R,** 160, **KC,** 194, 200
Devine, Dan, 88, 120

Diabetes Center, **C,** 113
Dickey Mansion, **KC,** 193–97 *passim,*
    200, 216
Dillingham, Jay, 232
Dimmitt, E., 22
Dimond, E. Grey, 221, 235, 270
Dimond, Mary Clark, 235
Dinges, Susan, 224
Direct Marketing Foundation of New
    York, 236
Director's Residence, **R,** 144
Dittrich, Theodore T., 202, 208, 209
Division for Continuing Education,
    **KC,** 209
Dixon, Nikki, 226
Dockery, Alexander, 37
Dockery-Folk Dormitory, **C,** 80. *See
    also* Housing
Doerr, J. Joseph, 227, 233
Dokoudovska, Tatiana, 224
Don Cossack Choir, **R,** 157. *See also*
    Music
Donnell, Margaret, 234
Donnelly, Governor Phil, 76
Dormitories. *See* Housing
Douthat, Captain R. W., 134, 137
Dowgray, John, 216, 229
Downing, Dan, 125
Doyle, Kevin, 226
Drake, E. A., 139
Drake, Richard, 210–11, 212, 213
Drama. *See* Theater
Drennan, Phyllis, 116
Driscoll, Glen, 243, 244, 245, 249,
    250–53, 256, 257
Dudley, Margaret, 212
Duncan, Clyde, 107
Duncan, Gustavus, 134, 135
Dunn, S. Watson, 112
Dwyer, Sam, 105

**E**

Earhart, Amelia, 157
Earls, Carol, 88
Eating Clubs, **R,** 166, 173
Echols, William H., 138–39, 141,
Eckles, C. H., 70
Eckles Hall, **C,** 71
Economics, Department of, **C,** 49,
    **StL,** 244
Eddy, William B., 215, 227
Edgar Snow Memorial Collection.
    *See* Snow, Edgar, Memorial
    Collection
Education, College of, **C,** 71, 99
Education, Division of, **StL,** 244
Education, School of, **C,** 49, 68, **KC,**
    209, 218, 227, **StL,** 252, 259
Edwards, Francis C. "Ike," 170
Edwards, George R., 62, 88
Edwards, Virginia, 261
Ehly, Eph, 223, 234
Ehrlich, George, 209
Eickhoff, Harold, 246, 247

Eisenbrandt, Leslie, 209, 217
Ekblaw, Sidney E., 200
Electrical Club, **R,** 146
Electrical Engineering, Department
  of, **C,** 81, **R,** 163; laboratory, **R,** 166
Ellis, Elmer, 92, 93, 95–96, 99, 102–3,
  106, 107, 163, 170–73 *passim*, 214, 216,
  242–43, 250, 267, 269, 270, 273
Ellis, Roy, 93
Ellis, Ruth, 95
Ellis Library, **C,** 119, 120, 269. *See also*
  Library
Elston, Sarah Gentry, 14, 80
*Emerging University, The. See* Touhill,
  Blanche
Emerson, George D., 134, 135, 138
Emersonian Club, **R,** 135
Emmons, Ardath, 106, 273
Engineering, College of, **C,** 24, 31, 70,
  81, 94, 105, 111, **R,** 132; laboratory,
  **C,** 120
Engineering Management, Depart-
  ment of, **R,** 187
Engineering, School of, **R,** 171, 172,
  184
Engineers' Club, **R,** 146
Engineers' Council for Professional
  Development, 163
Engineers Day, **R,** 166. *See also* St.
  Patrick's
Engineers Week, **C,** 45, 73. *See also* St.
  Patrick's
English, Earl, 81
English, Francis W., 96, 97, 242
English, Department of, **C,** 9, 35, 117,
  **KC,** 235, **StL,** 244
Enrollment, **C,** 9, 11, 20, 24, 28, 42, 45,
  50, 53, 65, 67, 75, 77, 80, 125, **R,** 132,
  133, 134, 136–39, 145, 148, 152, 153,
  154, 161, 162, 166, 170, 172, 173, 181,
  182, 185, **KC,** 197, 200, 204, 206, 208,
  213, 215, 216, 225, 230, 232, **StL,** 243,
  244, 250, 256, 259, **UM,** 273, 281. *See
  also* Black Students; Foreign Stu-
  dents; Minority Student
  Recruitment; Women Students
Epperson House, **KC,** 204–5, 206, 218
Epworth House, **KC,** 216
Esterhazy Quartet, **C,** 116, 117. *See
  also* Music
Etheridge, William C., 70, 81
Ethnic Awareness Center, **KC,** 228
Etskorn, K. Peter, 260
Eubank, Louis, 106
Eubanks, Eugene E., 233
Evans, James, 224
Evans, Karl, 118
Evening College, **StL,** 244. *See also*
  Continuing Education, Division of
Evening Division, **KC,** 209, **StL,** 243,
  245. *See also* Continuing Education,
  Division of
Evers, Charles, 178
Eversman, Walter, 186
Experimental Mine, **R,** 173

Extension Division, **C,** 34, 98, 106,
  267, **R,** 184, **StL,** 244, **UM,** 271, 273,
  274, 281. *See also* Continuing Education, Division of
Eye Foundation, **KC,** 222

F

Faculty Women's Club, **StL,** 249, 253
Fagan, Val, 226
Fagin, Margaret, 244
Fairchild, Arthur H. R., 35
Falsetti, Joseph, 112, 118
Family Study Center, **KC,** 228
Fane, Irvin, 72
Farmer, John, 118
Farmers Fair, **C,** 44, 45, 72
Farnsworth, Robert, 215
Fasel, George, 111
Faucett, Thomas R., 185
Faurot, Don, 62, 75, 88, 89, 123
Faurot Field, **C,** 121, 122
Faust, Martin L., 99
Fedder, Ed, 260
Federation of Graduate Clubs, 34
Feld, Selma, 212, 228
Ferguson, Oliver, 270
Ficklin, Joseph, 12
Field, R. M., 23
Field, Eugene, 22–23
Field Hockey, **StL,** 248. *See also*
  Athletics
Finch, James A., Jr., 95, 242, 270
Fine Arts Building, **C,** 96
Fine Arts, Division of, **C,** 64
Finley, Charles, 176
Fisher, M. M., 27
Fisher, Paul, 82
Fisher, Roy F., 112
Fisher, William, 223
Fleck, Joseph, 201
Fleet, A. F., 27
Folk, Joseph, 148
Football, **C,** 39–41, 62, 84, 88, 89, 100,
  120–22, **R,** 140, 141, 147, 148, 151, 160,
  168–69, 176, 186. *See also* Athletics
Ford, President Gerald, 187
*Foreign Affairs*, 232
Foreign Students, **R,** 178, **StL,** 260
Forestry, School of, **C,** 80
Fort, Tomlinson, Jr., 185
Fort Leonard Wood, **R,** 166
Fort Wyman, **R,** 131, 132, 136
Frame, Floyd H., 163
Francis, David R., 29, 31, 33, 60
Francis Fountain, **C,** 60
Francis Quadrangle, **C,** 33, 37, 51, 53,
  69, 70, 102, 107, 109, 112–15 *passim*,
  118. *See also* Quadrangle
Franzen, William, 252
Fraternities, **C,** 22, 24, 38, 45, 53, 87,
  107, **R,** 145, 148, 153, 165, 166, 178,
  179, **KC,** 198, 232, **StL,** 251. *See also*
  Greek System; Interfraternity
  Council; Pan Hellenic Council;

Sororities
Freedom of Information Center, **C,** 82
Freegard, Susan, 254
Freilich, Robert, 228
French, Eunice, 178
French, William J., 233
Friberg, Stig, 186
Froman, Jane, 64, 65
Frost, Robert, 64
Fuller, Harold Q., 166
Fulton, Charles H., 154, 160
Fulton Hall, **R,** 163

G

Gaines, Lloyd, 83
Galbreath, Tony, 121
Galloway, Beverly T., 46
Gardner-Hyde Dormitory, **C,** 80. *See
  also* Housing
Garrett, Leon E., 151, 154
Gator Bowl, **C,** 88. *See also* Football
General Assembly of Missouri, 3, 29,
  131, 137, 225, 267, 273
General Lecture Series, **R,** 157, 186
General Library, **KC,** 218. *See also*
  Library
Gentry, Eliza, 14, 69
Gentry, Sarah. *See* Elston, Sarah
  Gentry
Gentry Hall, **C,** 88. *See also* Housing
Geology and Mineralogy, Depart-
  ment of, **C,** 35
Geology Building, **KC,** 219
Geology, Department of, **C,** 31, **R,** 188
George, Melvin D., 276–79 *passim*
Geyer, Henry S., 3
GI Bill of Rights, 77, 162
Gill, John Holt, 135
Gillette, Mary Louise, 13
Gilliland, Charles E., 209
Gingerich, Newell, 70
Ginn, Rosemary Lucas, 65
Ginter, Adella, 107
Girls' Rifle Team, **C,** 54
Glee Club, **C,** 63, 64, **R,** 157, 186. *See
  also* Music
Glenn, William Ellis, 134, 135
Glick, Milton, 116
Gliddon, Reverdy, 212
Godwin, Linda, 118
Goldman, Morton, 209
Golf, **C,** 91, **R,** 154, 160, 169, 176. *See
  also* Athletics
*Good Seed, The,* **R,** 179
Goode, Wayne, 242
Gordon, Boyle, 18
Gorman, Linda, 118
Gottschalk, Victor Hugo, 145
Goula, N. E., 22
Grabowski, Bernard, 215
Graduate Center for Materials
  Research, **R,** 173
Graduate Studies, School of, **C,** 34,
  47, 105, 111, 112, 116, **R,** 166, 171, 172,

178, 184, **KC,** 211, 216, **StL,** 245, 256, 257, **UM,** 274
Graham, Robert, 80
Grant, William T., 211
Grant Hall, **KC,** 211, 225
Greek System: mentioned, **C,** 87–88, 108; Greek Day, **R,** 166; Greek Town, **C,** 88; Greek Week, **R,** 166, 179, **StL,** 249, 251; organizations, **C,** 22, 45, 94, 107, **R,** 145, 165, 168; 178, 179, **KC,** 197, 198, 209, 212, **StL,** 251. *See also* Fraternities; Interfraternity Council; Pan Hellenic Council; Sororities
Green, A. P., Chapel, **C,** 92
Green, Avis, 70
Greene, Eva Endurance Hirdler, 148–49
Gregory, Dick, 216
Griffiths, Martha Wright, 82
*Grit,* **C,** 49
Grobman, Arnold B., 242, 258–62, 277
Gross, Calvin, 217, 227
Groth, Aaron, 80
Guitar, Odon, 9
Gustin, A. L., Jr., 91
Gwynn Hall, **C,** 70

**H**

H&R Block Foundation, 236
Haag, Lena, 197
Haag Hall, **KC,** 201, 219
Haden, John J., 20
Hadley-Major Dormitory, **C,** 80. *See also* Housing
Hall, Adele, 233
Hall, Donald J., 233
Hall, Joyce C., 93, 233
Hall Family Foundations, 235
Halliburton, Richard, 157
Halligan, James E., 185
Hansen, Douglas, 107
Harbison, M. B., 22
Harriman, Averell, 200
Harris, Elmo Golightly, 141, 142
Harris Hall, **R,** 161
Hart, Dave, 121, 123
Hartley, Joseph R., 256–57
Haseman, Leonard, 81
Hashinger, Margaret, 211
Hasselmann, Karl F., 163
Hatch Hall Dormitory, **C,** 104. *See also* Housing
Havighurst, Robert, 227
Health Sciences, **C,** 111; library, **C,** 104
Hearnes, Warren, 113
Hearnes, Warren, Multipurpose Building, **C,** 113, 125
Hellmuth, George, 149, 242
Hellmuth, Obata, and Kassabaum, 242
Henderson, Norlan, 215
Hendricks, Everett, 200, 211, 223

Henning, Oscar, 163
Henry, Gwinn, 61
Henson, Paul, 227
Heritage Singers, **KC,** 217. *See also* Music
Hetherington, Clark W., 41
Hetherington, Richard W., 233
Hewitt, Kate W., 193
Heysinger, Jack D., 216, 233
Hicks, Frederick C., 35
High, Marathon, 200
Hill, A. Ross, 47, 49, 55, 151, 193
Hill, Henry B., 200
Hill, Shirley, 216
Hill Hall, **C,** 99
Hille, Stanley, 116
Hillis, Margaret, 234
Hills, Stephen, 5
Hindman, Darwin A., 106
Hines, Anthony, 116
Hinkson Creek, 48, 87
Hirdler, Eva Endurance. *See* Greene, Eva Endurance Hirdler
History and Political Economy, Department of, **C,** 35
History, Department of, **C,** 35, 80, 96, **KC,** 212, **StL,** 244
*History of MSM,* 161
Hitchcock, Ethan Allen, 46
Hobo Day, **KC,** 198
Hockaday, Irvine O., 5
Hockey Puck, **R,** 173. *See also* Theater
Hodges, John R., 200
Hoffman, Donald, 218
Hohenschild, Henry, 139, 142, 143, 148, 149, 151
Holliday, Harold L., 206
Holmes, Chauncey D., 106
Home Economics, Department of, **C,** 45, 98; domestic economy laboratory, **C,** 44
Homecoming: mentioned, **C,** 41, 56, 61, 62, 88, 125, **StL,** 256; king and queen, **C,** 125; queen, **C,** 88, 125, **R,** 177
Honorary Knights of St. Patrick. *See* St. Patrick's
Honors College, **C,** 119–20
Horner Institute, 211
Horseman, Elmer, 209
Horticulture, Department of, **C,** 80
Horton, Guy M., 276
Hosmer, James K., 13
Hospital Hill, **KC,** 221–23. *See also* Medicine, School of
Housing: boarding clubs, **C,** 21–22, 24, **R,** 137; dormitories, **C,** 21, 42–43, 51, 53, 64, 69, 77–80, 87–88, 104, 111, **R,** 140, 144, 160, 164, 166, 173, 176–77, 184, **KC,** 206, 209, 213; temporary, **C,** 77–80, **R,** 162
Houston, Mark, 226
Howard, Ernest E., 193, 208
Howard County, 3
Hudson, William W., 6, 7, 9, 10, 22

Huggins, G. Ellsworth, 103
Hultsch, Roland, 118
Humanities and Social Studies, Department of, **R,** 163
Humanities, Department of, **R,** 171
Humphrey, Robin, 224
Hurwitt, Rheta Sosland, 235
Hutchins, Ed, 111–12, 122
Hyland, William G., 232

**I**

IFC. *See* Interfraternity Council
Illingworth, Alfred S., 118
Independence Residence Center, **KC,** 229
*Independent, The,* **C,** 38
Independent Organization, **R,** 179
*Index, The,* **C,** 38
Institute of American Music, **KC,** 224. *See also* Music
Institute of River Studies, **R,** 182
Interfraternity Council (IFC), **R,** 166, 179, **KC,** 199. *See also* Fraternities; Greek System; Pan Hellenic Council; Sororities
International Club, **R,** 147
Ira Remsen Society, **R,** 159
Iron County, 131
Irving Literary Society, **R,** 135
Irwin, Will, 64
Itschner, Earnest T., 106

**J**

Jackling, Daniel C., 137, 149, 151, 163
Jackling Gymnasium, **KC,** 156, 170, 174
James, William, 173
Jazz Ensemble, **KC,** 223. *See also* Music
Jefferson City, 26, 103, 112, 144, 217, 225, 273
Jefferson Club, **C,** 93
Jefferson, Thomas, Award, **R,** 186
Jefferson Tombstone, **C,** 112
Jenkins, Darold, 62
Jenkins, Lee, 107
Jesse, Addie, 29
Jesse, Bredelle, 106
Jesse, Richard Henry, 22, 29, 34–35, 37, 39, 45, 47, 141, 151
Jesse Hall, **C,** 32–33, 55, 58, 67, 68, 76, 87, 91, 92, 102, 107, 126, 127, 268. *See also* Academic Hall
Jischke, Martin L., 188–89, 281
Johnson, J. Stuart, 172
Johnson, L., 22
Johnson, R. W., 19
Johnston, Eva, 80
Jonas, Harry, 233
Jones, Archie, 211, 224
Jones, C. Cliff, 227
Jones, J. Carleton, 55, 56, 80, 100
Jones, W. "Mack," 111, 118

Jordan Foundation, 262
Journal Club, **R,** 146
Journalism, School of, **C,** 38, 44,
    47–49, 66, 69, 70, 81–82, 83
Journalism Week, **C,** 117

**K**

Kahler, W. W., 94
Kahrs, Robert, 116
Kaiser, Edward, 111
Kalb, Marvin, 216
*Kangaroo,* **KC,** 199, 213
Kangaroos. *See* Athletics
Kansas City, 34, 83, 100, 106, 193, 194,
    200, 213, 214, 216, 217–18, 220, 225,
    232, 236, 247, 267
Kansas City Art Institute, 211
Kansas City Association of Trusts
    and Foundations, 214, 217
Kansas City Ballet, 224. *See also* Ballet
*Kansas City Call,* 83
Kansas City Conservatory of Music,
    211. *See also* Conservatory of Music
Kansas City Dental College, 193. *See
    also* Dentistry, School of
Kansas City Medical College, 200.
    *See also* Dentistry, School of
Kansas City Philharmonic Orchestra,
    194. *See also* Music
Kansas City School District, 228, 233
Kansas City School of Law, 200. *See
    also* Law, School of
*Kansas City Star,* 27, 47, 93, 218
*Kansas City Times,* 194, 215
Kappa Alpha, 145, 165. *See also*
    Fraternities
Kappa Kappa Gamma, 22. *See also*
    Sororities
Kappa Sigma, 145. *See also*
    Fraternities
Katz Pharmacy Building, 216
KCUR-FM, **KC,** 213, 228
Keathley, George, 235
Keeley, Mary Paxton, 49
Kelley, Clarence M., 232
Kelly, Frank, 232
Kelly, Mervin J., 163
Kelly, N. J., 94
Kelly, Patrick, 216, 228, 233
Kelly, Tom, 151
Kemner, Gerald, 224
Kemper, Enid, 118
Kemper, James M., 211
Kemper, R. Crosby, 41
Kemper, R. Crosby, Jr., 82, 118
Kennedy, Senator Edward, 221
Kennedy, Lyle, 211
Kennedy, Robert F., Memorial Sym-
    posium, **KC,** 230
Kenneson, Carolyn, 117
Kershner, Karl K., 154, 163
Kesey, Ken, 230
Kessler, Harry H., 187
Key, Billy, 176

KFRU, **C,** 70
Kiehl, Elmer R., 97, 98, 115
Kimel, William, 112
Kimpton, Lawrence, 93, 200, 210
King, Stephen B., 8
King, Vivian, 125
Kirkendall, Richard S., 118
Klapis, Ralph, 234
Klapp, William D., 118
Klausner, Tiberius, 224
Klemme, Arnold W., 106
Knight, Charles E., 279
Knight, Douglas, 186
Knoll, Richard, 224
Koeppe, Owen, 115
Kolker, Berndt, 209
KOMU-TV, **C,** 81
Krajicek, Dayton D., 220
Kuehn, David, 233, 234
Kuhlman, John, 108, 118
KUMR-FM, **R,** 186
KWMU, **StL,** 252, 261
Kyd, Stirling, 273

**L**

LaBudde, Kenneth J., 212
Labunski, Wiktor, 211, 223
Ladd, George E., 143, 145, 147–48,
Lamade, George, 49
Lamade, Howard, 49
Lambda Chi Alpha, 145. *See also*
    Fraternities
Lambert, Edward C., 81
Lathom, Wanda, 224
Lathrop, John Hiram, 3, 5, 6–8, 10, 11,
    13, 50, 51, 80, 100
Lathrop Hall, **C,** 42, 64. *See also*
    Housing
Latin American Club, **R,** 147
Law Barn. *See* Law Building
Law Building, **C,** 31, 269
Law Day, **C,** 98–99
Law Library, **C,** 98. *See also* Library
*Law Review,* **KC,** 207
Law School Foundation, **C,** 98
Law, School of, **C,** 17, 18, 19, 24, 26, 31,
    56, 71, 83, 98, 120, 123, 269, **KC,** 200,
    204, 207, 211, 227, 228
Laws, Samuel Spahr, 16, 21, 22, 23–27,
    41, 80, 100, 112, 115, 137
Laws Observatory, **C,** 9, 14, 16, 25–26
Leach, Sue, 177
Ledman, Alonzo, 107
Lefevre, George, 35
Lefevre Hall, **C,** 115
Leffingwell, Edward H., 8
Lehrer, James, 82
Leisenring, John, 223
Lengyel, Jack, 121, 123
Lennon, Max, 115
Lenox, Mary, 116
Levine, Daniel U., 227
Levis, Larry, 117
Levit, Martin, 212

Levy, Solomon, 212
Lewis, Fred, 211
Liberal Arts Building, **KC,** 197
Liberal Arts, College of, **KC,** 209, 212
Liberal Arts, Division of, **R,** 172, 176
Library, **C,** 13, 19, 26, 34, 51–52, 67, 68,
    85, 95, 97, 98, 105, **R,** 144, 146, 149,
    170, 173, 174, 179, **KC,** 194, 197, 212,
    218, 216, 235, **StL,** 243, 261. *See also*
    Bloch, Leon E., Law Library; Cur-
    tis Laws Wilson Library; Ellis
    Library; General Library; Law
    Library; Linda Hall Library;
    Lottes, John O., Health Sciences
    Library; Thomas Jefferson Library;
    Truman Library
Liebnitz, Paul, 215
Lightner, Lee M., 220
Linda Hall Library, **KC,** 201. *See also*
    Library
Lindberg, Donald, 105
Lindenmeyer, Ed, 62
Linville, Duana, 276–77
Litherland, Bea, 113
Litton, Jerry, 85
Lloyd, Samuel H., 154, 157
Lobeck, Charles, 112
Lodwick, Gwilym S., 105
Loeb, Isidor, 35, 50, 55, 80
Loeb, Marshall R., 82
Loeb Group Dormitory, **C,** 80. *See
    also* Housing
Londre, Felicia, 224
Long, Norton, 252
Long-Range Plan, **UM,** 279
Longmire, Martha, 211
Longwell, John H., 80, 97, 98, 106
Lorey, Edwin G., 172
Lottes, J. Otto, 104
Lottes, John O., Health Sciences
    Library, **C,** 113. *See also* Library
Lowe, Henry, 123
Lower, Elmer, 70
Lowry, Thomas Jefferson, 5, 24
Lowry Hall, **C,** 60
Lowry Mall, **C,** 119
L.S.V., **C,** 45
Lucas, Jean Baptiste Charles, 256
Lucas, Rosemary. *See* Ginn, Rose-
    mary Lucas
Lucas Hall, **StL,** 252, 256
Lynn, J. J., 205

**M**

Machine Shop, **R,** 157
Mackaman, Frank, 173
Madrigal Players, **R,** 186, 187. *See also*
    Music
Maestre, Sidney, 94
Mag, Arthur, 214, 232
Magrath, C. Peter, 188, 235, 262,
    278–80
Mahoney, John, 250
Mallory, Arthur, 243

Manchester, William, 81
*Maneater*, **C**, 85, 86, 274
Mangel, Margaret, 98, 113
Manheim, Ernest, 200
Mann, Clair V., 163
Manual Training Building, **C**, 31
Marbut, Curtis Fletcher, 35, 36
Marchello, Joseph M., 184–88 *passim*, 277
Marchello, Louise, 184, 189
Marching Mizzou, **C**, 39, 88, 122. *See also* Band
Margolin, Ruth, 228
Marillac College and Campus, **StL**, 258, 259
Mark Twain Building, **StL**, 247, 248, 256, 261
Marksbury, Mary Lee, 212
Marshall, Charles Edmund, 70
Martin, Deanna C., 235
Martin, Frank L., 47, 70
Martin, Shirley, 259
Martin, W. R., Jr., 107
Martinez-Carrion, Marino, 233
Marx, Bill, 121
Mason, Ronald, 216
Materials Science Research Center, **R**, 165, 171
Mathematics, Department of, **R**, 139
Matthews, George H., 11, 12
Matthews, Jack, 85, 110, 111
Maurois, Andre, 201
McAfee, James W., 94
McAlester, Andrew W., 18
McAlester Hall, **C**, 43
McAnerney Hall, **R**, 176. *See also* Housing
McCleary, E. H., 151
McCleary, Glenn A., 71, 98, 106,
McCoy, Layton, 215
McCune, Marie P., 216
McDavid, Frank, 80
McFarland, Robert H., 172
McGill, James, 279
McGlothlin, Don, 116
McGrath, Earl J., 209–10
McHaney, Powell, 80, 94
McIlrath, Patricia, 207, 209, 224, 227, 235
McIntyre, Bruce, 223
McIntyre, John, 224
McIntyre, Maybelle H., 104
McKee, Mary, 56
Mcleod, Frederick R., 212
Mcleod, John, 117
McLorn, Olive G., 103
McNeely, E. J., 94
McNutt, Vachel H., 149, 188
McNutt, Mrs. Vachel H. "Momma Mac," 149, 187–88, 271
McNutt Hall, **R**, 188, 271
McNutt, V. H., Foundation, 188
McRae, Austin L., 140–41, 145, 152, 153, 154
McReynolds, Senator Allen, 76, 80

Mechanical Hall, **R**, 144, 147, 153, 162
Medicine, School of, **C**, 9–10, 12, 18–19, 43, 68, 173, **KC**, 221–22
Memorial Stadium, **C**, 56–59, 61, 88–91, 100, 106, 113, 122, 125
Memorial Tower, **C**, 56–57, 59, 60–61, 66, 67, 91. *See also* Memorial Union
Memorial Union, **C**, 56, 61, 92, 99, 101–2. *See also* Memorial Tower
Menefee, George, 149
Merrill, Lindsey, 224, 233
Metallurgical and Chemical Society, **R**, 152
Metallurgical and Nuclear Engineering, Department of, **R**, 185
Metallurgy, Department of, **R**, 145
Meyer, Max, 66
Middlebush, Frederick A., 67, 76, 83, 92, 93, 94, 160
Middleton, Charles C., 104
Middleton, Mike, 107
Miles, Aaron, 171, 172
Miles Auditorium, **R**, 171
Military Science, Department of, **C**, 19–20, 39, **R**, 153, 171,
Military Ball, **R**, 160
Military Band, **C**, 20. *See also* ; Band
Millay, Edna St. Vincent, 64
Miller, Edward, 112
Miller, Frank, 106
Miller, Fred, 104
Miller, Merritt F., 17, 36, 37, 70, 80
Miller, Will, 116
Millsap, Marvin, 234–35
Millsap, Marvin and Rose Ann Carr, Memorial Trust, **KC**, 234
Milstead, William, 215
Mine, Experimental, **R**, 158, 173, 183
*Miner. See Missouri Miner*
Miners. *See also* Athletics
Mineral Engineering Building, **R**, 149
Mineralogical Museum, **R**, 145. *See also* Museum
"Miner's Minstrel," **R**, 148. *See also* Theater
Mines and Metallurgy, School of, **R**, 171, 184
Mining Building, **R**, 143, 163
Mining Engineering, Department of, **R**, 132, 162
Mining Experiment Station, **R**, 162
Minor, Andrew, 117
Minor, Benjamin B., 11
Minority Engineering Program, **R**, 177
Minority Student Recruitment, **KC**, 231. *See also* Blacks
*Missouri Agricultural College Farmer, The*, **C**, 38
*Missouri Alumni Quarterly*, **C**, 40, 47
*Missouri Alumnus*, **C**, 118
Missouri Archaeological Society, **C**, 61
Missouri College Newspaper Association, 248

Missouri Coordinating Board for Higher Education, 257
Missouri Cultural Heritage Center, **C**, 119–20
Missouri Geological Survey, **R**, 163
Missouri Intercollegiate Athletic Association, **R**, 176
Missouri Legislature, 3, 4, 6, 10, 11, 12, 14, 16, 23, 26, 28, 31, 34, 56, 79, 112, 131, 138, 142, 143, 144, 145, 163, 214, 227, 248, 267
Missouri Medal of Honor, **C**, 49
Missouri Metallurgical Society, **R**, 152
*Missouri Miner, The*, **R**, 152, 153, 178
Missouri Mining Association, **R**, 148
Missouri Mining Club, **R**, 146
Missouri Press Association, 52
Missouri Repertory Theatre, **KC**, 207, 224, 225, 227, 235. *See also* Theater
*Missouri Review, The*, **C**, 117, 118
Missouri School of Religion, 60, 67, 116. *See also* Religious Studies, Department of
*Missouri Statesman*, **C**, 9, 11, 13
*Missouri Student*, **C**, 85
Missouri Students Association (MSA), **C**, 85
Missouri Valley Conference, **C**, 41
*Missourian. See Columbia Missourian*
Mitchell, Henry, 215, 235
Mitchell, Roger, 116
Mobberley, James, 224
Model School. *See* Normal School
Modern Languages, Department of, **C**, 26
Monaco, Ed, 241, 242
Monroe, Haskell, 115, 281
Monroe, Jo, 115
Monsanto, 263
Moore, Norman, 114
Morelock, Thomas, 107
Morgan, John A., 211–12, 214
Morgan, Patricia, 212
Morgan, Speer, 117
Morgenthau, Hans, 200
Morrill Act, 14, 19, 131, 267
Morris, J. M., 138
Morris, J. U., 107
Mortar Board, **C**, 74, 85, **KC**, 232
Mortvedt, Robert, 208, 210
Mott, Frank Luther, 70
MSA. *See* Missouri Students Association
MSM Players Club, **R**, 156. *See also* Theater
*M.S.U. Independent, The*, **C**, 38
Mueller, H. E., 243
Muilenberg, Garrett, 163
Multimedia Auditorium, **KC**, 218
Mumford, Frederick B., 17, 36, 37, 56, 70
Mumford Hall, **C**, 56, 66
Museum, **C**, 16, 26, 31, 97, **KC**, 219. *See also* Mineralogical Museum; Museum of Art and Archaeology;

Natural History Museum
Museum of Art and Archaeology, **C,**
113. *See also* Museum
Music, **C,** 63, 64, 116–17, **R,** 134, 137,
147, 157, 186, 187, **KC,** 194, 199–200,
211, 217, 223–25, 234, 235, **StL,** 246,
247, 252. *See also* Performing Arts
Music Club, **KC,** 200. *See also* Music
Music, Department of, **C,** 96, 97, **StL,**
259
Music, School of. *See* Conservatory
of Music
Mystical Seven, **C,** 45, 74, 85

**N**

NAACP. *See* National Association for
the Advancement of Colored
People
Nagel, Elsa, 107
Nagel, Paul, 273
Nalle, William N., 131
National Academy of Sciences, 127
National Association for the
Advancement of Colored People
(NAACP), 83
National Association of Collegiate
Schools of Business, 227
National Association of Cosmopoli-
tan Clubs, 147
National Association of Land Grant
Colleges and State Universities,
278–79
National Defense Training Program,
75
National Register of Historic Places,
113
National Science Foundation, 81, 105,
164, 185
Natural History Museum, **C,** 26. *See
also* Museum
Naval ROTC, 75
Neff, Ward, 49
Neff Hall, 69, 82
Neihardt, John G., 95
Neill, Robert, 262, 270
Nelson, Donald Marr, 75
Nelson, Earl F., 98
Nelson Gallery and Atkins Museum,
194
Neufield, John, 207
New Horizons Campaign, **KC,** 236
*New Letters,* **KC,** 228
Newcomb, Ernest H., 193–94, 196,
197, 236
Newcomb Hall, **KC,** 194, 236
Nicholas, George, 112
Nichols, Miller, 216
Noback, Richardson K., 221, 233
Normal Department. *See* Normal
School
Normal School, **C,** 9–14 *passim,* 16, 24,
47, **R,** 137
Normandy Residence Center, **StL,**
241

Normandy School, District, 267;
Board, 241
North Campus, **KC,** 236, **StL,** 259, 263
Norwood, Joseph G., 12, 18
Norwood Hall, **R,** 143–45, 149, 154
Noyes, G. L., 56
Noyes Hall, **C,** 56
Nuclear Engineering, **R,** 164
Nuclear Reactor, **C,** 106, **R,** 164, 171
Nursing, School of, **C,** 43, 113, **KC,**
222, **StL,** 259

**O**

O'Keefe, Thomas, 186
Oakley, David, 186
Obetz, John, 224
Observatory. *See* Laws Observatory
Old Chem, **R,** 138, 142, 162, 173
Oldham, Marion, 83
Oliver, John W., 72
Olson, James C., 217–18, 232, 275–79;
administration of, 229, 230
Olson, Vera, 217–18, 276;
Olson, Ronald, 187
Omicron Delta Kappa, 209, 232
Onofrio, Al, 120
Optometry, School of, **StL,** 258–59
Orchestra, **C,** 116, **R,** 147, **KC,** 200.
*See also* Music
Order of the Golden Shillelagh, **R,**
184. *See also* St. Patrick's
Organization of Women Students, **R,**
177
Ormsby, H. H., 159
Orton Society, **R,** 159
Ounsworth, Marjorie, 211
Overby, Osmond, 113
Oxford Hall, **KC,** 216, 236

**P**

Pack, John W., 135
Palmer, Chase, 139
Pan Hellenic Council, **R,** 166, 179,
**KC,** 199. *See also* Fraternities;
Greek System; Interfraternity
Council; Sororities
Papick, Ira, 118
Papish, Barbara Susan, 109
Parizek, Eldon, 212, 233
Park, John T., 185, 188
Parker, Luman Frank, 151
Parker, Ralph, 105
Parker, William L., 43
Parker Hall, **R,** 149, 151, 152, 154, 157
Parker Memorial Hospital, **C,** 43
Paterson, Robert W., 99
Patterson, Robert, 227
Patterson, Russell, 211
Peay, Francis, 118
Peck, Raymond, 273
Peden, William H., 97
Penney, J. C., Awards, **C,** 81

Penney, J. C., Continuing Education
Building, **StL,** 253, 256
Performing Arts, **C,** 63, 64, 116–17, **R,**
134, 137, 147, 157, 186, 187, **KC,** 194,
199–200, 211, 217, 223–25, 234, 235,
**StL,** 246, 247. *See also* Ballet; Band;
Music; Theater
Performing Arts Center, **KC,** 225, 227
Perkins, Marlin, 70
Perry, John, 243
Pershing, General John J., 55, 63, 76
Peters, L. E., 22
Pharmacy, School of, **KC,** 202, 206,
222
Phelps, John S., 135
Phelps County, 131, 135
Phi Beta Kappa, 45, 46, 94
Phi Delta Theta, 22. *See also*
Fraternities
Phi Kappa Phi, 232
Phi Kappa Psi, 22. *See also*
Fraternities
Phillips, James, 215
Philo Society, **R,** 146
Philosophy, Department of, **C,** 35,
**StL,** 244
Physical Education, Department of,
**R,** 171
Physics and Engineering Building,
**C,** 33
Physics, Department of, **C,** 26, 31, 70,
**R,** 163, 185, **StL,** 244; laboratory, **C,**
32
Pi Delta Chi, 168. *See also* Sororities
Pi Kappa Alpha, 145. *See also*
Fraternities
Pickard, John, 35, 50
Pickard Hall, **C,** 35, 113
Piepho, Robert W., 233
Pierson, Elmer F., 231
Pierson Hall, **KC,** 215, 231, 232
Planje, Theodore J., 166, 171, 184
Players Club. *See* MSM Players Club
Playhouse. *See* University Playhouse
Poehlman, J. M., 81
Pogemiller, LeRoy, 211
Pogue, Jim C., 184
Polk, Tom, 107
Ponder, Henry and Alberta, 103
Popper, Robert, 233
Potter, C. E., 242, 243
Powell, J. B., 39
Power Plant, **C,** 31, 33, **R,** 163
Powers, Warren, 120
Pratt, George C., 7
Preparatory Department, **C,** 24, **R,**
134, 145–46, 148
Preservation Hall Jazz Band, **R,** 178
President's House, **C,** 9, 11, 16, 31, 40,
95
Presidential Research Award, 277
Price, Charles H., II, 82, 227
Priestly, J. B., 157
Proctor, Paul, 171
Project UNITED, **StL,** 252–53

Public Works Administration (PWA), 68
Pullen, Roscoe, 98
Purdy, Allan, 85, 111
PWA. *See* Public Works Administration

**Q**

QEBH, **C,** 85
Quadrangle, **KC,** 197, 237; white campus, **C,** 69. *See also* Francis Quadrangle
Quarles, James T., 64
Quintanilla, Luis, 201

**R**

Raitt, Jill, 116
Ralston, Jack, 224
Ratchford, C. Brice, 97, 98, 106, 111, 218, 232, 256, 257, 271, 273–75, 277, 278, 279
Ray, David, 228
Read, Daniel, 12–14, 15, 17–18, 23–24, 42, 132
Read, Mary, 15
Read Hall, **C,** 43, 45, 56, 69. *See also* Housing
Reed, Michael J., 233
Reid, William H., 106
Reinert, Paul, 93
Religion, School of. *See* Missouri School of Religion
Religious Studies, Department of, **C,** 116
Remmers, Walter and Miriam, 186, 187
Remmers Special Lecture/Artist Series, **R,** 186, 187
Rendina, Dorothy, 211
Renner, Richard, 111
Research Center, **R,** 171
Research Park, **C,** 106
Research Reactor, **C,** 106, **UM,** 271
Reserve Officers Training Corps (ROTC), 53, 75, 86, 111, 162, 178, 249; Building, **C,** 20; **R,** Day, 178
Revzin, Marvin, 221, 233
Reynolds, Donald W., 70, 104
RFK Symposium. *See* Kennedy, Robert F., Symposium
Rhynsburger, Donovan, 63, 64, 84
Rich, Ruth Anne, 224
Richards, Richard, 118
Richards, Walter Buck, 139, 141–43
Richardson, Ty, 226
Ridley, Jack, 160, 161, 177
Rifle Competition, **R,** 169. *See also* Athletics
Rinehart, Roy J., 202, 203, 209
Ripley, E. L., 13, 24
Rivermen. *See* Athletics
Robbins, Frederick A., 69
Roberts, Roy, 93

Robinson, Hamilton B. G., 211, 217, 218, 220, 221
Robotics, **R,** 185, 272
Rock Mechanics and Explosives Research Center, **R,** 172, 188
Rockefeller Foundation, 69, 97
Roland, Johnny, 120
Role and Scope, 182, 256, 257, 273, 278
Rolla, 14, 131–32, 137, 142–43, 144, 146, 149, 151, 153, 154, 156, 166, 177, 179, 267
Rolla Building, **R,** 132, 133, 134, 136, 138, 140, 144, 146, 163, 187, 189
*Rolla Herald*, 135
*Rollamo*, **R,** 149, 154, 156, 160
Rollins, A. W., 4, 22
Rollins, Curtis B., 22, 29
Rollins, Edward, 22
Rollins, James S., 3, 4, 12, 14, 29, 50, 51, 131
Rollins Field, **C,** 40, 41, 58
Roosevelt, Eleanor, 94, 209
Root, Oren, 12
Ross, Bill, 232
Ross, Charles G., 38, 47
Rost, William, 209
ROTC. *See* Reserve Officers Training Corps
Roth, Genevieve, 209
Rothwell, Gideon, 29
Rothwell Gymnasium, **C,** 41, 76, 78
Royall, Norman, 200, 208, 218, 219
Royall Hall, **KC,** 218, 219
Rudd, Charlie, 107
Rugby, **R,** 176. *See also* Athletics
Rusk, Howard, 68
Russell, George A., 228, 232–36, 277
Russell, Ruth Ann, 220

**S**

Sabates, Felix, 222
Salazar, Tony, 231
Saline County, 3
Salinger, Pierre, 216
Sanborn, J. W., 16, 17, 27, 70
Sanborn Field, **C,** 17
Sanford, Orin G., 194
Sapp, Virgil, 244
Sarchet, Bernard, 187
Satyrs, **R,** 152
*Savitar,* **C,** 38, 39, 72, 93; Frolics, 87
Scabbard and Blade, **R,** 159
Scasselati, Vincent, 224
Schearer, Laird, 185, 187
Schell, Elyzabeth, 103
Scheneman, Carl, 273
Schlechten, Albert W., 166
Schlundt, Herman, 36, 56, 67
Schlundt Hall, **C,** 56
Schoemehl, Lois Brockmeier, 249
Schoemehl, Vincent, 250, 262
Schoolcraft, Henry Rowe, 131
Schooling, Bess, 111
Schooling, Herbert, 111, 112–13,

116, 120
Schrenk, Walter T., 154, 161, 173
Schrenk Hall, **R,** 161, 173
Schulte, Henry, 41, 62
Schurz Hall Dormitory, **C,** 104. *See also* Housing
Schwada, John W., 103, 107, 109, 111, 269, 270, 271
Schwartz, Charles and Elizabeth, 70
Schwartz, Eleanor, 233
Schwartz, Norman L., 212
Schweitzer, Paul, 13, 20, 67
Schweitzer Hall, **C,** 43
Science Building, **KC,** 197, 202, **StL,** 278
Science, School of, **R,** 171, 172
Scientific Building, **C,** 14, 15, 16, 26
Scofield, Carleton F., 102, 211, 213–16
Scofield Hall, **KC,** 216
Scott, George C., 64
Scott, John R., 38
Scott, John W., 157–58
Scott, Sam, 213
Scott, Walter D., 70
Scurlock, John, 200
SDS. *See* Students for a Democratic Society
Seamon, W. H., 141
Seares, Frederick H., 36
Sears, Earnest, 81, 98, 127
Separatism, 160, 161, 162
Shack, The, **C,** 87
Shakespearean Club, **R,** 135
Shane, Fred, 64
Shannon, James, 5, 10
Shapley, Harlow, 36
Shepley, Ethan, 93
Shields Mansion, **KC,** 274
Shira, Robert B., 220
Shoemaker, Floyd, 97
*Showme,* **C,** 85, 86, 87
Shutz, Byron, 118
Shutz, Maxine, Good Teaching Award, **C,** 118
Sickman, Laurence, 232
Sigma Nu, 145. *See also* Fraternities
Sigma Xi, 45. *See also* Fraternities
Simmons, John "Hi," 62, 90
Simmons Field, **C,** 90
Simpson, Chauncey, 62, 75
Sinclair, Charles and Josie, 104
Sinclair Farm, **C,** 104, 271
Singleton, Charles W., 93
Six, Herbert, 211
Skidmore, Max, 233
Smarr, Larry, 118
Smith, Allen, 112
Smith, Chuck, 246, 247
Smith, David, 232
Smith, Donald, 229
Smith, E. A., 187
Smith, Robert, 113
Smith, Thomas R., 118
Smith, Tom, 94
Smith-Lever Act, 267

Smurfit-Alton Packaging Fellowship,
    **R,** 186
Snow, Edgar, 39, 235
Snow, Edgar, Memorial Collection,
    **KC,** 234
Soccer, **R,** 176, **StL,** 248. *See also*
    Athletics
Social Sciences and Business Admin-
    istration Building and Tower, **StL,**
    253, 255, 279
Social Studies, Department of, **R,** 171
Society of Alumni, **C,** 9
Society of American Military
    Engineers, **R,** 159
Society of Women Engineers, **R,** 168
Sociology, Department of, **C,** 31
Soils, Department of, **C,** 70
Sommers, Joan, 223
Sorby, Donald, 222, 233
Sororities, **C,** 22, 24, 38, 87, 94, 125, **R,**
    168, 179, **KC,** 209, 212, 232, **StL,** 251.
    *See also* Fraternity; Greek System;
    Interfraternity Council; Pan
    Hellenic Council
South Campus, **StL,** 259
South Mall, **R,** 173
Southwick, Martha, 117
Spaeth, J. Duncan, 194–96, 197
Speca, John, 200
Spector, Gene, 259
Speer, Hugh W., 200, 209, 216
Spencer, Helen, 227
Spencer, Kenneth A., 218
Spencer, Kenneth A., Chemistry
    Building, **KC,** 202, 219, 275
Spencer, Kenneth and Helen, Foun-
    dation, 218, 219
Spencer Theater, **KC,** 227.
Sports. *See* Athletics
Spotts, Carleton, 117
Sprinkel, Beryl W., 82
SSB Tower. *See* Social Sciences and
    Business Administration Building
    and Tower
St. Louis, 3, 18, 34, 83, 100, 106, 160,
    214, 241, 242, 244, 249, 250, 252, 257,
    258, 261, 263, 267, 276, 281
St. Louis Board of Aldermen, 250
St. Louis Board of Education, 250
*St. Louis Republic,* 47
St. Louis Symphony, 246, 252. *See also*
    Music
St. Patrick's, Day, **C,** 45, 87, **R,** 149,
    150, 157, 158, 161, 169, 179, 180, 181,
    186; Board, **R,** 177, 179; Coronation
    Ball, **R,** 157, 158; Honorary
    Knights, **R,** 179; Queen, **R,** 149
Stadler, L. J., 69
Stadler, Lewis J., 69, 256
Stadler Hall, **StL,** 69
Stafford, Richard, 80
Stalcup, Sparky, 88
Stankowski, Anton J., 41, 62, 106
Stanley Hall, **C,** 67

Star and Garter, **R,** 156
Stark, Nathan, 221
Starr, Martha Jane, 228
State Geological Survey, 144
State Highway Department, 165
State Historical Society of Missouri,
    52, 97, 269
Stauffer, Bill, 88
Stegeman, Charles, 224
Steuber, Bob, 62
Stewart, Norm, 67, 88, 122, 124
Stipanovich, Steve, 122, 124
Stoia, Eugene, 211
Stonehenge, replica of, **R,** 188
Straumanis, Martin E., 173
Strauss, Eugene M., 227
Strickland, Arvarh, 111
Strickland, William, 217, 222
Stucky, Duane, 114
Student Affairs Committee, **StL,** 247
Student Athletic Association, **R,** 141
Student Council, **R,** 148, 153, 158, 177,
    **KC,** 199
Student Health Center, **C,** 68
Student Theater, **KC,** 225. *See also*
    Theater
Student Union, **KC,** 206, 207, 213
Student Union Board, **C,** 94, **R,** 177
Students for a Democratic Society
    (SDS), **C,** 109–10
Studio Set, **StL,** 260.
Sturges, Hollister, 218
Subler, Craig, 218
Summers, David, 187
Sumnicht, Russell, 221
Sunderland Foundation, 218
Sundvold, Jon, 122, 124
Sutton, Richard, 219
Swallow, George C., 15–17, 24
Swartout, Harold, 106
Sweeney, Leo J., 212
Sweeney, Robert, 221
Swimming, **R,** 169, 176; meets, **R,**
    160; pool, **C,** 104, **StL,** 261. *See also*
    Athletics
Swinging Choraliers, **KC,** 223. *See
    also* Music
Swinney, E. F., 204
Swinney Gymnasium, **KC,** 203–4,
    229, 273
Switzler, William F., 11
Switzler Hall, **C,** 11, 17, 44, 70, 81
Szekely, Eva, 117


**T**

Tap Day, **C,** 74, 86, 112
Tarkow, Theodore, 111
Tate, Frank R., Mr. and Mʳ
Tate, Lee R., 56
Tate Hall, **C,** 56, 58, 67      , 269
Tau Beta Pi, 145
Tau Kappa Epsilon, 165. *See also*

Fraternities
Taylor, Carl C., 93
Taylor, Eleanor, 107
Taylor, General Maxwell, 93
Taylor, John, 212
Teachers College. *See* Normal School
Teel, Bob, 122
Tennis, **R,** 160, 169, 176. *See also*
    Athletics
Theater, **C,** 63, 64, 84, 96, 117, **R,** 148,
    154, 156, 173, 186, **KC,** 200, 206–7,
    224–25, 227, 235, **StL,** 246. *See also*
    Performing Arts
Theater, Department of, **C,** 64, 97,
    **KC,** 207, 224, 226, 235
Theta Sigma Phi, 94. *See also*
    Sororities
Theta Tau, 145
Thilly, Frank, 35
Thomas, Robert S., 7
Thomas Jefferson Library, **StL,** 250,
    254. *See also* Library
Thomas Jefferson Hall, **R,** 173, 176.
    *See also* Housing
Thompson, Dudley, 166, 171, 172, 182
Thompson, Lelia, 168
Thompson, William H., 257
*Tiger, The,* **C,** 38
Tigers. *See* Athletics
Tindall, Cordell, 71
Todd, Albert, 135
Todd, Robert B., 7
Todd, Robert L., 7
Tophatters Club, **KC,** 199, 200. *See
    also* Music
Topping, Seymour, 82
Torch and Scroll, **KC,** 209
Touhill, Blanche, 244
Townes, Morris, 121
Townsend, Loran, 71
Townsend, Vera, 118
Track, **C,** 41, 62, 90, **R,** 147, 160, 169,
    176. *See also* Athletics
Trani, Lois, 220,
Trani, Eugene P., 232, 233
Trenholme, Norman, 35
Trogden, William B., 87
Troutman, William, 200
Trova, Ernest, 259, 261
Trowbridge, Edwin A., 80
Trowbridge, Harry, 157
Truman, President Harry, 38, 83, 93,
    200, 209
Truman Campus, **KC,** 229
Truman Library, 229. *See also* Library
Truman Medical Center, **KC,** 221, 222
Trustee Professorships, **KC,** 233
Trustees, Board of. *See* University of
    Kansas City Board of Trustees
Trustees of the Nelson Gallery, 193
Tucker, Avis, 70
Tucker, Jean, 252
Tucker, R. J., 81
Tucker Prairie, **C,** 81

Tureman House, **KC,** 216
Turner, Emery, 244, 250, 257–58
Turner, William D., 157, 159
Twain, Mark, 46, 87
Twin, Edward, 221

**U**

U.S. Army Corps of Engineers, 182
U.S. Bureau of Mines' Mississippi
  Valley Experiment Station, 154
Uehling, Barbara S., 113, 115–16,
  119–20, 121, 277
Uffelman, Hans, 215
Union Literary Society, **C,** 8, 9
United Telecommunications Inc., 233
University Associates, **KC,** 211, 212,
  218, 233
University Center, **R,** 173, **R,** 212, 231,
  **StL,** 253, 256
University Choir, **R,** 186. *See also*
  Music
University Chorus, **C,** 116, **StL,** 246.
  *See also* Music
University Hall, **C,** 270
*University Magazine,* **C,** 38
*University Missourian,* **C,** 9, 17, 23, 38,
  49
*University News,* **KC,** 199
University of Kansas City Board of
  Trustees, 193, 194, 197, 198, 200, 206,
  208–18 *passim,* 227, 232, 233, 236
University of Missouri Board of
  Curators, 3–18 *passim,* 22, 23, 26, 27,
  29, 33, 40, 41, 47, 51, 55, 62, 65, 66, 67,
  70, 72, 77, 79–85 *passim,* 94, 95, 102,
  103, 109, 111, 112, 113, 118, 131–38 *pas-
  sim,* 141, 142, 143, 144, 148, 149, 151,
  152, 154, 160, 161, 166, 171, 172, 176,
  188, 208, 217, 219, 230, 232, 233, 242,
  257, 259, 267, 269, 270, 271, 273–78
  *passim*
University of Missouri Hospital and
  Clinics, **C,** 98, 114; Eye Clinic, 113.
  *See also* Lottes, John O., Health Sci-
  ences Library
University of Missouri Press, **UM,**
  97, 185, 271
University of Missouri Studies, **C,** 35
University Players, **KC,** 199–200, **StL,**
  246. *See also* MSM Players Club;
  Theater
University Playhouse, **KC,** 206, 208,
  209, 224, 226
*University Review, The,* **KC,** 200, 228
University Singers, **C,** 116, **KC,** 200,
  223, **StL,** 246, 247. *See also* Music
University Theater, **C,** 63. *See also*
  Theater
Unklesbay, A. G., 270, 271
Unruh, Adolph, 244
*Urban Lawyer, The,* 228

**V**

Vandegrift Mansion, **KC,** 216
Vanderbilt, Cornelius, 157
Veblen, Thorstein, 50
Veterans, **C,** 77–80, 84, **R,** 153, 161, 162,
  166, **KC,** 206
Veterans Hospital, 98
Veterans Service Committee, 80
Veterinary Medicine, School of, **C,**
  80, 104
Viles, Jonas, 35
Villa, Thomas, 250
Vincil, J. D., 144
Volker, William, 193, 197, 203
Volker Campus, **KC,** 218, 219, 222
Volker String Quartet, **KC,** 224. *See
  also* Music
Volz, Marlin M., 207

**W**

Wadsworth, Homer, 214, 217, 221
Wait, Charles E., 136, 138
Walker, Diana, 234
Walker, Mort, 86, 87
Walker, Pinkney C., 99
Wall, Herbert, 64
Walter Williams Hall, **C,** 69, 70
Walters, Everett, 251, 256, 260, 261
Walton, Sam, 72
War, **C,** 53, 55, 56, 77, **KC,** 202, 204, 206;
  Armistice, **R,** 153; Civil War, **C,** 6, 9,
  10, 11, 12, 13, 18, 19, 20, 24, 27, 40, 50,
  51, 82; World War I, **C,** 41, 55, 76, 80,
  **R,** 152, 153, 154, **KC,** 193; World
  War II, **C,** 76, 78, 80, 81, 82, 83, 91,
  95, **R,** 154, 161, 162, 167, **KC,** 200,
  203, 206, **UM,** 275
War Department, 153
War Surplus Buildings, **C,** 77–78, **KC,**
  206
Waring, Richard, 215
Warner, Don L., 184
Waters, Henry J., 37, 45,
Waters Hall, **C,** 37, 66
Wauchope, George A., 30, 35
Weaver, John C., 171, 172, 217, 218, 250,
  270–71, 273; Administration of, 274;
  Inauguration of, 109
Webb, Cecil, 107
Weide, Kenneth, 113
Weifenbach, William, 209
Weinberg, Gladys Davidson, 97
Weinberg, Saul, 97, 113
Weldon Spring Fund, 275, 277
Westermann, Edwin J., 212, 229
Western Dental College, 200, 202. *See
  also* Dentistry, School of
Western Historical Manuscripts Col-
  lection, 97, 271
Western Musical Conservatory, **R,**
  134, 137. *See also* Music

Westveld, R. H., 80
Whaley, Randall, 216–17, 271
Wheeler, Charles B., 232
Whitcomb, Michael, 116
White Campus, **C,** 43, 51, 56. *See also*
  Quadrangle, White Campus
White Recital Hall, **KC,** 227
Whitener, Joy, 244
Whitman, Dale, 116
Whittaker, Charles E., 211, 217
Whitten, J. C., 37
Whitten Hall, **C,** 43
Whitten's Walk, **C,** 37
Widenhofer, Woody, 120, 121
Widmar, Gary, 229
Williams, Charles H., 34
Williams, Charles P., 132–36, 160, 165
Williams, Hazel Browne, 212
Williams, Hosiah, 178
Williams, Rex Z., 165
Williams, Walter, 47, 66, 67
Wilson, Curtis Laws, 160, 161–62, 163,
  165, 170, 273
Wilson, James, 45, 46
Wilson, R. C., 41
Wilson, Vernon, 98, 105, 221, 269, 270,
  271
Wilson Fellows, **StL,** 249
Wise, James, 185
Wixson, Bobby, 178
Wixson, Douglas, 186
Wollard, Joseph D., 185
Wolpers Hall, **C,** 104. *See also*
  Housing
Women Students: mentioned, **C,** 65,
  87, **R,** 188, **KC,** 233; athletics, **C,** 41,
  43, 56, 68, 122, 124, **R,** 176, **KC,** 232,
  **StL,** 248, 258; enrollment, **C,** 12,
  13–14, 20, 24, 45, 75, 104, **R,** 134,
  145–46, 154, 167–68, **KC,** 204, 206;
  housing, **C,** 22, 69, 80, **R,** 137, 176–77
Women's Center, **KC,** 228
Women's Council, **KC,** 218
Women's Forum, **C,** 64
Wood, Horace W., 106
Wood, Minnie, 152
Woodill, Mindy, 177
Woods, Bob G., 116
Woods, Howard, 259
Woods Hall, **StL,** 259
Woodson, Warren, 5
Woodward, C. M., 29, 33
Workshop, The, **C,** 64, 84. *See also*
  Theater
World War I. *See* War
World War II. *See* War
Wrench, Jesse, 61

**Y**

Yanders, Armon, 112
Ye Tabard Inn, **C,** 81, 82
YMCA. *See* Young Men's Christian
  Association

Young, Jill, 125
Young, Lewis E., 148, 149, 151
Young, Robert, 242
Young Men's Christian Association
    (YMCA), **C,** 45, 47, **R,** 147, 149

Young Women's Christian Associa-
    tion (YWCA), **C,** 45
Yu, Wei-Wen, 187
YWCA. *See* Young Women's Chris-
    tian Association

**Z**

Zauchenberger, Herwig, 229
Zeta Phi. *See* Beta Theta Phi
Zoology, Department of, **C,** 35, 69, 70
Zuber, Marcus, 81

# PHOTO CREDITS

Agricultural Editor's Office (Cooperative Extension): 37 (bottom), 44 (top), 58 (bottom), 72

Mrs. Thomas W. Botts, 90 (bottom)

College of Engineering, **C,** 105

*Columbia Daily Tribune,* xii, 102 (top, photographer Leight), 106 (top, photographer Jim Noelker), 122 (bottom left, photographer Rees), 125 (top, photographer Jeff A. Tayler, bottom, photographer Jim Noelker), 126 (photographer John La Barge)

*Columbia Missourian,* 83 (top)

Ellis Library/Special Collections, 86 (top right)

Esterhazy Quartet, 117 (photographer Carole Patterson)

Don Faurot, 89 (top)

James A. Finch, 97, 270 (top right)

Mrs. Dorothy Gladwill, 60

Honors College, **C,** 119 (bottom)

Kappa Kappa Gamma Archives, **C,** 22 (center)

Barbara Jahn King, photographer, 268, 269 (bottom)

Michael Middleton, 107

*Missouri Alumnus,* xiv, 92, 101, 104, 106 (bottom), 108 (top), 111 (top, bottom), 112 (top left, bottom), 113 (bottom), 114 (bottom), 115 (top, bottom), 118 (bottom), 120 (bottom left), 122 (top left and right), 123 (top), 269 (top, photographer Larry Boehm), 273 (top), 280

Missouri Historical Society, 12 (top), 67 (bottom, photographer Glenn S. Hensley), 70 (top, photographer Glenn S. Hensley), 74 (photographer Glenn S. Hensley), 75 (photographer, Glenn S. Hensley), 93 (top left)

*The Missouri Review,* 118 (top, cover photograph courtesy of Jet Propulsion Lab, Pasadena, CA)

Museum of Art and Archaeology, **C,** 113 (top)

James and Vera Olson, 276 (top and bottom)

William E. Partee Center for Baptist Historical Studies, 7 (top)

Mrs. Clarence M. Pickard, 70 (bottom)

*Rolla Daily News,* xi, 179 (bottom, photographer Joel Goodridge), 180 (bottom)

State Historical Society of Missouri, 3 (bottom), 4 (top, bottom left, bottom center, and bottom right), 5 (top, bottom), 6 (top right and bottom), 9 (gift of Mrs. Ruth Rollins Westfall), 10 (top), 12 (bottom, gift of Mrs. Ruth Rollins Westfall), 14 (top, center, and bottom), 15 (gift of Mrs. Ruth Rollins Westfall), 16, 19 (bottom, gift of Mrs. Ruth Rollins Westfall, top), 20 (top left, gift of Albert Glenn Cooper, top right), 21 (bottom), 22 (bottom), 23 (top, gift of Laura Matthews), 24 (top left and right, gifts of Harry King Tootle), 25 (top, bottom), 28, 30 (bottom, gift of Trenton Boyd), 32 (top, center, bottom), 35 (top center and top right), 37 (top), 41 (top), 42 (top), 43 (top, bottom), 45 (top and center, gifts of Robert L. Price, bottom, gift of H. F. Nelson), 47 (top left), 48 (bottom), 49 (top, gift of Mary Paxton Keeley), 51, 53, 54 (top, bottom), 55 (bottom), 56 (center), 57 (top, bottom), 58 (top), 61 (left, photographer Leon Waughtel, gift of Roy King), 66 (bottom), 76 (top, loaned by Mr. and Mrs. Thomas W. Botts, bottom, gift of Mrs. George A. Rozier), 80, 131 (top, bottom)

*St. Louis Post-Dispatch,* 54 (top and center), 73 (top), 79 (top), 155, 169 (top)

University Archives, Columbia and UM, 3 (top), 6 (top left), 7 (bottom left and right), 10 (bottom), 11, 17 (bottom), 18, 22 (top), 23 (bottom), 26, 27 (top), 29 (top, bottom), 30 (top), 31 (top, bottom), 33 (top, bottom), 34 (top, bottom), 35 (top left), 36 (bottom), 38, 39 (bottom left and bottom right), 40 (top), 41 (bottom), 44 (bottom), 46, 47 (top right, bottom), 48 (top), 49 (bottom), 50, 56 (top, bottom), 59 (top and bottom), 61 (right), 62 (top), 63 (top, center, bottom), 64, 66 (top), 67 (top), 68 (top, bottom), 69 (top, bottom), 71 (top, bottom), 73 (bottom), 77, 78 (top, bottom), 79 (bottom), 82 (top, bottom), 84 (top, center, bottom), 85, 86 (top left, bottom left), 87, 88, 89 (bottom), 91, 93 (top right and bottom), 94 (top, bottom), 95 (top, bottom), 96 (top, bottom), 98, 99, 100, 102 (bottom), 103, 108 (bottom), 109, 110 (top, bottom left and right), 112 (top right), 116, 119 (top), 120 (top left), 121 (top, bottom), 123 (bottom), 124 (top left and right, bottom), 271 (bottom)

University Archives, Kansas City, 39 (top), 193 (top, bottom), 194 (top, center, bottom), 195 (top left and right, bottom), 196 (top, bottom), 197 (top, bottom), 198 (top, bottom), 199 (top, bottom), 200 (top), 201 (top left and right, bottom left and right), 202 (top, bottom), 203 (top, bottom), 204 (top, bottom), 205, 206 (top, bottom), 207, 208, 209, 210, 211 (top, bottom), 212 (top, bottom), 213 (top, bottom), 214, 215, 216 (bottom), 217 (top, center, bottom), 218 (top, bottom), 219, 220 (top, bottom), 221, 223 (bottom), 226 (bottom), 227 (top, bottom left and right), 228 (top, bottom), 229, 230 (top, bottom), 231 (top left and right, bottom left and right), 232 (top, bottom), 233 (top), 234 (bottom), 236, 237

University Archives, Rolla, 132 (top, bottom left and right), 133, 134 (top, bottom), 135, 136 (top, center, bottom), 137, 138 (top, center, bottom), 139 (top, bottom), 140 (top, bottom), 141 (top, center, bottom), 142 (top, bottom), 143 (top, center, bottom), 144, 145, 146 (top, bottom), 147, 148 (top, bottom), 149 (top, bottom), 150 (top, center, bottom), 151 (top right and bottom), 152 (top, bottom), 153, 154 (top, bottom), 156 (top, bottom), 157 (top, bottom), 158 (top, bottom), 159, 160 (top, bottom), 161, 162, 163 (top, bottom), 164, 165 (top, bottom), 166 (top, center, bottom), 168, 169 (bottom), 170 (top, bottom), 171 (top, bottom), 173 (top), 174, 175 (bottom), 176 (bottom), 178, 179 (top), 180 (top left and right), 181 (top left and bottom), 182 (top, bottom), 183 (bottom), 184 (top, bottom), 270 (top left)

University Archives, St. Louis 241, 242, 243, 245, 246 (top), 247 (bottom), 249 (bottom), 250 (left and right), 251 (bottom), 252 (bottom), 253 (top right, bottom right), 254 (top left and right), 256 (bottom right), 257, 258 (top), 259 (bottom), 261 (top right, bottom right)

University Communications Office-University of Missouri–Kansas City, vi, 200 (bottom), 216 (top), 222, 223 (top), 225, 226 (top), 233 (bottom, © 1986 Chuck Kneyse), 235, 275

University of Missouri–Columbia School of Medicine, Office of the Dean, 270 (bottom)

University of Missouri Hospital and Clinics Public Relations, 114 (top)

University of Missouri Intercollegiate Athletics, C, 40 (bottom), 62 (bottom), 90 (top), 120 (top right)

University of Missouri–Kansas City Audiovisual Services, 273 (bottom), 274

Univerity of Missouri–Kansas City Conservatory, 224 (photographer Michael Rush), 234 (top, photographer William Cofer)

University of Missouri-St. Louis Office of University Communications, 244 (Steve Mutchler-Photographics), 246 (bottom, photographer Daniel T. Magidson),

247 (top, NEWS Photo-News, Washington, D.C.), 248 (top left and right, bottom), 249 (top), 251 (top left and right), 252 (top, Leon Photography), 253 (top left, Leon Photography, bottom left), 254 (bottom, Leon Photography), 255, 256 (top and bottom left, Leon Photography), 258 (bottom, photographer Daniel T. Magidson), 259 (top), 260, 261 (top left), 262 (top, bottom), 263 (photographer Marcus Kosa, Mind's Eye Ltd), 277, 278 (photographer Cedric R. Anderson), 279

University of Missouri–Rolla News and Publications, iv, 151 (top left), 172 (top, bottom), 173 (bottom), 175 (top), 176 (top), 177, 181 (top right), 183 (top), 185 (top, center, bottom), 186 (top left and right, bottom), 187 (top, bottom), 188 (top, bottom), 189 (top left and right, bottom), 271 (top), 272 (top, bottom)

University Relations, 83 (bottom)

Western Historical Manuscript Collection, 8, 13, 17 (top), 20 (bottom), 21 (top), 27 (bottom), 35 (bottom), 36 (top), 42 (bottom), 65